THE GOLDSMITH'S HANDBOOK

THE GOLDSMITH'S HANDBOOK

CONTAINING

FULL INSTRUCTIONS

FOR THE

ALLOYING AND WORKING OF GOLD

BY

GEORGE E. GEE

Published by

Gyan Publishing House
5, Ansari Road
Daryaganj, New Delhi-110002
Phone: 011-47034999, 9811692060
E-mail: books@gyanbooks.com

Distribution Network
gyanbooks.com
India, USA, Canada, UK, Australia

ISBN: 978-93-6433-052-7 (PB)
First Published, 1881

2nd Impression 2024

Printed at: Gyan Press, Delhi.

THE GOLDSMITH'S HANDBOOK
AUTHOR: GEORGE E. GEE

THE

GOLDSMITH'S HANDBOOK

CONTAINING

FULL INSTRUCTIONS

FOR THE

ALLOYING AND WORKING OF GOLD

INCLUDING

THE ART OF ALLOYING, MELTING, REDUCING, COLOURING, COLLECTING, AND REFINING; THE PROCESSES OF MANIPULATION, RECOVERY OF WASTE, CHEMICAL AND PHYSICAL PROPERTIES OF GOLD; WITH A NEW SYSTEM OF MIXING ITS ALLOYS; SOLDERS, ENAMELS, AND OTHER USEFUL RULES AND RECIPES.

BY GEORGE E. GEE

GOLDSMITH AND SILVERSMITH, AUTHOR OF "THE SILVERSMITH'S HANDBOOK"

SECOND EDITION, CONSIDERABLY ENLARGED

LONDON

CROSBY LOCKWOOD & CO.

7, STATIONERS' HALL COURT, LUDGATE HILL

1881

PREFACE TO THE FIRST EDITION.

HAVING been frequently applied to by gold-workers and others, with reference to certain difficulties relating to their trade, which they were unable to overcome mechanically; the idea presented itself to the mind of the Author, that a work *practically* treating on the "Uses and Applications of Gold," having special regard to the business of the goldsmith and jeweller, would be a useful auxiliary to the artificer also, by affording him a constant means for consultation and instruction.

From an intimate connection with this craft or art, of a very practical nature, extending over a period bordering upon twenty years; and having held during nearly the whole of that time a position of trust and responsibility with several leading manufacturing firms; also from his experience as a jeweller's manager, he is not only enabled to place before the reader the results of his own personal experience, but also that of others who have been under his direction and control.

And further, having given considerable attention to the intricacies of the trade generally, he has, as a natural consequence—in common with others—met with many difficulties connected with it; besides other obstacles which are to be found in the path of the younger craftsmen. These however have been ultimately overcome by the exercise of patience, careful observation, and perseverance. To guide, therefore, the workman and young apprentice, and, as far as possible, to prevent them from experiencing similar perplexities by pointing out their chief causes and the remedies, as well as to supply some additional information which will, it is hoped, contribute both to their efficiency and advancement, is the aim of the writer.

Directions for mixing gold, solders, enamel, &c., are here given of a thoroughly experimental character. The processes of colouring, collecting, refining, and some other modes of treatment of the precious metal are also described, and for accuracy they can be safely depended upon.

The Author has endeavoured to avoid, as much as possible, technical expressions; having regard all through to the main object of this little volume, namely, the benefit of that class of practical gold-workers who take an interest in the daily business of their life, to which, perhaps, chance or choice has called them; but who unfortunately may be unable to improve their position, from the want of a higher and more comprehensive knowledge of their calling. He has, therefore, tried to make the matter plain and intelligible to all who may give it their attention. Especially does he desire that such of his fellow workmen who are steadily devoting their energies to this art, in any of its several branches, may through this instrumentality acquire a knowledge of facts, and a set of useful rules with which they have, perhaps, hitherto been unacquainted.

It only remains to be added that the greater portion of this work has appeared in the form of articles in the *Jeweller and Metal-worker*, a well-known and valuable journal, published in the interests of the trade indicated by its title. Much additional matter has however been here introduced, and the whole carefully revised; so that it may become, as it were, a manual of reference and a guide to the jeweller's workshop.

PREFACE TO THE SECOND EDITION

THE Author, in presenting a second and enlarged edition of this work to his readers, has much pleasure in stating that the additional information, as given in the form of an Appendix, is thoroughly sound and practical, and that good commercial successes may be accomplished by following the directions therein given.

The new matter consists partly of the results of some of the Author's numerous experiments and researches into the subject upon which he writes, and partly of the details of modern processes of working in daily practice in his manufactory, such processes having been rendered perfectly successful; and a hope is here indulged that such knowledge will be found available for service in assisting the labour and promoting the interests of the melter, the colourer, and the gold-worker generally.

The title of the work, too, has been changed from "The Practical Gold-worker," to "The Goldsmith's Handbook," in order to make it uniform with its companion volume, "The Silversmith's Handbook."

G. E. GEE.

58, TENBY STREET NORTH, BIRMINGHAM.
July, 1880.

CONTENTS.

CHAPTER I.

History and Sources of Supply.

a 3

CHAPTER II.

Properties of Gold.

CHAPTER III.

Various Qualities and Alloys of Gold.

CHAPTER IV.

Melting and Rolling.

CHAPTER V.

Coining.

CHAPTER VI.

Manufactured Articles.

CHAPTER VII.

Solid Wire-Drawing.

CHAPTER VIII.

Manufacturing Processes.

CHAPTER IX.

Engraving and Chasing.

CHAPTER X.

Solders and Soldering.

CHAPTER XI.

Various Processes of Colouring and Finishing.

CHAPTER XII.

Collecting and Refining waste Gold.

CHAPTER XIII.

Tables of Specific Gravities, Alloys, &c.

CHAPTER XIV.

Useful Hints.

APPENDIX.

Results of Experiments and Researches.

Details of Modern Processes.

THE

PRACTICAL GOLD-WORKER.

CHAPTER I.

Gold; its History and Sources of Supply.

To aid the advancement of scientific knowledge, and to give assistance to the manipulator or worker in the precious metal, is the object of the writer of this book; as well as to enable the artisan and the uninitiated to acquire a general knowledge of the history, and useful appliances of the chief material connected with the goldsmith's art. In the first place, with the idea that the subject may be interesting to the general reader as well as to the practical man, we propose to review the ancient history of gold, together with its modern progress and usefulness as regards ornamental art. The last-mentioned matter will be amply discussed hereafter, when the processes and treatment of the precious metal will be explained, together with all that can, in common fairness to the trade of a

B

manufacturing goldsmith, be published. This information will be derived both from actual experience, and from the study of the works of most of the leading authors who have written upon the subject.

Gold of all metals is the most imperishable, and consequently the most noble and beautiful. It is, therefore, identified with everything that is intrinsically valuable and outwardly rich. It is the most solid of all the metals, and when in a state of perfect purity consists of particles so fine in the grain and so closely united, that they can hardly be separated. When unalloyed it does not suffer any diminution or loss by melting; it does not tarnish in the air, neither is it subject to rust if laid by, but always retains its natural appearance; no acid or salt of any kind will affect it in the least degree; it has moreover a beautiful characteristic yellow colour, and is justly distinguished from all other minerals by the name of "the king of metals," or the "royal metal."

The history of gold abounds in so much that is interesting, that we have thought it worth while to trace a little of its ancient production and applications. Gold has been known from the remotest age. The sacred writers used to identify it with everything that was precious, and speak of it as the metal of supreme excellence. The first mention of it in the pages of the Old Testament is in the Book of Genesis (chap. ii. 10—12): "And a river went out of Eden to water the garden; and from thence it was parted, and became into four heads. The name of the first is Pison: that is it which compasseth the whole land of Havilah, where there is gold; and the gold of that land is good." The Book of Genesis is supposed to have been written by Moses about 1,500 years before the birth of Christ; gold, then, upon the evidence of Scripture, has been used upwards of 3,300 years. The first mention of its being employed for the purposes of ornamental art is found in the same book (Genesis chap. xxiv. 22): "The man" (this was Abraham's servant) "took a golden earring of half a shekel weight, and two bracelets for her (Rebekah's) hands of ten shekels weight of gold." A golden skekel, according to our present currency, would be worth about £1 16*s.* 6*d.* The same book also informs us that articles or ornaments of jewellery were worn by the Jews, of almost every description now to be seen in the nineteenth century. In Genesis also (chap. xli. 42) we read of other things of the same kind, the manufacture of which was known to the ancients: "And Pharaoh took off his ring from his hand, and put it upon Joseph's hand, and

B 2

arrayed him in vestures of fine linen, and put a gold chain about his neck." As far as we have been enabled to ascertain by reference, gold is mentioned in the Bible in all upwards of three hundred times, in connection with various things with the manipulation of which the old Jewish patriarchs must have been tolerably conversant; for we read of jewels, crowns, bowls, knops, bars, pillars, hooks, flowers, rings, chains, bells, plates, tablets, ouches, and talents of gold; also cherubims, candlesticks, mercy-seats, ephods, breast-plates, and calves, all of which were of gold; there were besides settings of gold, tables covered with gold, houses embellished with gold, while the throne itself is said to have been overlaid with pure gold. Further, all Solomon's drinking vessels were made of this metal (1 Kings x. 21): "And all king Solomon's drinking vessels were of gold, and all the vessels of the house of the forest of Lebanon were of pure gold; none were of silver: it was nothing accounted of in the days of Solomon." So abundant does it appear to have been in his time, that it is reported that he received 666 talents of gold (equal to about 27 tons) in one year.

Gold has been known and used by every nation, both uncivilised and civilised, from the earliest period down to our own time. Among the old

Egyptian monuments it is found, and semi-barbarous nations also used it in the form of dust as the principal medium of exchange. When America was discovered by Columbus, gold was well known to its inhabitants; the Chinese have used it from time immemorial; the Medes and Persians were remarkable, even more than other Asiatics, for their love of gold; jewels of costly descriptions were employed to indicate the rank of the wearer, and this custom is still continued in the East at the present day. Africa too has long been celebrated as the land of gold-dust, and it is supposed that the Ophir whence Solomon obtained so much was a country on that coast. To show the sacred value, in ancient times, the Egyptians placed on gold, it was represented by a circle with a dot in the middle: this circle, amongst that nation, being the symbol of divinity and perfection.

Gold is found in America, and mines exist in California, Mexico, Brazil, British Columbia, Peru, Central America, Granada, and several other localities in South America. At present the United States of America contribute more than one-third of the total supply of gold.

The metal is never met with in a pure state in nature, being always alloyed with silver and sometimes with copper; the proportion varying greatly in the different gold mines of the world. In Californian and some other mines of America, the purity is not quite equal to our standard; nevertheless, this does not alter the fact that America is the richest gold-producing country of the whole world at the present time.

California is the largest field in America, producing gold to the value of £13,000,000 per annum; Mexico and South America contribute £1,000,000. (We are indebted for these statistics to "Cassell's Technical Educator—Mineral and Commercial Products.") Previous to 1847 (the year of the discovery of gold in California) the average produce of the whole world was far short of that now yearly produced by California. Professor Tomlinson, in his "Useful Arts and Manufactures," said: "Yet so comparatively small were the gatherings of the precious metal, that in reckoning the average produce of all parts of the New and Old World for a series of years previous to 1847, it did not amount to the annual value of five millions sterling."

In Australia, gold is found in New South Wales, Victoria, Melbourne, Sydney, Reedy Creek, Geelong, and numerous other places; but the places just mentioned are the most important and extensive producing districts in that country. New Zealand is also a gold-producing country. That of Australia and New Zealand is remarkable for its pureness, being considerably above our present English standard, and containing only about three per cent. of alloy, or fifteen grains to the ounce.

The year 1851 was a year of special interest to the English people, and memorable to this country in more respects than one. It was in that year that the first International Exhibition of Industry was opened in Hyde Park, and it was in that year also that Australia first began to reveal her long-hidden treasure. The first discovery in our Australian possessions was made near Bathurst, situated about one hundred miles west of Sydney, New South Wales. A gentleman of the name of Hargraves, who had for some considerable time been familiar with the geology of the district, by way of experiment, took several baskets of soil from the ground and washed the contents, when they were found to contain gold. The experiment was repeated with the assistance of a body of men, and the result fully justified his expectations and rewarded him for his labours. This brilliant discovery soon however became known, and gold-digging became a flourishing industry. Mining operations were carried on by emigrants from all parts of the world, and in a short space of time similar results to those already achieved in

California followed. At the present time the gold-producing districts of Australia, with New Zealand, contribute one-third of the total supply. The purity of the Australian gold as taken from the bowels of the earth, as we have already remarked, is greater than that of any other country in the world.

In Asia, the Ural Mountains contain some rich gold districts; they are situated on the borders of Asiatic Russia. Tibet, in the Chinese Empire, also furnishes gold. The islands of Sumatra and Ceylon, in the Indian Ocean, likewise contribute to our store; so do Borneo and Japan, in the Pacific Ocean. Other parts of Asia yield small supplies, such as the rivers of India, China, Sumatra, and Asia Minor, but the total supply is not very important when compared with other places, the annual value not exceeding half a million sterling; the chief districts being the Ural Mountains and the East Indies.

In Africa, gold seems to have been found from the very earliest ages; and along the coast of Caffraria the sands abound in gold-dust. This district is reputed to be the oldest and richest of the sources known to the ancients; it is supposed, as already mentioned, that the Ophir of the ancients was part of this coast, the place where King Solomon obtained so great an abundance of gold

(1 Kings x. 11): "And the navy also of Hiram, that brought gold from Ophir." The chief sources here are Guinea and the Gold Coast; the latter includes the district between Darfur and Abyssinia, where the principal portion is found. A small quantity is found in the sands of the rivers Gambia, Senegal, and Niger; "and although," says Professor Tomlinson, "Africa is at once pointed out by her 'Gold Coast' as yielding the precious metal, the whole supply from that continent is not estimated at more than 5,000 lbs. weight annually." The value then of the whole produce of this continent will not exceed a quarter of a million sterling per annum. Africa, in this respect, has lost her ancient position and has become the poorest quarter of the hemisphere in the yield of the precious metal.

Having now spoken of most of the gold districts we come nearer home, and it will, no doubt, be interesting to our readers to know, not only what are the gold-yielding localities of Europe, but also in our own country. In Europe, the Ural Mountains, dividing Asiatic from European Russia, furnish the largest quantities of gold. It is also to be found in the sands of the Rhine (in Prussia), the Rhone (in France), the Tagus (in Spain), the Danube (in Turkey), and many other rivers, but it is rarely considered worth working, because it exists in these respective places in too small a quantity to pay expenses. The provinces of Asturias and Granada, in Spain, formerly furnished a large amount, the mines being very rich and valuable, but they are now entirely neglected. Italy is not altogether destitute, for it is known to exist in the neighbourhood of the Alps, and in the sands of some of the rivers. At Edelfus, in Sweden, it has also been found. The Carpathian Mountains, in the Austrian Empire, also furnish the precious metal. The richest and largest mine on the continent of Europe, with the exception of Russia perhaps, is in Hungary: this and the Ural Mountains furnish the chief European supply.

Our own country is not without her gold districts, for small quantities have been found in Cornwall. In the reign of Queen Elizabeth extensive washings for gold were carried on at Leadhills, Lanarkshire, Scotland. It has also been found at Glen Turret in Perthshire, at Cumberhead in Lanarkshire, and more recently large quantities have been found in Sutherlandshire. Ireland, towards the close of the last century, supplied a large quantity of gold, but the yield lasted only for a short period; it was found at Arklow, in the county of Wicklow. Pieces were found by the people varying from the smallest particle to twenty ounces in weight. Gold has also been found at Dolgelly, in North Wales, and energetic proceedings have been carried on there. Nevertheless, we shall have to look in the future, as in the past, to the great gold-producing countries of America and Australia for a sufficient supply of the precious metal for the use of our artistic workers. The total annual gold supply of Great Britain and Ireland would not be sufficient to keep ten of the largest Birmingham firms fully employed manufacturing their usual 9-carat quality of goods for one week. We have said that in ancient times Africa was the great gold country of the world. In more modern times, till as recently as the year 1847, Mexico, in North America, and Chili, Peru, and Brazil, in South America, produced most of the gold used for the currency and in the goldsmith's art; but the discoveries in California and Australia have established a field, the productions of which will not for a considerable time, at least, be exhausted.

Gold always exists in nature in the metallic state, there being no evidence to the contrary. It is found in the form of gold-dust and nuggets in earth deposits; these deposits being formed by the breaking-up of old rocks containing gold, under the influence of storms and torrents, which have swept the metal, together with soil and other matters, into deep receptacles, leaving it often at the bottom of rocks and in the bends of rivers. The lowest of these deposits are generally the richest on account of the specific gravity of the metal; but it is sometimes found upon the surface of the earth, and the Californian gold was discovered in this way.

The metal is found in veins, in pyrites (firestone), in granite rocks, and in layers or strata of clay, gravel and pebbles, sometimes at a considerable distance below the soil. It is also obtained in considerable quantities mixed with sand and gravel on the surface. In North America it exists in loose deposits in beds of gravel from nine inches to three feet in thickness, and from three to six feet from the surface of the ground. In California, it consists chiefly of *alluvial gold*, to which reference has already been made. In Australia gold quartz (a semi-crystallised rock, chemically termed hydrate of silicon) is more common, the precious metal in these lumps of rock appearing in the form of branchlike fragments. Here it is also found in some abundance in various-sized nuggets, and more plentifully in the form of gold-dust.

Gold-dust abounds chiefly in the sands and beds of rivers. On the coast of Africa, it is said that the negroes dig out the earth, rich in gold-dust, to a great depth. In Ireland gold has been found in masses, some lumps being of great size. The nuggets found in Australia often exist in large masses, one specimen having been found weighing 46 ozs. The mines of Russia contain large masses of gold; on the southern portion of the Ural Mountains (Asiatic side), in 1842, sands of immense richness were discovered; and at the period of which we speak, an enormous mass of gold was dug up weighing about eighty English pounds. This splendid mass was afterwards placed in the collections of the Corps des Mines, at St. Petersburg. Some six years previous to this a large piece of this metal was found in the same neighbourhood, weighing upwards of 22 lbs. troy. According to some writers upon this subject, it is not, however, a usual thing to find masses of such proportions in the Ural districts of Asia or Europe; the metal more commonly existing in small grains or fragments, and the yield averaging from thirty to seventy grains of gold per ton of soil.

We have already said that in Australia, one of the great modern gold-producing countries, massive lumps are to be found in considerable quantities;

only the other day a friend showed us a beautiful nugget which he himself had discovered in that place, which is now worn as a scarf pin, and the purity of it no jeweller could dispute.

There are several ways of separating the gold from the ore at the different mines throughout the world. The most simple method is that of washing the sands of rivers, that is the alluvial deposits which have been washed by floods and storms into deep gullies. There are numerous processes of washing in vogue, and these are adopted to suit the resources of the gold-diggers. In South America, and other countries having sands rich in gold-dust, this washing is performed in shallow iron or zinc pans; the earth being put in and well stirred up with water, the light earthy matters suspended in the water being afterwards poured away from the gold. This process is repeated until all the particles of earth are removed, leaving the gold-dust visible to the naked eye in minute grains at the bottom. Another method which has found some favour amongst gold-diggers, is the employment of shallow wooden troughs, lined with coarse cloth at the bottom; these troughs, which are of some length, must be placed in a slightly-inclined position; the auriferous sands are then thrown into the trough, a gentle stream of water is allowed to run in, and from its inclined position, the fine sand is washed away, leaving behind the small particles of gold in the tissues of the cloth, which are recovered by washing in water. In other cases, ordinary sloping boards, of common deal in its rough state, are taken, and shallow grooves made across them; the soil is then thrown upon the planks, the coarseness of which, together with the grooves, form collecting-places for the gold, which, on account of its very high specific gravity, sinks into the crevices thus provided, while the lighter matters are washed away by the stream of water employed for the purpose.

At the gold-diggings of California and Australia, where these rich sands and alluvial deposits exist to a great extent, a *rocker* commonly called the "Burke rocker," or cradle, has been generally employed; this rocker will wash from seven hundred to one thousand bushels of gravel or sand a day; the cost of the machine complete being about twenty-five dollars (English money, £5 4*s.* 2*d.*)

Most of the gold of the United States is worked up into jewellery, and not in the coinage; a large trade being done at Newark, Philadelphia, Providence, Rhode Island and numerous other places. Professor Bloxam, in his work on metals, thus describes the cradle used at the Californian gold-diggings: "This is a wooden trough about six feet long, resting upon rockers, and at the head of it is a grating upon which the alluvial deposit to be washed is thrown. This end of the cradle is about four inches higher than the other, so that a stream of water entering it flows through and escapes at the lower end, left open for this purpose, carrying the earthy substances with it, and leaving the particles of gold, with a small quantity of earthy matter, in the trough. These are swept out into a pan, dried in the sun, and freed from the lighter matters by blowing upon them." It must be understood that these are not the only methods of gold-washing, the process being slightly different at nearly all the gold mines.

At the mines in Russia iron sieves are most generally used, fitted upon sloping boards upon which cloth, or some other substance, is placed; these receive the deposit and are placed under a gentle current of water, which, being well stirred, the fine sand and gold-dust fall through on to the cloth beneath, and are thus recovered. These processes cannot be employed when the gold exists in iron pyrites, quartz, or other similar rock, being only adapted to the washing of alluvial deposits, sands, &c. In any of the previous operations the digging for gold is attended with little expense;

but where it is disseminated through auriferous iron pyrites, quartz rock, &c., a considerable outlay generally attends the operation. Expensive crushing machines and stampers have to be employed for the purpose of breaking up the rough hard material which contains the gold. Sometimes the ore is very hard; so that before submitting it to the action of the stamping or crushing machine, it has to be well burnt and quenched in water, in order to render it morè brittle, and consequently easier to crush. The stamping and crushing is done in water, and is continued until the ore is reduced to a very fine powder, when the gold is separated by one or other of the processes already explained; or, it may be extracted by amalgamation with metallic mercury, which dissolves and collects it. The surplus mercury may be removed by putting the amalgam into a coarse flannel bag and well squeezing it, when a great portion of the mercury will run out, leaving the remainder a solid mass in the bag. The remaining mercury may be got rid of by placing the substance in an iron pan or box, and heating it over a gentle charcoal fire, which renders it volatile.

CHAPTER II.

Properties of Gold.

HAVING now pointed out the places where gold is to be found, and the way in which it is extracted or separated from the ore, we leave this part of the subject, and purpose in what follows to deal with the precious metal as a commercial product. In this we hope to give some practical information which will no doubt be useful to our readers, more particularly to working jewellers.

Pure gold, on account of its very rich colour and non-liability to tarnish in air or water, either by oxidation or from the action of sulphuretted hydrogen, is used for a variety of commercial and ornamental purposes. Being very solid it has a high specific gravity, one other metal only being superior; this metal (platinum) being the heaviest known substance; it is, however, not much employed in commerce. The specific gravity of gold is 19·2, but by hammering it becomes 19·5. It will be well to explain, before proceeding further, the meaning of the term specific gravity; in order to remove from the minds of those of our readers who are unacquainted with chemical phraseology and technical expressions, any doubt which may exist as to the true nature of its meaning. The specific gravity of a substance is the proportion it bears in weight to that of an equal bulk of water. Specific gravity is, then, the difference subsisting between the weights of equal bulk, or given dimensions, of liquids or solids. For example, if we take two pieces of gold wire, each of exactly the same size and length, and place them separately in the opposite pans of a pair of scales, the scales will exactly balance, the gold wire being identical in weight, and therefore of the same specific gravity. If we now remove one of the pieces of gold wire and substitute one of silver of exactly the same size and length, by balancing the scales again we shall at once see that the gold wire is much the heavier; and the difference between the two metals shows their relative specific gravity.

Water, in consequence of its lightness in comparison with the metals, and the ease with which it is obtained pure, is adopted as the standard of specific gravity. Taking water as the unit, we write after it the figure 1, or 1,000; these numerals may represent grains, pennyweights, or ounces. The metals employed by the jewellers in the manufacture of their articles or wares would be numerically expressed thus:—

Water, sp. gr. (specific gravity)		1 or 1,000
Spelter	do.	7·2 or 7,200
Copper	do.	8·96 or 8,960
Silver	do.	10·5 or 10,500
Gold	do.	19·5 or 19,500

The weight of gold is nineteen and a half times that of water of the same bulk, silver ten and a half times heavier, and copper nearly nine times, as indicated by the above table.

Perfectly pure gold, or fine gold, as it is more generally called, cannot be procured in commerce, in consequence of the long chemical refining process which would make it too expensive for manufacturers of jewellery, according to present competing prices. The different qualities are expressed in carats; the finest gold, which should be quite free from any alloy, is commonly expressed as 24, but the fine gold of commerce consists only of about $23\frac{3}{4}$ to $23\frac{7}{8}$ carats, and this is quite good enough for ordinary practical purposes. Fine gold consists of irregular minute grains of a dull yellow colour, but it can be made bright by heating and boiling in hydrochloric acid; however, this is only a matter of taste, and does not make the slightest difference to the working of the metal; in fact, some masters give a preference to the dead colour. So far as our own experience goes, we unhesitatingly say that for manufacturing purposes the one is quite as good as the other. The melting point of fine gold is 2,016° Fahrenheit, and it appears of a greenish shade when fused in the pot; when heated to the above degree it reflects like a mirror. Fluxes will change the colour of gold; borax makes the colour rather paler, whilst saltpetre deepens it. The chemical nomenclature of fine gold, and of the other metals used in jewellery with it, are represented as follows:—

Name of Element.	Symbol.	Equivalent.
Gold (aurum)	Au.	197·0
Silver (argentum)	Ag.	108·0
Copper (cuprum)	Cu.	31·7
Spelter (zinc)	Zn.	32·6
Hydrogen (a gas)	H.	1·0

These various elementary bodies have symbols of a very simple character, which are generally formed by taking the initial of their names; but in cases where two or more elements are the same, some other letter must be taken for distinction; the symbols, therefore, of metals represent or express their chemical names.

The *equivalent* of a metal is only another name for atomic weight: and these equivalents are at present practically recognised by the principle of the atomic weight of hydrogen being taken as the standard unit of 1. In order to assist the reader we will illustrate this. It is well known that pure water consists of two elements or bodies, hydrogen and oxygen, and that these ingredients or gases do not exist in equal or variable, but in quite fixed, proportions; every atom of water contains eight times the amount of oxygen to that of hydrogen—therefore, hydrogen being the lightest, it is taken as 1. *Equivalent chemical weight*, then, expresses the different proportions, by weight, in which substances, whether solids or fluids, chemically unite with each other. For example, one part by weight of hydrogen, goes as far in combining with eight of oxygen to form an oxide, as 108 of silver, or 197 of gold; and these equivalents will not neutralise the eight of oxygen more effectually than the one of hydrogen does, but just the same, and produce a similar compound. The same remarks apply to all the other equivalents of elements. If we take, to show this more clearly, one grain of hydrogen and eight of oxygen, exactly nine grains of water are formed; but if we were to take two grains of hydrogen and eight of oxygen, and submit them to the same treatment, the same amount of water would be formed as before, and the surplus hydrogen found uncombined. So it is with gold: if we were to take more than the 197 equivalents of gold to eight of oxygen to form oxide of gold, the surplus in this case, as in the above, would be found uncombined; therefore to form oxide of gold we say eight oxygen, 197 gold.

Fine gold is of a very malleable temper. It spreads under the hammer more than any other metal, and may be worked into almost any form or design by the hand of a skilful workman. There is no metal that can be extended so much by hammering or rolling, as pure gold. "One ounce," says Smith in his "School of Arts," "beaten into leaves, would cover ten acres of ground." "It will so yield to mechanical force," says Lutschaunig, "that it may be reduced to the 200,000th part of an inch in thickness." For manufacturing purposes these extremes are seldom or never reached. Practically the limit to which fine gold is now reduced as regards thinness is in the gold-beater's art, where it is so wrought that a hundred square feet of it weigh only one ounce, and this would cover only the 480th part of the space mentioned by Smith. The metal employed by the gold-beater should be pure, or very nearly so, but it generally consists of about 23 carats. The various colours which this kind of gold presents, are obtained by alloys with silver and copper in different proportions. The pale leaves consist of twenty-three parts of fine gold and one part of silver; the deep-coloured leaves, approaching to a tint of red, contain twenty-three parts of fine gold and one part of best Swedish copper; the fine orange-coloured more commonly met with, contain half-part of silver, and half-part of copper to twenty-three of fine gold. Too much silver in the alloy is an obstacle to the gold-beater, in consequence of its hardening properties, therefore its use should be avoided as much as possible.

Gold-beaters' gold is prepared by taking the right proportions of fine gold and alloy, and melting the mixture in a crucible; it is then cast into small oblong ingots, each about three-quarters of an inch in width, and one and a half inch in length, and weighing about two ounces. Each ingot is afterwards rolled very thin between two reversible polished steel rollers, the gold being often annealed in order to render it soft, as it has a tendency to become hard under this process; by this means it can be reduced with little expense into a very fine riband, of not more than one-eight-hundredth of an inch in thickness. It is then cut into lengths about one inch square. A number of these are taken and secured by a most useful contrivance. With a sixteen-pound hammer, having a smooth convex face, the gold is then beaten until its dimensions are considerably extended, when it is cut as before, hammered again, and if necessary the process repeated until it is of the proper thinness for transfer to the books in which it is sold to the public. These usually consist of twenty-five leaves each, when trimmed being about 3¼ in. square, and costing to the trade from 1*s.* to 1*s.* 3*d.* the book.

The uses to which this gold is now put, even in everyday transactions, are more numerous probably than the majority of workmen through whose hands it regularly passes in the different stages of manufacture contemplate; suffice it to say, that almost every article, both in business enterprise and domestic life, is beautified and enriched by its application at the hands of studious and skilful artisans. Even the paper upon our walls, our china, tea-trays, book-edges, and covers, signboards, sewing machines, and in fact, almost every article and trinket of our household, is decorated more or less with this metal. We have also printing in letters of gold, gold lace, and by no

C

means the least, our best picture-frames are all embellished with it; and although the various uses thus described may appear to the uninitiated as rather comprehensive and costly, the gold would not indeed, if recovered from a whole host of such articles and trinkets, and melted, amount to more than two pennyweights, or of the value of 8*s.* 6*d.* We have deemed it desirable to supply this information, which may, perhaps, be considered beside the chief branch of our subject, viz. the uses of gold and its connection with the jewellery trade and the money or currency, in order to show the widespread usefulness of the precious metal; and the very extreme of malleability to which it is reduced in order that it may be applied to so vast a circle for purposes of ornamentation, and that at a comparatively reasonable cost.

Fine gold is quite as remarkable for its ductility as its malleability. The ductility of a metal is the possession of that property of yielding to mechanical force which renders it capable of being drawn into wire successively through a series of graduated holes in a steel plate, called by wire-drawers, a draw-plate; if the metal be perfectly ductile, wire of almost any thinness may be thus obtained. Pure gold is at the head of all metals for ductility; it is stated that wire-drawers have extended from an ounce of gold, a thread 230,800 ft. long.

The inlaid vessels, and work in gold *filigree* from India, are examples of the great ductility and admirable mechanical qualities of this noble metal. In India the greatest perfection seems to have been attained to in the art of drawing gold wire, as witness the gold-embroidered housings of the elephant and howdah, as exhibited by Her Majesty in Hyde Park, 1851. And further, this filigree is produced so fine in that country, that in England there are no competitors in the market as manufacturers of so fine and real wire-work. The vast majority of London and Birmingham filigree is not at all similar to the real filigree-work of India: the London and Birmingham wire being thicker, round wire, flattened, with a milled or serrated edge, and afterwards so placed upon the different designs for the filigree of the edge to show itself; whilst the Indian is wire *considerably* thinner, doubled and twisted into a fine cord of extreme delicacy. The extreme point of ductility is never practised in England, there being no advantage gained in the commercial world, the finest wire required for manufacturing purposes being either for the purpose of filigree, or gold lace. For the latter it is drawn very fine, and afterwards flat-

C 2

tened between a pair of steel rollers to any size, to suit the object in view.

There is reason to believe that the ancient Israelites had some knowledge of the ductility of this metal, and that the art of making round wire was known to them (Exodus xxxix. 3): "And they did beat the gold into thin plates, and *cut it into wires*, to work it in the blue, and in the purple, and in the scarlet, and in the fine linen, with cunning work." It is not said to what extent these wires were reduced in thinness, and no object but one purely experimental would aim at the extension of an ounce of fine gold into a wire the length we have mentioned; indeed we much question whether the most experienced wire-drawer of the present school would accept an order such as the above, even at his own price. The drawing of a pennyweight of gold by mechanical force into a wire 11,540 ft. long, and a single grain into a wire 480⅚ ft., is a difficulty not to be easily overcome. We have some practical knowledge of the art of wire-drawing, and we distinctly say, that unless the wire was previously coated very strongly with silver, any attempt on the part of the workman to produce such a length must result in failure. If the object can be attained, which we much question, then the silver may be removed from the surface of the wire, by dissolving with nitric acid; and although the acid has no effect upon pure gold, still, in consequence of the thread of gold being so extremely fine and delicate, it must be done with very great care to prevent the wire becoming disunited.

The tenacity of a metal is its strength and toughness—that property which prevents, when mechanical power is exerted, the easily tearing asunder of the metal, the separation of the particles when excessive force is applied, and the giving way when supporting any particular weight. In this respect gold is not at the head of the list; for while a piece of gold wire of the thickness of No. 14 size Birmingham wire gauge will support a weight of $150\frac{3}{4}$ lbs. avoirdupois, a wire exactly the same dimensions in silver will support 187 lbs., and a similar one of iron 549 lbs. Thus, the position that gold occupies with regard to its tenacity and toughness, is not equal to that of its ductility and malleability.

CHAPTER III.

Various Qualities and Alloys of Gold.

FINE gold is too soft to stand the wear and tear of ordinary use, hence arose the necessity for the incorporation of some other material to give it increased hardness. The following table gives the relative value of the different carats, and the proportion of alloy to be added, taking 24 as the unit of fine gold:

Qualities of Gold.	£	s.	d.	Alloy to be added.
24 carats.	4	5	0	None.
23 ,,	4	1	5½	1 carat.
22 ,,	3	17	11	2 ,,
21 ,,	3	14	4½	3 ,,
20 ,,	3	10	10	4 ,,
19 ,,	3	7	3½	5 ,,
18 ,,	3	3	9	6 ,,
17 ,,	3	0	2½	7 ,,
16 ,,	2	16	8	8 ,,
15 ,,	2	13	1½	9 ,,
14 ,,	2	9	7	10 ,,
13 ,,	2	6	0½	11 ,,
12 ,,	2	2	6	12 ,,
11 ,,	1	18	11½	13 ,,
10 ,,	1	15	5	14 ,,
9 ,,	1	11	10½	15 ,,
8 ,,	1	8	4	16 ,,
7 ,,	1	4	9½	17 ,,
6 ,,	1	1	3	18 ,,
5 ,,	0	17	8½	19 ,,
4 ,,	0	14	2	20 ,,
3 ,,	0	10	7½	21 ,,
2 ,,	0	7	1	22 ,,
1 ,,	0	3	6½	23 ,,

The above value represents the ounce troy, and is quoted at the mint price of purchase. The purchasable price of fine gold from refiners will be a little higher than that given in the above table, on account of the expenses in refining; in large quantities, say over 10 ozs., it will cost from £4 5*s.* 3*d.* to £4 5*s.* 6*d.* per ounce; in smaller quantities, it will cost from £4 5*s.* 6*d.* to £4 6*s.* per ounce; therefore, if 1 oz. of fine gold be required, it will cost £4 6*s.* nett, from all houses.

In judging of a piece of work of alloyed gold, the value (if with a view of sale) must not be calculated merely upon the amount of fine gold the piece of work contains; for, in that case, the calculation as to the real value will be wrong and misleading; because in the alloy there is a certain proportion of silver, and as this metal is rather expensive, a loss would occur by the transaction. For example, if we take the proper proportion of fine gold existing in an ounce of 18-carat gold, at the mint value as given in the table, £3 3*s.* 9*d.*, to obtain that amount of gold from the refiner in the best market it will cost £3 4*s.* 3*d.* (the increase being due to the expenses in refining), in order to produce that fine state of division required for alloying. Now, in order to produce 18-carat gold,

5 dwts. or 6 carats of alloy, must be added to the quantity of fine gold of the above value; if we say half silver and the other half copper, at the lowest trade price it will cost 9*d.*; so to practically produce an 18-carat alloy of gold it will cost £3 5*s.* per ounce to the manufacturer of jewellery before he actually introduces it into his workshop. All other alloys should be calculated after the same manner, and we should say an ounce of 8-carat gold is worth £1 10*s.*

The use of 22-carat gold as our national standard of value for the coinage is well known, but a few additional particulars will not be irrelevant to that branch of the subject upon which we are now entering. Gold coins, when first introduced into the currency of England by Henry III., were of fine gold, that is to say of 24 carats. Edward III. was the first English king who used gold coins of an inferior standard, in the form of 6*s.* pieces, nearly equal in size to the present sovereign, and consisting of $23\frac{7}{8}$ carats. A coin called a noble followed, worth 6*s.* 8*d.* Edward IV. reduced the standard to that of 18 carats. The next change was made by Henry VIII. raising it to 22 carats. From that time until the reign of Queen Elizabeth the currency underwent various changes; but it was then again fixed at 22 carats, and it has so continued with about one exception down to the present time. All English gold coins are nominally and intrinsically worth the sums they represent. This is so when they leave the Mint, and have not been subjected to the wear and tear of circulation.

Besides the standard fineness for coins, there is also a legal weight, fixed according to the regulations of the Mint. Thus in England a pound troy of the standard metal is worth £46 15*s*., so that if a single pound troy of standard gold were taken to the Mint to be coined, after forty-six sovereigns and one half-sovereign had been manufactured out of it, a portion of gold of the value of 5*s*., not used up in the coins, would remain. The same quantity will coin 44½ guineas, of the value of 21*s*. each; hence the value of standard gold is £3 17*s*. 11*d*. per ounce.

The coinage of gold is conducted with great exactness by the officers of the Mint, with respect to weight; and the extreme accuracy with which they are compelled to work will be shown by the following extract from the first schedule of the Coinage Act, 1870.

The imperial weight in grains only is here given:

Coin.	Weight.	Remedy.
Sovereign . . .	123·27447	0·20000
Half-sovereign . .	61·63723	0·10000

The *remedy* is the difference allowed to the Deputy-Master of the Mint, between the standard and real weight of the manufactured coins; which in a sovereign is only one-fifth of a single grain; and to this limit he has invariably confined himself, as the trial of the Pyx fully proves. This test, which is one of the most ancient customs (the first-known writ for a trial of the Pyx dating from the reign of Edward I.), was made on Wednesday, July 21, 1875, at the Goldsmiths' Hall, according to the provisions of the Coinage Act, 1870. Although this is a trial of great importance to the authorities at the Mint, and also to the public, especially to the manufacturing goldsmiths, who are constantly melting up the coin of the realm for manufacturing and commercial purposes, it is a matter in which the latter take little or no interest. To the former the verdict is of great interest, because, if favourable, it is an honourable commendation of the officers of the Mint, for the faithful performance of their onerous duties during the past year; and also a perfect guarantee to the public and the goldsmiths, that the large amount of additional gold coinage annually manufactured and circulated is fully up to the legal standard, both as to fineness and weight.

The standard fineness for gold coins is 11-12ths

fine gold and 1-12th alloy, or millesimal fineness 916·666, the remedy being millesimal fineness 0·002 = 1-500th of a grain. The guinea is of the same standard as the sovereign in fineness, but differs in weight, hence its value of 21*s*. A guinea weighs 5 dwts. 9½ grs.; and a sovereign 5 dwts. 3¼ grs. and a fraction of a grain; of which 4 dwts. 22¾ grs. and 4 dwts. 17 grs. respectively are fine gold. Since the reign of George III. guineas have not been coined for circulation. There is also a difference in the colour. Guineas look yellow, while the modern sovereign shows a deep red tint. This denotes an alloy of silver in the former, and one of copper in the latter. Our gold coins are now always alloyed with copper, with the exception of those manufactured by the colonial mint at Sydney, in Australia, for which silver is employed. These can easily be distinguished from English coins by their greenish-yellow cast, even without a close inspection of the impression of the die, which is slightly different upon the obverse side; whilst upon the reverse, besides other distinctive features, it has the word *Australia* stamped upon it.

These coins are of the same standard in fineness, weight and value as English coins, and usually pass without observation among commercial men. We have heard some persons express doubts as to the genuineness of a coin the colour of the Australian sovereign, as regards its value; but they have been those through whose hands no large number of coins have passed, and who are unacquainted with the variety of colours gold may be made to present to the eye; if there be any real difference between the Australian and English sovereign, the former has the advantage on account of the extra silver it contains; silver being more expensive than copper. That characteristic deep red colour to be seen in a new English gold coin, is produced when it is submitted to the very highly-polished dies of the coining-press, when it comes out perfectly bright and of a beautiful lustre.

Previous to the reign of Charles II. all the coin of the realm was made by hand—by forging or hammering pieces of gold to the proper thickness required for the coins, then cutting squares a little larger than required for the different sizes. The corners were afterwards removed from the squares, and rounded to the size, when they were adjusted to the weight of the money desired to be put into circulation. These round blank pieces were then placed between two hardened and tempered steel dies, containing the pattern of the intended coin; the upper die being struck with a hammer, the impression was produced. This method of making the coins was far from perfect, in consequence of the difficulty in placing the dies exactly opposite each other, and also from the uncertainty of the blow producing a perfect impression on the blank piece of gold intended for the coin. The coining-press, introduced into England in the beginning of the last century, remedied this long-experienced defect.

Our present gold coins are as nearly perfect as possible as regards artistic design, taste, and workmanship, and as such, are well known all over the world.

Twenty-two-carat gold, besides being made into coins, is very largely used in the manufacture of wedding-rings, which must be of this quality. So keen is the competition in this branch of industry that a wedding-ring may now be purchased from the manufacturer for a very little above its real value in gold; and it is by no means an unusual thing at Mr. Aston's manufactory in Birmingham, when trade is busy, to work up in this manner a thousand pounds' worth of gold per week. This quality of gold is very expensive to use for such a purpose; consequently the working loss would be very great in a manufactory carrying on business to the above extent; indeed, it could not possibly be estimated at less than £2,000 per annum. Of course, we mean that this amount goes into the polishing dirt, floor sweep, washing waters, &c. However, there is one decided advantage which the wedding-ring makers have over other jewellers, viz. that the material—the coin—is sent with the order, and no doubt the manufacturers in several other branches of jewellery—not to say all—would like the same system or custom of trade established with them.

Wedding-ring makers have to pay a duty upon their manufacture of 17*s.* per ounce, 1-6th being remitted for loss in finishing; because it is compulsory that this quality should, when made into wedding-rings, be *Hall-marked*, and this has to be done when the articles are in a half-finished state; therefore, for every six ounces you pay for five, and so on. For this reason it is usual to melt down the coin of the realm, and for more purposes than one it is an advantage to wedding-ring manufacturers to do so, for they can then depend upon the quality, and also effect a saving of from 4*d.* to 5*d.* per oz.—a gain to a large firm not to be lost sight of, in these days of eager competition. Twenty-two-carat gold is also used in the manufacture of mourning-rings, but to a more limited extent than the above. In some instances, watch-cases are made of 22-carat gold; but English watch-cases more commonly consist of 18-carat gold. Watch-cases (English) bear the mark of Goldsmiths' Hall as a guarantee of their quality, and are manufactured duty free.

Twenty-carat gold does not occupy a very prominent position in the jeweller's workshop, the demand for it being so limited that it is rarely if ever asked for. As a consequence, it is not largely manufactured into articles of jewellery. Sometimes, however, this quality of gold is used by coloured gold-workers, when different colours or shades are required in decorative designs, and when these colours cannot be produced in inferior gold. For this purpose it is both elegant and ornamental. Brown gold may be made by taking twenty parts of fine gold and four parts of copper; puce gold by taking twenty parts of fine gold and four parts of silver; these ingredients must be well incorporated. In Ireland 20-carat gold is a legal standard, and has been so from the year 1784, in the reign of George III. This standard was established, principally, to encourage the manufacture of watch-cases and jewellery, it being at that time illegal to manufacture articles of this description inferior to 22-carat gold.

Eighteen-carat gold is the second English standard, and of this quality all our best jewellery is made. It is largely manufactured into all kinds of personal ornaments, as it is an alloy rich in quality; the beauty of its colour moreover not being much altered by wear. In England this standard is used in the manufacture of watch-cases, which, if of proper fineness, bear the Government hall-marks. There is now no duty on the manufacture of watch-cases of any description. Mourning-rings too are made somewhat extensively of this quality; wedding-rings also to some extent.

Mourning and wedding-rings, if of 18-carat gold, or of the higher standard to which we have already referred, must pay duty upon the manufacture of 17*s.* per oz., 1-6th part, as usual, being remitted for waste in finishing. It is compulsory that these articles should be hall-marked, and bear the stamp of the properly-authorised officials of the town in which they are made. In Birmingham the title of the guild is "The Guardians of the Standard of Wrought Plate." It has exclusive jurisdiction over all the gold made into the above articles in the town of Birmingham, or within 30 miles of it.

Eighteen-carat gold, from the peculiar nature of its alloy, can be wrought into almost any article of exquisite beauty and delicate workmanship; if properly cast, it is both malleable and tenacious. It is also exceedingly ductile. A hardness is imparted to this quality of gold which admirably adapts it to the manufacture of jewellery of the highest order. There is, perhaps, a difficulty in preparing 18-carat gold, not experienced in some other alloys; this defect soon shows itself when submitted to the breaking-down mill, by little cracks all over the surface of the bar of gold; and when this appearance presents itself, it is by far the most economical plan to re-melt it at once, than to go on with the breaking-down; for when the process of slitting is attempted, the gold will all fly into little fragments, and the probability is that some will be lost. The prevailing opinion in the trade is, that this want of unity or amalgamation of the particles of the gold and alloy is due to the copper which is employed. Our experience teaches us—having tried every kind of copper, from the bean-shot down to the best refined Swedish wire, for the purpose of producing 18-carat gold rather cheaper—that we have invariably found that there is not so much in the quality of the copper as in the quantity used. This we wish to state for the benefit of the goldsmiths' trade. Formerly we used a rather large proportion of copper, in order to effect a saving of about *3d.* per oz., but the misfortune to which we have just alluded sometimes presented itself, and after trying all sorts of copper, with no certainty of permanent success, we thought of the plan of alloying with more silver and less copper. In this we succeeded, and now never meet with a bar exhibiting the defects after rolling just described.

It is the most economical plan, when these defects appear, to reduce the bar to the regular 9-carat quality. It is only right to state that we always found 18-carat gold, alloyed with bean-shot copper, a more difficult and harder alloy to work with than when the refined wire was used. One great drawback in shot copper (which is very injurious in alloying, particularly in this quality) is, that it may contain lead or tin; and half a grain of either in an ounce of this gold will prevent it from working. This quality of gold is now always manufactured fully up to the standard fineness, every design possible being hall-marked; and where this is not possible, the guarantee of the manufacturer is given with the article, who, if a respectable person, can be thoroughly depended upon. Previous to the year 1798 it was illegal to manufacture from this quality of gold; now, however, some thousands of ounces are made annually into all sorts of articles. Some of these are ornamented with a variety of colours, which may be produced by the following methods of alloying :—

Colours of Gold.

Yellow Gold—pure or fine gold, 24 parts.

Red Gold—fine gold 18 parts, copper 6 parts.

Green Gold—fine gold 18 parts, silver 6 parts.

Blue Gold—fine gold 18 parts, iron 6 parts.

White Gold—fine gold 12 parts, silver 12 parts.

Platinum, or fine silver, may be employed for white gold. Red and white are generally employed for flowers, green for leaves, while the stems or sprays may be made of yellow or fine gold. Blue gold may be used for special purposes of ornamentation. This latter alloy requires great practical knowledge, as it presents many difficulties in its preparation ; these are best overcome first by melting the gold, and then introducing some iron wire into the molten mass, until the proper quantity of alloy is formed. Then the crucibles must be withdrawn, and the composition poured out into an ingot-mould prepared for its reception. This alloy must not be quenched in water, but allowed to cool; the ingot of gold to be perfect should exhibit no signs of porosity ; if it turns out of the ingot-mould in proper condition, it must be well hammered upon the edge, and annealed, in order to render the grain more close and prevent it cracking in the rolling-mill. This process may be wisely repeated upon the surface, and the ingot again put through the fire. The gold is then ready for the breaking-down mill, and may be safely wrought into wires or sheets of different sizes.

Fifteen-carat gold is another alloy largely used in the manufacture of coloured jewellery. This quality, to our mind, is second to none with respect to works of art in jewellery, both in regard to taste and appearance, as well as durability. It can be made to look quite equal to the finest gold, and in addition it is easy of manipulation; almost any article can be easily made from it, whilst the hardness which nine parts of alloy imparts, is not such as to prove a hindrance or a difficulty in the manufacture, but unites with it that amount of strength and durability which is so essential in costly articles of jewellery. These advantages make articles of this gold wear much better than when made of a softer material; they also keep their form and shape a considerable time longer.

According to the provisions of the Assay Act of 1854, 15-carat gold can now be assay-marked as a guarantee of proper fineness, but it is not compulsory unless requested by the purchaser. There is no duty on its manufacture, neither is there on that of 18-carat gold into chains, studs, lockets, charms, fancy rings, &c. Purchasers of 15-carat goods should beware of an inferior quality of gold introduced into the trade and called 15-carat, bearing a stamp something similar to the hall-mark; however, this is not the hall-mark, but the private mark of the manufacturer. Nevertheless, the general public who are conversant with the prices at which these articles are sold, will at once see that this is not done with the intention of representing the quality as equal to 15-carat, by a glance at our table of values for the various qualities. We shall now give an account of the different qualities in general use.

Thirteen-carat gold is called common when speaking of coloured golds, for the reason that it is about the lowest quality that can be conveniently coloured to look rich and beautiful. A slightly inferior quality (12½-carat) can be coloured, but 13-carat is about the usual kind employed in all respectable coloured-gold houses. In Birmingham a very large quantity of gold is weekly employed in manufactures of this quality.

Some firms manufacture nothing else. It is largely made into chains, lockets, pins, studs, sleeve-links, solitaires, pendants, bracelets, rings, brooches, and filigree ornamentation. In fact, almost every article we can mention has it in some part of its composition. If the reader were to take a walk down any of the principal streets of Birmingham, viz. New Street, Bull Street, or High Street, the vast majority of articles of coloured gold jewellery exhibited in the shops that met his eye would be of this quality, and marked as 15-carat fine gold. The retail purchasers are, of course, in most instances, ignorant of the true value of gold and the art of alloying; and some, on the representations of the shopkeepers, who often know no better, believe that they are buying full 15-carat gold of the proportion expressed in the Act of 1854. It is a difficult matter, too, even in this enlightened age, in which the secrets of the goldsmith's craft are freely and openly expressed, to convince them of the error of their belief. Some manufacturers profess to have secrets in the art of producing good colours for their wares; and there is, no doubt, a motive for this, namely, the producing a demand for the articles of special firms, well known for excellence of finish, over all others. To understand perfectly the art of alloying gold and silver is of very great importance, and an advantage to manufacturing goldsmiths, besides having a tendency to produce profitable results, more than any thing (if the practical part be understood properly) connected with the art of the goldsmith.

Twelve-carat gold is the best of the bright golds, and is so called to distinguish it from the coloured; although any of the qualities that are described in speaking of coloured gold may be made bright by a little variation in the mixture of alloy. The demand for articles in this gold is not at present of an extensive nature; no doubt because the finish of coloured gold looks more costly and beautiful. No gold inferior to 12-carat will colour to present that appearance which characterises the higher qualities. Twelve-carat gold finished bright has a fine rich sparkling appearance, and when the workmanship is good is very imposing; it is a good quality to work upon, being tolerably soft and ductile, as well as possessing good malleable properties. The quality generally manufactured is a little under the standard fineness, and therefore cannot be hall-marked. Gem, fancy, and other rings, when made of the full standard quality, bear the government stamp as a guarantee of its purity.

Ten-carat gold sustains all the characteristics of the former quality, both as regards facility of manufacture and finish; there are no hall-marks for this kind of gold, and it is very seldom manufactured fully up to the standard, unless specially asked for. A large quantity of goods is made of this quality in Birmingham.

Nine-carat gold is regularly manufactured into all kinds of bright goods, and this quality, when made fully up to the standard of fineness, is hall-marked. The demand for it is largely increasing. It is chiefly employed in the manufacture of keeper and fancy rings. A good trade has recently sprung up in the manufacture of solid gold chains of this class of gold. After all, the quality which is most extensively employed in every possible description of manufacture, is usually below this standard, probably it is about 8½ carats; and if alloyed according to the following table will stand the aqua test perfectly well. Nine-carat of the mixture of alloy we have given in the table, will stand more than ordinary treatment from the hands of the workman, and may be touched and removed from the annealing-pan while still red hot, without injury to any subsequent manipulation of it; it may also be quenched at any degree of heat in pickle or water, if any advantage is likely to accrue from it; but we strongly object to the continuous quenching of gold alloys at every subsequent process of annealing—partly because every time the metal is quenched in sulphuric acid pickle a portion of alloy in these low qualities is dissolved.

This improves the quality of the gold, by which the manufacturer does not receive any benefit, but is actually a loser. Moreover we shall see that, when we come to the processes of soldering, this pickling or boiling-out is perfectly indispensable.

Nine-carat alloys, if alloyed with too much spelter, will not present the characteristics we have just named in respect to treatment; if shaken or touched while hot, they are very brittle and difficult to work; consequently they take longer in working, and therefore the same quantity of goods cannot be produced in a given time with these alloys, as with those we have just described. The great point in the manufacture of gold articles should be to get the greatest amount of real work out of the smallest amount of material, so as to make the least possible waste or scrap for remelting; for this reason we say that the alloys which mostly tend to this object are the best for jewellers to use in their manufactures.

Eight-carat gold is sometimes used in the manufacture of jewellery, and is often styled 9-carat No. 2, in some of the workshops where this quality is somewhat extensively employed. In order tc stand the aqua test it must be alloyed with more

D

silver than ordinary 9-carat gold, and when finished appears rather paler to the eye; this may be a partial guide as to quality, but not always a sure one; if properly alloyed it works exceedingly well in any process of preparation, from the ingot bar down to the finished articles; but, of course, judgment must be used by the workman as to the proper periods for annealing; if this be neglected the gold will become hard and brittle, and, as the process of preparing proceeds, it will break and fall to pieces.

Seven-carat gold is generally termed common gold, and is about the lowest quality manufactured; it requires extra care in working, on account of the very large proportion of silver it contains, which increases the fusibility of this alloy. Care must necessarily be taken in annealing and soldering. The increased proportion of silver is requisite to enable the articles manufactured from it to stand the gold test of aqua-fortis. Gold chains of this quality are now very seldom made. It is mostly used by *Locket* makers in cheap work, where the backs and fronts are gold, and the edges, &c., are plated. The common alloys of gold have a much lower fusible point than those of a superior quality.

Pure silver has a brilliant white colour, and is the whitest of all the metals; none surpass it in lustre; and in hardness it ranges between pure gold and pure copper. It is more fusible than copper or gold, melting at a bright red heat or at 1,873° Fahrenheit. It is commonly used for the purpose of alloying gold in its pure state, but if too much be added it makes the gold pale.

Pure copper has a reddish appearance, and is the only metal of that colour; it is both malleable and ductile, hence it is used as an alloy for gold. In fusibility it stands between silver and gold. It is a very useful metal, a large number of cheap alloys being manufactured from it.

Composition is a mixture of copper and zinc, and is used by jewellers in alloying. Some of them profess to have secrets with regard to colour, which is produced by different proportions of the composition.

When it is necessary to form hard gold, this metal may be safely employed, although it will not be wise to use too much, about 4 dwts. to the ounce of fine gold being ample; if, as we have already observed, too much be added, it will make the gold brittle and unworkable. With less silver and more composition an alloy is formed equal in appearance to one of 2 or 3 carats higher, but it is very difficult to work, and after being some time in wear it changes colour. This alloy cannot be attempted in very inferior qualities as it will not stand the acid.

Spelter is another name for zinc, and is so-called because it is supposed to be deprived of its impurities. It is a bluish-white metal, highly crystalline and brittle; melting at about 773°, and at a red heat, rises into vapour. As it burns it is converted into a white flock-like substance. This is the protoxide of zinc, which is carried up in the current of warm air. The employment of zinc in gold alloys should be sparing, and must be added when the other metals are in a state of fusion, first heating it with the tongs over the crucible. Spelter does not harden gold, if used as we have recommended. It is generally purchased in cakes, and when required for use pieces are chipped off with a cold chisel.

We shall now give a table of the proportions of the various metals incorporated in the gold alloys used by jewellers:—

Table of Alloys.

23	carat,	½ part	copper,	½ part	silver,	23 parts	gold.
22	,,	1	,,	1	,,	22	,,
20	,,	2	,,	2	,,	20	,,
18	,,	3	,,	3	,,	18	,,
15	,,	6	,,	3	,,	15	,,
13	,,	8	,,	3	,,	13	,,
12	,,	8½	,,	3½	,,	12	,,
10	,,	10	,,	4	,,	10	,,
9	,,	10½	,,	4½	,,	9	,,
8	,,	10½	,,	5½	,,	8	,,
7	,,	9	,,	8	,,	7	,,
Compo.		16	,,	8 parts spelter.			

The above table represents the full standard quality of every alloy; if it be needful to make an inferior alloy, which is often the case in the manufacture of jewellery, the same calculation in respect to the inferior metals will do, but a small portion of fine gold must be deducted till it brings the alloy down to the value required.

We have been at some trouble in order to make our information complete, and have carefully arranged the following table:—

Specific Gravity Table.

Qualities.	Alloy.	Gold.	Total.
24 carat	None	19·5	19·5
23 "	·40	18·68	19·08
22 "	·81	17·87	18·68
20 "	1·62	16·25	17·87
18 "	2·43	14·62	17·05
15 "	3·55	12·18	15·74
13 "	4·29	10·56	14·86
12 "	4·70	9·75	14·45
10 "	5·48	8·12	13·6
9 "	5·88	7·31	13·2
8 "	6·32	6·5	12·82
7 "	6·86	5·64	12·5
Silver, pure	—	—	10·5
Copper, pure	—	—	8·96
Composition	—	—	8·37
Spelter	—	—	7·2

It is our intention to continue this matter a little further, so as to render these details as complete as possible for the workshop, in case the above differences in weight should not be understood by some. When a piece of work is desired of a certain size and weight, of a different quality to that usually worked up, the following table of weights will be found useful:—

Table of Weights.

Qualities.			Oz.	Dwts.	Grs.
24 carat of given dimensions will weigh			1	0	0
23	,,	,,	0	19	12
22	,,	,,	0	19	0
20	,,	,,	0	18	0
18	,,	,,	0	17	12
15	,,	,,	0	16	0
13	,,	,,	0	15	0
12	,,	,,	0	14	12
10	,,	,,	0	14	0
9	,,	,,	0	13	12
8	,,	,,	0	13	0
7	,,	,,	0	12	12
Silver	,,	,,	0	10	12
Copper	,,	,,	0	9	0
Composition	,,	,,	0	8	12
Spelter	,,	,,	0	7	12

These relative weights are sufficiently near for every practical purpose, and it is hoped, intelligible enough to be of assistance to such as deal with these valuable alloys.

The last-mentioned table will, it is hoped, prove of special service, not only to the practical goldworker, as a safe guide in the production of correct weights in the various qualities; but likewise to the manufacturer and the merchant, by affording them an easy method of estimating the value of an article required to pattern, in *any of the qualities* manufactured. For example, an article weighing in 9-carat gold 1 oz. would in 18-carat gold weigh 1 oz. 4 dwts.; thus showing conclusively that the extra quantity of raw material imparted to an article under the above conditions, must be taken into consideration when giving a quotation of cost. The principles which govern the above table, when fully comprehended, will be found both simple and advantageous.

CHAPTER IV

Melting and Rolling.

HAVING described the specialities of gold, and the qualities used in its manufacture, we have now reached a point very important and interesting to the jewellery trade; and we may as well state that it is our desire to go through a kind of apprenticeship in respect to the processes employed in the manufacture. We hope that the information thus afforded, besides being valuable to the practical workman, by giving him facilities which will result in the more successful performance of his work, will prove useful to the manufacturer also by imparting to him that with which he has been hitherto unacquainted. We shall lay most stress upon those processes of Art-workmanship and management, in which we venture to believe we have been more successful than most of our compeers.

In order to describe minutely the processes or methods of working with the precious metal, we shall commence with the first proceeding in the course of the manufacture, viz. the preparation of the alloy and its subsequent treatment in the crucible. The state of purity of gold and silver, when purchased from the refiner for the purpose of alloying, has already been sufficiently explained in this volume. The copper used is various. In the jewellery trade the refined grain-copper is commonly preferred, costing 2*s.* per lb., a prejudice existing against the employment of the bean-shot: but this is not altogether warranted, as bean-shot copper may be safely used in all the varieties of bright gold alloys. As regards the workable qualities of its alloys, they are all that could be desired, therefore we cannot understand this prejudice.

From an economical point of view its use is a saving, its cost being about £5 12*s.* per cwt., or 1*s.* per lb. In purchasing the materials for alloying, where a fair average trade is being carried on, there is an advantage in purchasing copper in large quantities; but in gold and silver the reverse is the case. Irrespective of the disadvantage of the cash lying idle, gold being always bought for cash, some of its particles are so fine and minute, that every time it is touched or moved about, some portion is sure to be lost; the portion may, perhaps, be very small indeed, but when we take into consideration the extremely valuable nature of gold in the above state, the loss in the course of a year may be something amazing. For these and other reasons which could be adduced, we recommend the purchase of gold at the time it is needed, and sufficient only for the purposes required.

In preparing the mixture of gold, silver, and copper for the crucible, care should be taken in weighing them accurately, in order to prevent improvement or deterioration in the qualities of gold constantly in use. In melting all qualities it is a wise plan to place the lightest of the metals to be melted at the bottom of the crucible—viz. the copper first, the silver next, and the gold last; by so doing the melter is more likely to get a perfect amalgamation of the metals, as the gold, being the heaviest, is sure to find its way towards the bottom of the pot. When spelter is employed it must not be put in until the other metals are melted; being of so volatile a nature, it would be all evaporated before the mixture of alloy was properly incorporated, consequently the bar of gold would fall short of its original weight, the quality would be improved, and the manufacturer would be unable to compensate himself without re-melting with an addition of alloy.

Plumbago crucibles are the best for all practical

melting purposes, and with care will last from twenty to fifty times; if new, a very small quantity of charcoal powder should be put into the pot with the mixture of alloy. This coats the surface of it, and prevents the metals from adhering to it. When the gold is at the point of fusion, fling on to it about a table-spoonful of pure and perfectly fine vegetable charcoal. The layer of charcoal which forms upon the surface of the gold in the crucible protects the mixture from the action of the air, which would refine the gold, by destroying some of the alloy. When perfectly fused, the mixture must be well stirred with an iron stirrer (consisting of a long round piece of iron sharpened at the point), which should previously be made red hot, to render the whole mass uniform in quality. The pot is then quickly withdrawn, and its contents poured into a suitable ingot-mould, previously warmed and greased to prevent adhesion. The warming of the mould is quite indispensable; but if made too hot, the metal on being turned into it will spit and fly about; besides incurring great loss of gold, dangerous results may thereby happen to the person in charge; the same remark applies when the ingot-mould is cold; therefore, this part of the process must not be neglected, but carefully attended too. The ingot-mould, we may state, is hot enough when it will just stand touching with the hand for a second or so. In nine cases out of ten, if the gold is properly heated in the melting and cast all right with the charcoal flux we have recommended, the working qualities in its subsequent treatment will be found all that could be desired for any purpose whatever.

When it is desired to produce very tough gold, use as a flux a table-spoonful of charcoal as before, and one of sal-ammoniac, adding it to the gold on the eve of melting; the sal-ammoniac burns away while toughening the gold, leaving the charcoal behind to perform the functions already indicated. The employment of the mixture of sal-ammoniac will bring the ingots of gold up bright and clear; it will also prevent them from splitting or cracking at the rolling-mill, and in subsequent working; if proper attention has been paid to it, the gold will then be found tough and pliable. This does not, however, apply to every kind of alloy, but it may be affirmed of those we have described, and can be safely and thoroughly depended upon.

The furnace used by most jewellers is the ordinary wind furnace, built of brickwork, which is admirably suited for such purposes; a size convenient for every requirement is of the following dimensions: eight inches square inside, and sixteen inches deep from the grate which supports the fire.

For producing tough gold, the employment of common salt as a fluxing agent is sometimes strongly recommended. There is not, however, much to be said for its use, as it produces a very liquid flux, and is not half so clean as the one we have recommended. In the casting, unless very great care is exercised, it runs into the ingot-mould with the gold, producing a brittle-like substance, and this forces itself into the bar of gold, the surface of which becomes irregular and full of holes; on this account alone, in preparing clean and smooth bars of gold, it is objectionable. The same may be said of borax, but that is still largely used in the jewellery trade for melting purposes. Nevertheless we are confident, from long practical experience (the result of many years' study and practice, during which time we have worked up many thousand ounces of gold), that there is no better flux than the mixture of *sal-ammoniac and charcoal*, for *every* possible purpose required, in the subsequent treatment of the different qualities of gold; and that for toughness, cleanliness, and producing good workable properties it cannot be surpassed.

In melting scrap-gold from the workshop, care

should be taken to see that it is quite clean, and free from organic matter, wax, &c. To effect this it is a good plan to heat the scrap in an iron ladle until all wax or grease is removed; this should be done before the workman weighs his scrap into the warehouse, and should be a special rule of every establishment. It has a great tendency (with other things of which we shall speak hereafter) to reduce the working loss which is almost unavoidable. This kind of scrap is best re-melted by itself, and the same flux may be employed as has been recommended for new gold; if the bar of gold should split in rolling, it is due to the presence of some foreign metal, such as lead or tin, or it may be iron or steel. Then remelt the bar with two parts carbonate of potash and one part of nitrate of potash (saltpetre); the saltpetre will draw the iron or steel into the flux, leaving the alloy of gold free. If lead or tin should get into the gold, very serious results follow—a very small portion being sufficient to split a large bar and render it totally unworkable and exceedingly brittle; when broken the grains appear close and pale. Bichloride of mercury (corrosive sublimate) is the best flux to use when these defects make their appearance; in the proportion of two parts charcoal to one of corrosive sublimate, when all will go right again.

Sandiver is also a very useful flux when iron or steel gets in the gold. Such gold, when re-melted, always loses in weight, some of the alloy being lost on account of the many small pieces of gold of which the scrap consists. This, of course, improves the quality; therefore, it is necessary, in order to keep the gold of one standard, to add some small portion of alloy, either silver or copper; but as the scrap may contain a little solder, copper will be the best to use. The following calculations may be relied upon for the different qualities:—

Table of Calculations.

Wet-coloured scrap,	3 grs. of copper	per	ounce
12-carat scrap	6	"	"
10 "	9	"	"
9 "	12	"	"
Hall-marked make no addition whatever			

All qualities of scrap should be well sorted and undergo the action of a magnet before re-melting, and the greatest care exercised in keeping every quality separate.

Sometimes in re-melting scrap-gold it is necessary to make some addition, either in fine gold or alloy, for the purpose of improving or reducing the quality. This happens when different qualities of goods are required on the spur of the moment, and it may not be convenient to procure fine gold at the time sufficient for the purpose; this is very often the case with beginners who have embarked in business with a limited capital, which may already be partially invested; to such persons the advice we now give may prove serviceable. There may be possibly existing at the time in the workshops, a large quantity of scrap of the regular quality; and if the proper rules for alloying, in reference to reducing and improving the qualities, were understood thoroughly, use might be made of it in the above direction; not only to the pecuniary interest of the man of business, but also to the advantage of all parties concerned. We shall be as simple and as concise as possible in our modes of calculation, and will employ the usual arithmetical signs. In preparing the scrap for reducing, great care must be taken in selecting it free from solder or other impurities, otherwise the calculation, as regards extreme accuracy, will be thrown out; and sometimes this is of importance, but more commonly speaking, when the quality is not for hall-marking, the difference likely to be made is of very little importance. The numeral 20 in the following tables will always be consonant, because it represents the number of pennyweights in an ounce of gold. The multipliers and divisors will be different, and will vary with the quality of gold required. As an example, suppose we want to find how much *pure gold* will be required to be added to 1 oz. of 9-carat scrap, in order to raise it to 15-carat gold, we should proceed thus :—

$$20 \times 15 = 300$$
$$20 \times 9 = 180$$
$$300 - 180 = 120$$
$$120 \div 9 = 13 \text{ dwts. } 8 \text{ grs.}$$

Therefore to every ounce of 9-carat scrap we shall have to add 13 dwts. 8 grs. of fine gold to make 15-carat gold. The divisor 9 does not represent the quality of scrap about to be improved, but is the difference between the quality manufactured and the numeral 24, which represents the number of carats in an ounce; consequently, when it is desired to improve the scrap, the divisor will always represent the difference between the quality *as improved* by the addition of fine gold and 24. When it is desired to reduce the scrap, the reverse will be the case; the divisor will always indicate the quality to be made. In order to prove the accuracy of the above mode of calculation, we will give the following proof :—

oz.	dwts.	grs.		£	s.	d.
1	0	0	of 9-carat scrap will be worth .	1	13	0
0	13	8	of fine gold @ 85*s.* 6*d.* will cost .	2	17	0
1	13	8		4	10	0

oz.	dwts.	grs.		£	s.	d.
1	0	0	of 15-carat gold is worth, with alloy .	2	14	0
0	10	0	" " .	1	7	0
0	3	8	" " .	0	9	0
1	13	8		4	10	0

Let us take another case as an illustration of what we mean. Suppose it is desired to reduce some scrap in quality, no alloy being suitable to be found in the alloy-book, we shall have to make a sort of guess-work, or haphazard calculation. If we adopt the system we are recommending, it will become very simple. To reduce 18-carat scrap in order to make 15-carat gold, we shall proceed as follows :—

$$20 \times 18 = 360$$
$$20 \times 15 = 300$$
$$360 - 300 = 60$$
$$60 \div 15 = 4 \text{ dwts.}$$

To every ounce of 18-carat scrap must be added 4 dwts. of alloy. This case clearly illustrates the difference in the divisor between reducing and improving the quality. If it is of importance to know how much mixture of alloy should be added to an ounce of fine gold in order to produce qualities of inferior standard, the numeral 24 becomes consonant, thus to produce 18-carat :—

$$20 \times 24 = 480$$
$$20 \times 18 = 360$$
$$480 - 360 = 120$$
$$120 \div 18 = 6 \text{ dwts. } 16 \text{ grs.}$$

Therefore, in making 18-carat gold, to every ounce of fine gold a mixture of alloy consisting of 6 dwts. 16 grs. must be added. The above examples represent almost every case, and any others which may arise out of them may be safely calculated, taking these as the basis or starting-point.

Practically, this system of mixing gold alloys presents a feature of considerable importance to manufacturing goldsmiths; where time and accuracy are valuable principles of business; as it possesses all the advantages of simplicity, correctness, and expedition combined.

To avoid misconception, and therefore, if possible, to prevent mistakes, by those adopting this system in the preparation of their various qualities, we have considered it desirable to extend our remarks, by giving a more comprehensive view of the principles which govern this method of calculation; because it may be assumed the numeral 120 divided by 9 produces 13 dwts. 3 grs. Now this is erroneous, as the following tables fully prove:—

$$480 \times 15 = 7{,}200$$
$$480 \times 9 = 4{,}320$$
$$7{,}200 - 4{,}320 = 2{,}880$$
$$2{,}880 \div 9 = 320 \text{ grs.}$$

$$
\begin{aligned}
20 \times 15 &= 300 \\
20 \times 9 &= 180 \\
300 - 180 &= 120 \\
120 \div 9 &= 13\tfrac{3}{9} \text{ dwts.}
\end{aligned}
$$

$$
\begin{aligned}
20 \times 15 &= 300 \\
20 \times 9 &= 180 \\
300 - 180 &= 120 \\
120 \div 9 &= 13{\cdot}333 \text{ dwts.}
\end{aligned}
$$

The first of these three examples is calculated in grains, the second in pennyweights and fractions, and the third in decimals; but in each calculation the effect is precisely the same, being equivalent to 13 dwts. 8 grs., as shown in our first example, and thereby proving most conclusively that the remaining 3 after division is not grains, but a fraction of a pennyweight; in order to reduce the remainder to grains multiply by 24, and again divide by the divisor 9, when the proper solution of the problem will be effected In all these examples, whether calculated in grains, fractionally or decimally, the principle is unalterable.

When the mixture of gold and alloy is properly incorporated (to effect which a good white heat is essentially necessary), it must be carefully cast into bars of gold, the sizes of which vary according to the branch of the jewellery trade in which they are used. Locket-makers usually cast their bars broad and thin, so as to get as large a surface as possible; and experience has taught the necessity of this, in order to avoid a large amount of waste in outsides and edges. Chain-makers generally cast those which they use long and tolerably thick, which when rolled, produce long strips of wire, and these are admirably adapted in every way to the art of chain-making. They are, perhaps, as much prized by the workman who operates upon them, as if he had the satisfaction of knowing that they were a part of his accumulated wealth.

The pouring of the gold into the ingot-moulds is an art which requires some little skill and practice. The flux floating upon the surface of the gold in the crucible, may be prevented from passing into the ingot-mould with the gold by using a thin piece of flat wood held in the left hand: poplar wood is the best, because it burns very slowly.

After the process of melting, the bars of gold should be accurately weighed, in order to ascertain how much has been lost in performing the work. If this operation should prove satisfactory, they must next be well filed upon the edges and corners to remove all loose and scraggling pieces, which would otherwise, in the subsequent process of rolling, be lost. After the completion of this latter process, the bars are again placed in the scales, and their weights entered in the mill-book, for the purpose of being sent to one of the rolling-mills to be rolled into sheets or wire, as may be necessary.

This is effected by submitting them to the action of large steel rollers moved by steam power. As the bar passes through, the rollers are pressed closer together by powerful screws; it is again passed through many times, with an additional pressure of the screw every time, until the gold has become hard and requires annealing. This process is performed by placing the metal upon a movable sheet of iron in a muffle, or oven, heated by flues; after this operation the bar is submitted to the same process of rolling, changing the rollers until the desired thinness is obtained. Such are the processes for the reduction of the bar into flats or sheets.

In producing strips of gold, previous to their manufacture into wire, the bar is first rolled to about No. 10 or 11 of the Birmingham wire-gauge, annealed, and then submitted to the action of a pair of circular, cutting-rollers, having a number of regular-sized grooves in each roller; the projecting portions overlap each other, so as to form knives or cutters. The size of the strips thus produced corresponds exactly with that of the grooves in the rollers. These strips may be severed from the bar with a pair of vice-shears, but it is not so clean and regular as the above method. The following table shows the cost of gold-rolling:—

Ozs.	s.	d.	Ozs.	s.	d.	Ozs.	s.	d.
3	0	6	39	2	11	70	5	2
9	0	9	40	3	0	71	5	2
10	0	10	41	3	0	72	5	3
11	0	11	42	3	1	73	5	3
12	0	11	43	3	1	74	5	4
13	1	0	44	3	2	75	5	4
14	1	1	45	3	3	76	5	5
15	1	2	46	3	4	77	5	6
16	1	3	47	3	5	78	5	6
17	1	4	48	3	6	79	5	7
18	1	4	49	3	6	80	5	8
19	1	5	50	3	7	81	5	9
20	1	6	51	3	8	82	5	10
21	1	7	52	3	8	83	5	11
22	1	8	53	3	9	84	6	0
23	1	9	54	3	10	85	6	0
24	1	10	55	3	11	86	6	1
25	1	11	56	4	0	87	6	1
26	2	0	57	4	1	88	6	2
27	2	1	58	4	2	89	6	3
28	2	2	59	4	3	90	6	4
29	2	3	60	4	4	91	6	4
30	2	4	61	4	5	92	6	5
31	2	5	62	4	6	93	6	6
32	2	6	63	4	7	94	6	6
33	2	6	64	4	8	95	6	7
34	2	7	65	4	9	96	6	8
35	2	8	66	4	10	97	6	9
36	2	9	67	4	11	98	6	10
37	2	9	68	5	0	99	6	11
38	2	10	69	5	1	100	7	0

Above 100 ozs. 6*s*. 3*d*. per 100 ozs.

CHAPTER V.

Coining.

THE finest or richest alloy of gold is employed by the gold-beater in the preparation of leaf-gold, and also by the artificer in artistic embroidery, massive ornamental work, and, in fact, in every work of art which can be improved in beauty by the addition of this highly-prized metal. The chief uses of leaf-gold have been already explained; therefore the next quality of fineness, to which we shall direct particular attention, is the national standard of value in this country—the circulating medium of exchange, or our coinage, the manufacture of which consists principally of sovereigns and half-sovereigns; and as the processes employed in this branch of metallurgy are instructive and interesting, we will briefly describe the work carried on at the Royal Mint.

First of all, the gold is sent from the Bank of England to the Mint in ingots of about 180 oz. each. Every ingot is tried by the Bank assayer, and also by the Mint assayer, in order to ascertain how much each bar differs from the standard (22-carats) of absolute purity or fineness. When the proper fineness has been ascertained, and the mixture of alloy prepared (which is now always copper), the total quantity of gold and alloy, in proper proportions, is taken and divided into lots of 1,200 oz., for the purpose of being melted into bars. The crucibles used by the master melter are about nine inches deep, by seven inches across the mouth; and are made of graphite or plumbago. These are well heated previous to the introduction of the ingots of gold and alloy, in order to prevent cracking or flying, which, should it happen, would be serious, when so large a quantity of metal had been added. To ascertain whether a pot is cracked or not, it is well to introduce a cold bar of iron and let it touch the bottom, when if any crack exists it will at once be visible. If the heating of the crucible has produced no ill effects, the bars of gold and alloy, which have already been prepared, are put in, and thoroughly melted, being finally well stirred with an iron stirrer; the whole mass is then poured into ingot-moulds, sixteen being placed side by side in a frame; the pot will hold sufficient metal to fill four ingots holding 300 ozs. each; consequently, four pots of gold will fill the whole of the ingot-moulds.

When the ingots have become cold, either by quenching or in the ordinary way, they are stamped with certain letters or figures, and two pieces for assay are cut from each. These two pieces are sent to different assayers, the result of the test being afterwards given to the Master of the Mint, and if found correct, the master melter has properly discharged his duty.

The sizes of the bars are about 24 in. long by 1·375 broad, and about 1 in. thick. When the Master of the Mint is satisfied as to the correctness of the test, they pass into the hands of the weighers. The scales employed are so strong, and at the same time so delicate, that a single grain will give the turn, even when loaded with 1,000 ozs.

The bars of gold, when thus accurately weighed, are rolled at the rolling-mill in the manner previously described, then cut into lengths of 18 in. each, again rolled until they are 1·829 inches in width, and 0·053 in thickness, being then equal to rather less than 2 in. in width, and 1-19th of an inch in thickness. This process must be carried out with great care, it being very necessary that all the bars should be of the exact size. The long flat strips of gold thus made are cut up into circular blanks of the size and dimensions of sovereigns and half-sovereigns, by the cutting-out presses. At the Mint twelve of these presses are in daily operation, the mechanism of which is extremely accurate.

Some of the blanks are taken occasionally and tested as to the proper size and weight, in order to see if the cutting-out presses are properly doing their work; and if they are correct, the cutting-out proceeds. Subsequently, about 720 oz. of blanks are taken and put into a bag, and carried into the weighing room, where can be witnessed at work several machines of truly marvellous beauty in construction, and of extreme accuracy. They weigh every blank separately, and even go so far as to separate the lighter or heavier coins, in a manner one would suppose the intelligence of man alone could effect—throwing those of the proper weight into one receptacle, those too heavy into another, and those too light into a third. These machines are fed by a workman, whose duty it is to place a pile of gold blanks in a kind of trough made on purpose to receive them, and then leave the machine to discharge the other duties attendant upon the process; the blanks fall one by one into little slits at the bottom of the machine. There are three provided, and to determine which of the three slits shall receive the coin, the machine previously weighs it. These machines will weigh

E 2

and separate about twenty-three blanks in a minute.

The heavy ones are afterwards passed through another wonderful machine, which files away the edges until the proper size and weight are produced. The next process is the testing, in order to ascertain whether there are any cracked ones among the bulk (a result of air-bubbles, caused through imperfect melting). A boy performs this operation. He grasps two handfuls of blanks, and rings each one on a block separately; by the nature of the ring or sound he can at once tell whether it is defective. If so, it is placed aside with the light blanks for re-melting. Those which are good are then submitted to the action of an edge-compressing machine, at the rate of about 700 per minute; where they are slightly reduced in diameter, and thickened at the edge. By this time they have become hardened and require annealing; after this is done, they are boiled out in diluted sulphuric acid pickle (oil of vitriol), in the proportion of one of acid to fifteen or twenty of water, and this produces a fine rich gold colour, by removing the black oxide of copper from the surface; after rinsing well in clean water, they are dried in box-wood sawdust. The principal part of the business then takes place—the coining—by which is produced the design upon the obverse and reverse sides; and also by which that beautiful bright colour to be seen upon a new sovereign is effected. The sulphuric acid pickle leaves a dead or matt appearance, and the parts which appear so bright when the coin is newly circulated are made so by the pressure of two highly-polished steel dies, one for each side of the coin; the blank being placed between the dies, one blow is sufficient to stamp the whole of it, including the two surfaces and the edge.

All the gold coins now issued from the English mint bear a milled or serrated edge, which is produced by ridges on the inside of the collar holding the blank, when it is being struck between the dies. This milling is so true that it would be a very difficult task for the counterfeiter to imitate it by filing. It is further adopted to afford an immediate detection of any attempt to deteriorate the coin by clipping or filing; and the greatest attention is consequently paid by the Mint authorities to this part of the work, in order to baffle the ingenuity of the would-be tamperer with the coinage. During the stamping the coins fall from the coining-press into a tray underneath, where they are again examined one by one, to pick out defaulters. The good ones are then removed to another room, where a small number of sovereigns or half-sovereigns are indiscriminately selected, weighed, and assayed, as a final test of the thorough accuracy of the whole manufacture. The sovereign, when completed and ready for circulation, is almost exactly ·868 of an inch in diameter; 1,869 sovereigns standard gold (22 carats) weigh exactly 40 lbs. troy weight; the legal weight of each can thus be very easily determined. Reduce the 40 lbs. to dwts., and divide the product by 1,869; if we then reduce the remainder to grs. and again divide, we shall have the weight of 5 dwts. $3\frac{171}{623}$ grs., which is equivalent to 123·27,447 grs., the exact weight of a sovereign. It is calculated that there are in circulation in the United Kingdom sovereigns and half-sovereigns to the value of 100,000,000 sterling.

As coins are subjected to considerable wear, through frequently passing from hand to hand, the amount of loss occasioned is worthy of some little consideration. Of course this amount will be in proportion to the length of time the coins have been in wear. To provide against this, the English Government allows a sovereign to be a legal tender till it is reduced not below 122·5 grs. (5 dwts. $2\frac{1}{2}$ grs.), the difference between this and the full standard weight being the remedy allowed by

English law for abrasion or loss by wear. Consequently, when English gold coins fall below this standard, they cease to be a legal tender. The depreciation of a coin depends upon its hardness, wearing much more when soft, and also upon the rapidity of its circulation. The above law, however, is not strictly carried out. The remedy for abrasion would be a little more than three-quarters of a grain for each sovereign, or decimally ·774 grain.

CHAPTER VI.

Manufactured Articles.—Locket-Making.

THE next branch of the subject, in treating of the uses of gold, we have to notice, is that relating to the jeweller, which includes the various works of art connected with the trade of a manufacturing goldsmith.

One of the first things that would be likely to strike the stranger in visiting a jeweller's workshop, would be the methodical manner in which it is fitted up. He would also probably observe the neat and compact arrangements provided for the workmen, consisting of convenient tables or benches for the easier performance of the work. The jeweller's board commonly provides sittings for four workmen, the outline of which is nearly half-circular; holes are sawn or scooped out from the semicircular side to form places for the requisite number of men, and these hollowed places, with their appendages, form what is technically termed the jeweller's "skin." This "skin" consists of a piece of leather fastened securely underneath the two arms of the board, and round the semicircle, so as to form a receptacle into which the filings or articles accidentally dropped by the workmen may fall; and also to serve as a convenient place for tools.

Many master-jewellers have now substituted iron pans or trays for these leather skins, which, in many cases, are better, as the lemel can easily be separated from the scrap. This is done by means of a small movable box provided in the bottom of the pan, with a perforated top, through which the lemel can at any time be swept by the workman; the lemel, to a considerable extent, where these trays are in use, being prevented from getting too much upon the tools; as a few seconds now and then, will suffice to sweep it through the perforated part of the tray into the box underneath. No contrivance of this kind is attached to the ordinary leather skin, and the lemel continually accumulating upon the handles, and in the crevices, of the tools (which are sometimes rendered moist through constant handling) is a source of inconvenience to the workman and a loss to the employer.

In the centre of this hollowed place there is secured, in the woodwork of the board, a small wedge-shaped, projecting piece of hard wood called the "peg;" and upon this the artisan performs all his work; and beneath this peg is the skin or tray of which we have spoken. Each workman sits at one of these peculiar-shaped places, and in close proximity to him is a bent gas-pipe, filed slanting at the mouth, and working upon a swivel. This is constantly burning, the flame being indispensable in the jeweller's art, for soldering purposes. These peculiar-shaped benches are generally arranged down one side of the workshop, and the heavier tools, lathes, rollers, draw-benches, &c., down the other side and middle; but where a separate shop can be provided for these latter, it is generally done.

We shall now endeavour to explain, from practical knowledge, the processes employed for producing modern jewellery of various kinds, comprising the personal ornaments of the rich, and such as is stored in the warehouses of the merchants and manufacturers who trade in it.

The qualities of the gold used in the manufacture of jewellery having been previously described, we shall at once proceed to allude to the manufacture of lockets, a branch of industry finding employment for a great number of hands; and, considering the rapidity with which orders are now executed compared with what they were a few years ago, an account of the work cannot, we think, fail to be interesting to the reader. A very large quantity of what are generally termed gold lockets consist of gold only on the tops and bottoms, or fronts and backs; and this is so delicate that it has to be strengthened underneath with base metal; in some cases it is as thin as No. 1 when doubled in the jeweller's metal-gauge. Being so thin, of course great care is required in manipulation, especially when the graver is being used. The rims are made of plating, as also are the loops and rings, the fronts and backs being all the gold they contain. These lockets are being made by the workman at about 1*s.* 3*d.* to 1*s.* 6*d.* each. This is, undoubtedly, caused by the low prices at which manufacturers find it necessary to sell them. The prices quoted above include everything incidental to the complete locket—plating, polishing, glasses, engraving, &c.—except the two blanks of gold to form the front and back of the locket.

To form lockets of this description, plain, oval, or other shaped blanks are cut out by the press: these are prepared in large quantities, and kept in stock ready for the different workmen to make use of at any time. The blanks, before going into the hands of the regular locket-maker, have to be stamped into shape: this is done by submitting them to the action of a pair of dies, which form the requisite design. The dies are strongly secured in the stamping-press, and the striking-up, as it is called, is generally entrusted to a jeweller's stamper, who performs the work at so much per gross.

These blanks being slightly raised, are now ready for the workman, who generally performs his work in a very dexterous manner.

We have as yet only spoken of the fronts and backs of lockets; but there are also the rims, rings, flats, and other parts, which we must now describe. These latter parts, as we have already stated, consist of "gold plating," and they are purchased in the form of wire from the plating warehouses. The rims are made by cutting the wire into lengths (the preparation of this will be referred to hereafter) suitable for the different sizes of the lockets required. They are made by boys, in large quantities, so that they may be ready to hand at any moment.

When the wire has been cut into lengths, the ends of the pieces are turned together and soldered, and afterwards shaped as desired upon a mandrel; they are then ready to receive the prepared gold parts. Each workman has a heap of fronts, backs, rims, &c., upon the board before him. He then begins to put the locket together; and it is almost marvellous to see how skilfully the operator handles his tools, and the rapidity with which the work is executed.

One of the most delicate operations to be performed in locket-making, is the preparing and fixing of the hinges, or joints. To do this properly and neatly is the aim of a good workman; but the appliances being numerous, the skill of the artisan is promoted. To adjust the hinges two rims are selected, care being exercised to see that they fit closely together, without which it would be impossible to make a nice-fitting joint. Small lengths of tube having been previously prepared, of different sizes suitable for hinges, the workman now takes a small round file (rat's-tail) about the size of the tube which is to form the joint, and makes a little groove with it in the centre of the edge of the two rims; this files away the substance of the two rims to where the gold fronts and backs go on; and the groove or hollowed surface is afterwards filled up by the hinge itself. It is then filed until the tube fits it nicely, when the proper length is cut off with a fine saw; a piece of steel wire is next put through it, and it is again sawn into three pieces. These pieces are then laid in the groove, and soldered, two pieces to one side of the rim, and one to the other; this is the work almost of an instant, so expert do the workmen become at this branch of the trade. The soldering of the hinges, to prevent filling, or tacking, requires great practical knowledge and judgment, in its execution; to the inexperienced, jeweller's rouge, or some whiting (a little of either), when put inside the tube, and where the saw has gone through, will prevent the solder flowing in those parts; but the most practical solderers perform their work without these precautions.

Having now performed the work of making rims and joints, the next process is the fastening on of the rings, which is a very simple operation, and can easily be effected even by a boy. A piece of steel wire (called in the trade a "spit") is taken, of the size required, and the rings wound upon it; this may either be done in the lathe, or at the peg: if the latter operation is resorted to, the spit must be held in a pair of hand-vices; the coil, or lap, as it is more commonly termed, is then sawn through on one side only, longitudinally. A large number of rings are thus very soon prepared; they are then closed with two pairs of pliers, and slightly filed at the joints. They are now ready to be soldered upon the rims, which is done either by securing them in their place with binding-wire, or by arranging them upon a slab of pumice-stone, in half-dozens or dozens at a time. This latter plan is certainly the quickest, when a proper piece of pumice-stone is provided for the purpose; a little pallion of solder is given to each, and a keen blast of the blow-pipe fastens securely a large number in a few minutes. The flats, and other parts of the inside of the locket, are prepared after the manner just described.

We now come to that part which completes the process of putting together, in these cheap lockets —viz. the adjustment of the fronts and backs to the already prepared framework. This is done with soft solder, and is performed in the following manner:—The flats of the rims, and the edges of the gold plates that are to come in contact, are slightly rubbed on the file, or stone, to provide a level and clean surface; the workman then takes up a back or front, and, with careful precision, secures it to a rim. This may be done with very fine binding-wire, or otherwise, as desired. When a quantity of these have been fitted, they are placed upon a bunch of matted wire (old binding-wire, and called the "devil"), ready to be soldered; a solution of chloride of zinc is then put round the part to be united, and also a few pallions of solder, when a gentle blast from the soldering-jet completes the operation. The better class of work, however, is hard-soldered, that being wholly composed of gold; but the processes of the metallurgy are similar to those we have described. The lockets, after being touched up a little by the workmen, are ready for the polisher, whose work we shall consider under another branch of this subject.

Common lockets have generally plain or engraved surfaces; but in the better class, the ornaments in the centre are raised, and diamonds and other precious stones are sometimes set in them; and in some cases also extend round the borders of the lockets. In order to vary the designs as much as possible, ornamentation is now produced by the "stamp," as well as by "hand;" and it is chiefly due to this advantage that the locket manufacturers are enabled to display such a variety of patterns. The parts made by hand are called settings, and are all "wrought," with the exception of the teething, this of late being more commonly performed by the press, instead of by the hand as formerly. These settings are placed upon the lockets according to the designs required, a number at a time, and then hard-soldered, a process which firmly secures them in their places. In the manufacture of *bright* gold lockets, where hard-soldering is adopted, silver solder is now always used. The process is performed in this way:—The parts to be united are made quite clean, free from grease or oxide; and a solution of borax being prepared by rubbing a piece upon a slate, to which a few drops of water have been added, the ornaments or settings are dipped into this solution, and at once transferred to their proper place upon the article in process of manufacture; and while others are being prepared in the same manner, these will have become dry. This operation tends to prevent moving during the process of charging, and also acts as a preventitive to rising in soldering; we may add that a little sandiver rubbed in the borax solution will prove an unfailing precaution against the latter. A quantity of very small pellets, or pallions, of solder are then cut, which, being picked up one by one on the point of a camel-hair pencil moistened in the borax solution, are put in their proper places, and the flame directed by the blowpipe from the gas-jet, soon unites the joints as firm as a rock.

The ornaments, or, more properly speaking, settings, which are to receive precious stones or other jewels, are placed upon the lockets, with their teeth uppermost, the gems most suitable to form the designs being put in proper order between them. The tops of the teeth are so bent or turned over, that they fully encircle the stone, and thus hold it securely in its place. This system is called "colleting," and by it, beautiful effects are often produced. The best method of setting, or the one most admired, is called "fancy setting." It consists in drilling holes for the gems, and then with the scorper hollowing away a portion of the metal around the holes to fit the stones, and also in the direction the gems are to extend; at the same time the bringing up of four little beads or caps is effected, which act as claws, and form an efficient security for each gem. This kind of setting, as applied to lockets, is very beautiful. We have partially described the duties of the "setter," and if he can perform the latter process satisfactorily for a first-class jeweller, he is considered a workman of no mean order; it is not at all unusual to meet with good collet-setters, who are also good makers, but a maker is very seldom met with who can fancy set. There is another method called Roman setting, but it is not applicable to this branch of the trade.

The processes adopted by modern jewellers

in manufacturing ladies' gem-rings, bracelets, brooches, seals, &c., are, in their general detail, analogous to those already described—certain parts being raised by the stamp, and others being wrought, or made by hand; these are all put together piece by piece by the workman, until the article is completed. A very good impression of a locket, or any other article with a flat ornamental surface, may be taken by the workman (and the design kept for future reference) in a few minutes, by wetting some note-paper with the tongue and smoking the article over a gas-flame; when it must be pressed upon the paper, and a perfect impression will thus be produced, fully showing the nature of the ornamentation, &c.; the impression can further be made permanent by drawing it through milk, and afterwards drying the paper.

It will now be necessary (in order to proceed step by step) to give some information respecting solders, which will enable the workman neatly to execute his work, for a great deal depends upon the solder, as well as on the skill of the artisan, in producing clean and invisible joints. Some jewellers know but little of the degree of heat necessary to melt the various metals and their alloys. As a table supplying this information will no doubt be welcome, the following is given of the standard metals:—

Daniell's Table.

Fine gold will melt at		2,016	deg. Fahr.
Pure copper	„	1,994	„
Fine silver	„	1,873	„
Pure spelter	„	773	„

The next table, prepared from Daniell, will correspond with the alloys we have previously given, and thus supply a want long felt by the goldsmiths; not only for the treatment in the crucible, but more particularly in the subsequent manipulation; whilst in the processes of annealing this table will also prove of some practical advantage, by showing that it is essentially necessary to vary the heat in some of the qualities to prevent scorching while they are upon the fire:—

Our Table.

23-carat gold will melt at		2,012	deg. Fahr.
22	„	2,009	„
20	„	2,002	„
18	„	1,995	„
15	„	1,992	„
13	„	1,990	„
12	„	1,987	„
10	„	1,982	„
9	„	1,979	„
8	„	1,973	„
7	„	1,960	„
Composition	„	1,587	„

This table clearly demonstrates the fact that

it is unwise to place metals upon the annealing-pan without careful attention being paid to them, when their points of fusion are widely at variance with each other. If a piece of 18-carat wire and one of 7-carat, of exactly the same description, were placed upon the pan in the muffle, without due regard to the above facts, and left until the 18-carat had acquired a good red heat, upon the withdrawal of the pan it would be found that the 7-carat had been overheated, and the nature perished, so as to render it further unworkable.

The list of silver solders as expressed below will in practice be found to answer admirably for every purpose with the alloys we have recommended. When using 7-carat or common gold, a very easy one is required; this has been considered, and every reliance can be placed on the solders here given, and their suitability approved, by their point of fusion to the qualities under manipulation:—

Silver Solders.

Description.	Fine Silver.	Copper.	Spelter.
Hard solder . .	16 parts	3½ parts	½ part
Medium solder .	15 ,,	4 ,,	1 ,,
Easy solder . .	14 ,,	4½ ,,	1½ ,,
Common hard .	12½ ,,	6 ,,	1½ ,,
Common easy .	11½ ,,	6½ ,,	2 ,,

Fusing Point.

No. 1. Hard solder .	. 1,866	deg. Fahr.
No. 2. Medium solder	. 1,843	"
No. 3. Easy solder .	. 1,818	"
No. 4. Common .	. 1,826	"
No. 5. Common easy	. 1,802	"

The fusibility of these solders will be a little higher than those given, because of the volatility of the zinc in melting, which increases the point of fusion when being used, for which allowance should be made. Any of them may either be used in pallion or filed into dust, as may be preferred. The former is more extensively employed by jewellers; and the latter by gold chain-makers, for which purpose it is more suitable, as it enables those who use it to get through more work in a given time. The pallion may be also used in the manufacture of chains—in fact, it is commonly preferred by curb-makers; and in the manufacture of Brazilian or snake chains its employment is compulsory. The object of zinc in silver solders is to increase their fusibility; it also, by its evaporation in the process, increases the strength of the joint by toughening the solder; but the use of too much is an obstacle in the way of the workman, and ultimately proves far from satisfactory to the purchasers of that class of jewellery: firstly, by the addition of too large a proportion of spelter to silver solders, they become brittle and partly unworkable, especially when the parts united with it have to bear a strain, as they break easily, and consequently have to be re-soldered. This may happen several times over; when this is the case it operates injuriously to the interest of the workman. Secondly, the above description in time eats away, and articles that have been soldered with it become disunited. We have seen chains, after having been some time in wear, sent to be repaired, without a particle of solder upon the joints. This was caused by the solder having contained too much spelter in the first instance; and even where this is not the case, the soldering places are liable to go black whilst lying in manufacturers' or merchants' stocks, if allowed to get damp or exposed to the acid vapours of their places of business; this kind, therefore, proves very unsatisfactory, and no possible advantage can be gained by any one from its use.

CHAPTER VII.

Solid Wire-Drawing.

ONE of the most important applications of gold is in connection with the art of chain-making; and there being in that branch of manufacture an unusually large amount of gold employed, it will be necessary to enlarge upon it, especially as it comprises the whole art of wire-drawing, the principles of which, when fully comprehended, are a source of assistance to the workman so engaged. When this wire-drawing, as applied to the manufacture of gold chains, is properly executed, there is every reason for the expectation of the best work throughout, at least so far as some patterns are concerned. In Birmingham wire-drawing is extensively practised, and that town is justly celebrated for it.

Perhaps it will not be out of place to give here a short history of it and a few facts bearing upon the process.

The malleability of gold must have been known long before its ductility, for we never read of the ancient gold-workers turning to any account this latter property. It has been suggested by Beckman, a German chemist, that gold and other wire were first formed by beating out the metal, and then cutting it into thin strips, which process is entirely borne out by Scripture, in the account of the preparation of the sacerdotal dress of Aaron, for which see Exodus xxxix. 3. Wire-work seems to have been rarely practised by the ancients, and their mode of making it was upon the anvil. It seems to be seldom mentioned in their writings; there is no allusion whatever to the *draw-plate*, the principal tool of the modern wire-drawer, even in later works upon the subject. The persons who fabricated wire by means of the hammer were termed wiresmiths. The introduction of the draw-plate for wire-drawing purposes, was made about the year A.D. 1350. It is said to be the invention of one Richard Archal, a Frenchman, but it was long before the ancient method of the hammer and anvil was entirely superseded.

In England wire appears to have been made by hand, or wrought, until the year 1565; at that time a Saxon (Christopher Schultz) came to this country, and introduced the draw-plate and its

F

applications for making iron wire, which had previously been introduced from the continent.

The alloys of gold for chain-making purposes should be exceedingly malleable and ductile, and the tougher the gold is, the better will it be able to stand the kind of treatment to which it will be subjected. According to the modern process, when it is ready for the wire-drawer, it is in the form of square strips, of the sizes Nos. 10, 11, or 12 of the Birmingham wire-gauge, unless otherwise ordered. The preparation of these strips has been explained when describing the process of rolling. The wire-drawer, in the ordinary performance of his work, submits them (after removing any rough surface left in the process of slitting) to the action of a pair of wire-rollers moving by hand power: these have nearly half-round grooves in them, and are diversified in size; during the revolution of the rollers, the grooves in the upper barrel meet those of the lower, so that when a strip of gold has passed through them, a piece of wire is at once produced almost round. This process is repeated until it has passed through all the grooves, the latter being regulated by screws; the gold has then become hard, and requires annealing: when this has been done the wire is pointed, and then comes the operation of the draw-plate, which usually consists of a piece of steel about 10 in. long, 1½ in. broad, and ⅛ in. in thickness. These plates are the best for all practical purposes, but others will do for small operations. They contain about 10 conical holes of different sizes, and following each other very regularly. By passing the metal through these holes successively, a wire of any size can easily be obtained. We are now speaking of round wire; but there are other kinds used by chain-makers, which will be considered in their order.

In the preparation of round wire, and also of some others, when different sizes are required in the manufacture of an article, it is advantageous to cut off certain lengths equal to the quantity of material required for it. During the process of drawing the gold, it is a very convenient method, and at the same time one which presents a great advantage to the workman, not only by enabling him to prepare the whole of his work at one time, which saves labour; but by giving him the opportunity to utilise the whole of his gold profitably if at piece-work.

By way of example, we will give a practical account of the matter, which will be well understood by the trade. If we were going to make a graduated curb Albert, the old plan would be to

F 2

draw down the wire until the largest or centre size was reached, wind off the links, draw it again to the next size and again wind off, and so on until all the sizes had been prepared. To wind the wire properly it would require annealing between every size, and to do this after every hole would be a continual source of hindrance to the workman. According to the method we suggest (and we believe we were the first to introduce it into the Birmingham trade), this inconvenience would be dispensed with, because we should draw all the wire first and so dispose of that branch of the business. This would be done in the following manner. Presuming there would be five sizes in the chain, that would be two inches to each size. When the wire had reached in dimensions the largest size, cut off a length of nine inches; afterwards cut off all the other wires in the same manner, as the drawing proceeds; nine inches of wire makes two inches of chain, consequently, in the above example, all the wires will be required of equal length; but when seven sizes are put in a chain, six inches will suffice for the first size, and seven inches in the subsequent ones. On a large scale a decided advantage is gained by this method, both in time and patience. Most other chains may be prepared upon this principle; and besides being found more convenient to the workman, a greater number of articles will be obtained out of the same material.

These wires are wound upon oval steel spits of various sizes, to form links, and afterwards, on being put into proper shape by the workman, become that well-known article, the "graduated curb."

The holes in the draw-plates are regulated when worn, by hardened steel punches of a conical form; they must not taper too suddenly, but gradually down to the point; if they are pointed too sharply they will leave no bearing on the draw-plates, the holes will pull out, and the wire will be very irregular in size, in some cases varying more than a size in one piece of wire; therefore the more gradual the taper of the punches the better, and the more certain will be the wire produced from them.

Wire is drawn by the wire-drawer into various shapes, the principal of which are hollow for jewellery and gold chain-work; these will be duly considered. Primarily the solid wires claim our attention, all of which can easily be prepared, far more so than the hollow ones, for the latter at times present features of great difficulty; and the best workman is often subjected to a good deal of trouble and annoyance in their manufacture.

Square wire is prepared in a similar way to round in the first process by the wire-drawer—the breaking-down; and afterwards, by submitting it to the action of the draw-plate; here the first difference in its form or shape commences to take effect. The plate through which the wire has to pass contains square holes instead of round, as in the previous case; these holes may be made of any size, regulating them by a steel punch, which, of course, must also be square. The exact size of the wire is obtained by knocking the punch into the plate from the back side of it, so as to open or enlarge one of the holes of the draw-plate, and afterwards by drawing the wire through it. When the holes are too large, the draw-plates are battered upon the front with a convex-faced hammer, and the punches applied from the proper side to regulate them, in the way just described; a bearing is thus produced upon the surface of the plates which protects the holes, and this renders the wire regular in size. The plates in use for these purposes being always soft, by constant wear and a continual alteration of the holes, the draw-plates will in time become hard and require annealing, after which process they should be allowed to cool gradually, by covering them with ashes.

Solid oblong and half-round wires, as well as

several other fancy wires, are all similarly prepared, with this exception, that each wire has its own draw-plate, corresponding exactly with the form required.

In the preparation of oblong and half-round wires it is usual to pass the wire through a pair of flattening rollers, so as to enable it the more easily to take the first hole of the draw-plate to which it is then submitted; by these means both wires are more quickly prepared. Oblong wire is sometimes made by square drawing, and then flattening it by the rollers; there is one advantage gained by so doing, namely, an oblong of almost any shape can soon be effected, and that without the use of numerous draw-plates of that pattern.

Hollow Wire-drawing.

The process of hollow wire-drawing is more complicated than that of solid, consequently, more than usual care is required in its production. Solid wire can easily be reduced in size by means of the draw-bench, a contrivance working with a windlass. In the case of hollow wire, it is commonly pulled through the draw-plates, by lapping it once round the person of the operator, and then swinging the body forward in the opposite direction of the draw-plate; this method prevents plier-marks, and also preserves the shape of the wire intact, by dispensing with the use of draw-tongs, and this is of some importance in fancy wire-drawing. Another good plan is to run the wire, as it leaves the draw-plate, upon a drum, turned with a perpendicular handle, which is secured to it horizontally. The wire is drawn through the draw-plate and wound upon the drum by a rotary action; whilst for facilitating its removal, the drum is slightly conical in form. After this proceeding, if the wire remains unfinished, it is at once transferred to a skeleton frame, corresponding with the outer dimensions of the drum, and revolving upon a perpendicular pin; the process is repeated as many times as circumstances permit, or until the proper size is produced.

The wire requires annealing repeatedly in all the processes of drawing, but experience and judgment will dictate how often it should be done; some golds will stand much rougher treatment than others, therefore, there are no fixed periods for this proceeding.

In preparing hollow half-round wire, the process commences according to the principles already laid down for round wire. Small half-round wire, in hollow may be first drawn two sizes smaller in the round than required when finished in half-round; that is to say, if the half-round were required to finish 18 size in the jeweller's metal-gauge, it should be drawn to 16 round wire in the same gauge, and subsequently flattened to size 3 by passing it repeatedly through a small pair of jewellers' flattening rollers; it is then well annealed, and greased ready for the application of the draw-plate. The gold (being now in the form of a flat narrow strip or riband) is pointed by cutting it with a pair of hand-shears, a little from each side of the strip at the end, so as to form a point for admission into the draw-plate; the wire is then pulled through a round hole, large enough to admit the point of a small steel punch, which acts as a doomer to the wire in its passage through the hole of the plate. One half-round plate is next taken, and the wire drawn successively through it until the desired size is made; though usually two holes are sufficient to obtain good half-round wire of the hollow kind.

Fancy wires of other descriptions are prepared in the first instance exactly as we have described; but there is a change of the process in finishing. Oblong wire would only require a very slight draught in the half-round draw-plate, just sufficient to make a set upon the edges of the wire;

it is then consigned to the oblong draw-plate. In its passage through the latter, it is supported by a small tapered punch of the same dimensions as the aperture in the plate; this produces a wire exactly the same shape as the aperture, only hollow instead of solid. Oblong wires will require to be of the same size in the round, in order to produce a tolerably sharp impression when they are finished.

Hollow square wire is made by taking two oblong wires and drawing them through a plate containing square holes, between which is inserted a round piece of steel wire, which keeps them in their proper places, and renders their impressions sharp and equal. Square wire must be two sizes larger in the round than is required in the square, as it finishes two sizes smaller in the latter; this is everywhere the case in the preparation of plain square wire. These observations also apply to fluted wire made in hollow; and other fancy wires may be obtained by carrying out the general rules here laid down.

Ornamental wire is produced by the flattening rollers bearing various patterns of artistic work, all of which have been originated in the modern school of goldsmiths. The subsequent processes of manipulation are precisely similar to those already given as regards general detail; and include the chief features in the art of wire-drawing as it pertains to the precious metal.

For the purpose of making gold chains any of the above wires may be taken and wound upon pieces of iron or steel, of different forms and shapes, according to the contemplated design; the iron or steel being removed, the coil of gold is sawn longitudinally, to form links, and these when put together in a multitude of ways, and soldered, complete the operations of the person called the "maker." Chains, like all other work, require to be repeatedly boiled in diluted oil of vitriol during the processes of soldering, in order to remove the black surface, or oxide, which is continually presenting itself; and which would operate injuriously in any additional soldering, if not removed, as the borax forms itself into a hard, glassy flux, and so becomes objectionable.

In concluding these remarks upon the manufacture of gold wire, we will give an explanation of the method adopted by "plating" manufacturers, but as this is not essential to our present subject, we shall only briefly refer to it.

CHAPTER VIII.

Manufacturing Processes.—Gold-plating.

GOLD-PLATING, like gold itself, consists of various qualities, and is valued at from two to fifteen shillings per ounce. It is commonly prepared in the following manner: a bar of gold of the quality desired and one of metal (composition or gilding metal will do) are taken and made perfectly flat under the stamp or press; when this is done, the two bars are cleansed, by scraping or filing the surfaces which will subsequently come in contact; this process is of importance, and must be continued until every particle of black is entirely removed. Of the two, filing is to be preferred, because the file-marks have a tendency to assist the complete amalgamation of the metals. Some thick borax is next prepared, and well rubbed over the surfaces. The two bars are well secured together by strong iron wire, and are then ready to be united into one. There being several methods of effecting this, it will be necessary to describe them. First, the process known as *sweating* should be explained. The two metals, when perfectly secured, are placed in a "muffle," and made red-hot; the heat is increased until they are almost at the point of fusion. At this period the operation requires very careful watching, and when the metals have become united, the whole is withdrawn, and the amalgamation is complete.

The second and best method, the one also, as far as we know, most adopted, is that of joining the two metals together by soldering. The whole process previous to the soldering is exactly as before. The metal bar being larger in every respect than the one of gold, the extended surfaces, therefore, of it provide a support for the pallions of solder, which are placed along one side and half-way along each end. The whole is then subjected to a powerful heat in the muffle, and the solder flows between the bars, thoroughly cementing them together. When this is seen to run down the side and ends not charged, the operation is complete, and the gold can be rolled, hammered, or otherwise manipulated.

For the purpose of making 9-carat plating, such as is used by locket-makers, a bar of 9-carat gold would be selected. The relative thickness of the two metals would be, perhaps, in the proportion of

1 to 20, and would cost about *2s.* per oz. To produce wire, flat, tube, &c., the metal is all rolled flat, when it may be stamped, spun, cut into strips, suaged, or doomed, and thus made into wire, or otherwise attenuated to any extent. In any of these processes the gold will follow the reduction of the baser metal, still retaining to a considerable extent the relative proportion of thickness between them. In the case of wire-drawing, we may remark that the holes of the draw-plates must be closely watched, in order to detect and remove scratches, &c., which would be a serious obstacle in the manufacture of good gold-plating.

Round wire-plating is made by cutting flat strips from the rolled metal, then by suaging or dooming, and afterwards drawing them until the outer edges meet. A thin riband of pallion solder may then be placed inside the joint and cemented, when the surplus solder must be removed; a continuation of the drawing process will render the wire fit for every purpose that may be needful.

Some gold-plating, however, is left with the joints of the wire unsoldered. In using wire of this kind much care has to be exercised, in order to prevent the joint being seen on the surface of the work, which would spoil the sale of it. With this class of goods the process of polishing is a very delicate operation, and must not be entrusted to an inexperienced workman.

Leaving this branch of the subject, we shall now extend our remarks in the direction of those processes which come immediately after the making of the articles, the first of which is polishing; and this will only be dealt with as it applies to the manufacture of *real* gold jewellery. No doubt, those who manufacture plated wares will glean sufficient information from the description here given, to be of some service to them.

Polishing.

Polishing is usually done by girls at the lathe, with a circular brush made of stiff bristles, and revolving upon a horizontal spindle. The brush finds its way into the small interstices of the work, and, if skilfully employed, does not injure the most delicately-constructed articles. All polishing is commenced in the first instance by rubbing down, or smoothing the surface of the work, with some kind of hard material, which entirely obliterates all file-marks, all roughness of workmanship, and other imperfections left by the maker. The substance employed by the polishers in effecting the above object, is a mixture of pumice, emery, and crocus, prepared with oil to the consistence of a thick paste, and applied in very small quantities to the revolving brush and also to the work. If the work is required to be very finely polished, after the first coarse marks have been removed, another mixture must be used, consisting of finely-powdered rottenstone and oil: this preparation removes the polishing-marks produced during the first operation. A special brush must be used with the last mixture. If a higher degree of polish is required, still finer materials must be employed, but such is very seldom the case in the jewellery trade. Touching the work upon the buff, to which a little rouge and brown candle-grease have been added, after the former processes have been employed, produces a high degree of polish. In fact, the whole process consists in entirely removing scratch after scratch, until nothing in the shape of marks is visible to the naked eye.

Some kinds of jewellers' work have to be exceptionally treated, on account of the extreme delicacy of make. The Water-of-Ayr stone is very commonly employed by jewellers in polishing. The inside of rings is polished upon a "chuck," tapered down almost to a point; and the application of a small portion of cotton-wool to hold the mixture makes an effective polishing-tool. Threads are also somewhat largely used in this process;

for the inside of the links of chains they are highly advantageous, and, indeed, cannot be surpassed. The work should be well boiled in diluted sulphuric acid, in the proportion of one part of acid to twenty parts of water, previous to polishing; so as to render it quite clean, and, being bright at the commencement of the latter process, it will continue so throughout; a slight rub now and then with a piece of cotton waste will remove the grease enveloping it, and thus inform the workman as to the necessity of continuing the operation. When the polishing is completed the work is washed out in a hot solution of soda, soap, and water, and dried in warm boxwood sawdust. The common washing soda is used on account of its cheapness, its cost being about 2*d.* per lb.; and 1 oz. of it to a pint of water will be found in almost every case sufficiently efficacious.

Enamelling.

Enamelling is much practised in this country, and as the application of this art to jewellery heightens its beauty, a few details connected with it may be necessary to complete the account of the various processes employed in the production of the jeweller's work. The artistic work of the goldsmith is also considerably enhanced by the use of enamel; and much skill and taste are absolutely requisite on the part of the workman, not only in the mechanical processes, but likewise in the preparation and arrangement of his colours, in order to produce the highest possible hue or tint. In fact, it is almost requisite that he should be an artist as well as a workman, to properly carry his craft to perfection.

It has been much more extensively employed since the year A.D. 1800, owing to the discovery of gas. This, and as a consequence, the use of coke, have given rise to improved appliances, rendering the operation less costly, and easier to perform. The extent of the patronage which the art has received has also tended to this result.

We shall refrain from going into the history of ancient enamelling and painting as it was formerly practised in Italy, where art study was almost a fundamental principle of education, and confine ourselves to simply giving an outline of the mysteries of the craft, and its adaptation to the present school of enamellers. Our remarks, therefore, being purely descriptive, are more particularly intended for that class of gold-workers which we shall call the "uninitiated," or *non-practical* in this art.

It is almost impossible for a good gold-worker to

be also a good enameller; yet it is necessary that the former should understand in some measure the principles of the craft of the latter.

Enamels are vitreous or glassy substances, used by metal-workers for producing various designs for useful or ornamental purposes. They are of two kinds, opaque and transparent, and have certain conditions to fulfil, viz. they must preserve a hard glassy appearance after fusion; they must adhere very firmly to the gold; they must fuse at a temperature below that of the substances to which they are applied; they must be insoluble in water and the ordinary acids, and remain unaffected by the action of the atmosphere; lastly, they must stand annealing and colouring, without becoming injuriously affected.

Enamels as applied to metals have a transparent colourless base, called fritz, or flux, and when required for use a colour is readily given to it by the addition of metallic oxides, of which the following formulas have been selected as the most useful:—

Fritz No. 1.

Red lead	.	10 parts
Flint glass	.	6 "
Saltpetre	.	2 "
Borax .	.	2 "

Fuse this mixture well in a clay crucible for

some time, then pour it out into a jar of water, collect the residue and afterwards reduce it to a powder in an agate-ware mortar, and preserve for future use.

Fritz No. 2.

Metallic tin .	8 parts
Metallic lead .	4 „

Fuse this composition in an iron ladle at a dull red heat; carefully remove the oxide which will form upon the surface, taking care also to obtain it quite free from the pieces of metal which have escaped oxidation, and reduce as before to a fine powder. Then take of this:—

Calcine . .	4 parts
Silica . .	8 „
Saltpetre . .	2 „
Common salt .	2 „

Well mix and partly fuse in a clay crucible; the fewer number of times this is fired the firmer it will be

Fritz No. 3.

Broken crystal goblets . .	12 parts
Calcined borax . . .	4 „
Glass of antimony . .	2 „
Saltpetre	1 „

Melt this mixture after the manner recommended for No. 1. Break up and again melt, as this flux improves by repeated meltings. The above enamel fluxes are admirably adapted to form the bases of enamels for gold-work. They may be made more fusible by increasing the proportion of borax; and by the latter substance the fusibility of all enamels may be increased at pleasure; but too free a use of it is an obstacle to the work of the artist.

Fritz No. 4.

Flint glass powdered . .	16 parts
Pearl-ash	6 "
Common salt . . .	2 "
Calcined borax . . .	1 "

Let these ingredients be well melted together, and afterwards finely broken into powder, and preserved ready for the additional colouring mixture of enamel.

Fritz No. 5.

Silicious sand . . .	12 parts
Calcined borax . . .	12 "
Glass of antimony . .	4 "
Saltpetre	1 "
Chalk	2 "

Mix and fuse as before explained, grind into very fine powder and re-melt; this operation may be judiciously repeated several times. We have only at present described enamels, and given directions for the bases of them; variety of design in colour is produced by the addition of some metallic oxide, which effects the change according to the kind employed. These oxides should be used as sparingly as possible, because some of them will not stand the chemical process of colouring or even boiling without a bloom coming over them. A good black enamel may be made by taking the following ingredients :—

Black Enamel.

Fritz or flux No. 5 . . .	14 parts
Peroxide of manganese . .	2 ,,
Fine Saxony cobalt . . .	1 ,,

Blue Enamel.

Fritz or flux No. 4 . . .	24 parts
Fine Saxony cobalt . . .	5 ,,
Saltpetre	1 ,,

Red or Crimson Enamel.

Fritz or flux No. 3 . . .	8 parts
Purple of cassius	1 ,,
Or red oxide of copper . .	1 ,,

White Enamel.

Oxide No. 2	1 part
Fine crystal	2 ,,
Peroxide of manganese . .	$\frac{1}{16}$,,

Green Enamel.

Fritz or flux No. 1 . . .	36 parts
Oxide of copper . . .	2 ,,
Red oxide of iron . . .	$\frac{1}{16}$,,

Yellow Enamel.

White lead	2 parts
White oxide of antimony . .	1 „
Sal-ammoniac	1 „
Alum	1 „

For the last-mentioned, pound each of the ingredients separately in a mortar and well mix together; then carefully submit them to a heat sufficient to decompose the sal-ammoniac (chloride of ammonia); this colour can be tested in the melting, and will do when the yellow is properly brought out.

Enamels may be made deeper in colour by a further addition of oxide, than that given for producing the respective tints. For instance, if a very intense blue is required, add half a part of zaffre to the other ingredients. For black the same of protoxide of iron, zaffre, or black oxide of copper; but the latter is not so good as the others. For red, the red oxide of copper may be employed; and in yellow, the oxide of lead must be used. For green the protoxide of iron, and oxide of chromium may be sparingly added to the transparent flux.

Enamels may be prepared and kept ready for use by grinding them in an agate mortar, and then placing them under water in a covered vessel. Or, if preferred, they may be preserved until required, in the lump, as they are formed after the crucible operation; if the last-mentioned plan is adopted, then they must be broken with a rather sharp-faced hammer, and pulverised by means of the aforesaid pestle and mortar. When this has been done they are well washed in clean water, and this washing is continued until all extraneous matter has entirely disappeared. They are then ready for use.

The work which has to receive enamel has to be specially prepared: this is done in the following manner:—The pattern desired is first drawn on the work by the graver; the groundwork or part to receive the enamel is cut down very evenly, and this helps to heighten the effect; in the case of transparent enamels the groundwork should be extremely smooth and bright. After the work has been well cleaned by washing in a hot solution of soda, soap, and water, and dried, the enamel is applied—in very delicate cases with the point of a pen, in others a knife or spatula may be substituted with advantage; the work is then fired, and the enamel is laid on again as many times as required.

When the enamel is sufficiently fused the surplus part is rubbed off, the article is rinsed, and again fired in order to close the pores. Great judgment is required with regard to this operation, as too long an exposure to the heat of the furnace would completely ruin the entire work. Different shades of colour require different degrees of heat, and a knowledge of this can be acquired only by continual practice; such knowledge, however, is of the highest importance, because in some of the lower qualities of gold, the fusing point of enamel is so very near that of the gold that there is great danger of fusing the one along with the other. As we have said before, when the workman finds himself beset with these difficulties, a small addition of borax to the enamel will remove these defects in the operation.

Opaque colours require a slower and longer-continued heat than transparent ones, because the base generally contains lead, tin, or antimony. In transparent colours a sharp quick heat is most suitable, which must be proportioned to the extent of brilliancy required.

Opaqueness may be given to black enamel by heating the work to a dull red after it has passed through the usual process of cleaning: the oxide which forms upon the surface being black, imparts a kind of darkness to the colour.

In the case of transparent enamels, the ground-

G

work must be clean, smooth, and quite bright; the grooved surface being commonly run over with a polished, half-round scorper, to make the effect more intense and beautiful, the latter quality depending to a considerable extent on this being properly performed.

By varying the alloys of gold a great alteration may be made in the brilliancy of enamel; for example, in transparent yellow and green, the alloy of gold should be rather pale; in the case of red, the reverse should be the case.

The vertical lapidary's wheel is now much used by the artificer for the purpose of removing the surplus enamel; and by the application of wet emery it is rendered clear and smooth: this is much quicker and better than the old method. It is finished upon the buff by an application of putty-powder (oxide of tin), as it is both smoother and cuts faster than most other polishing mixtures. In England the enameller's is a separate and distinct craft, and is altogether an art in itself; never having been found to answer well where tried by ordinary manufacturing goldsmiths, the designs and colours having in their hands too much of sameness, when compared with those produced under other circumstances. The enameller, to take high rank in the art, must have some knowledge of designing, engraving, and chemistry; he must likewise understand the alloys of gold and their points of fusion, and the effects of colouring the work; he must also be tolerably conversant with the nature of the workmanship that is continually coming under his charge; and all this knowledge may be considered quite sufficient to raise the art to a distinct branch of study and practice.

In closing our remarks on the preparation of enamels, colours, and fluxes, and their mode of application to gold alloys, we desire to say that the rules or directions here given have been selected from very high authorities in the trade, and we trust they will be found equally serviceable to those desirous of gaining information concerning enamels and the art of enamelling. The exact work cannot well be described, and thorough success is to be achieved only by the exercise of good taste, and by long-continued practice and attention to the craft.

Where diamonds and other precious stones are employed as well as enamel, work pertaining to the latter is performed first. Engraving, chasing, colouring, and lapping, are all subsequent processes of the goldsmith's art.

CHAPTER IX.

Engraving and Chasing.—Engraving.

THE art of engraving on stone and metals by incised lines is so ancient that we cannot trace the historic period when it was not practised; suffice it to say, that among the collections of antique art in the British Museum, there are numerous examples of engraving, the work of the ancient Egyptians and other nations, executed on fine marble and also on precious stones. Besides, we know that engraved stamps or seals were used as official signatures in the very earliest times, for which we have only to refer the reader to the first books of the Holy Scriptures. Again, during the wanderings of the Israelites in the desert, we read that Bezaleel, of the tribe of Judah, and Aholiab, of the tribe of Dan, were set apart specially for the purpose of "devising and executing curious works in gold, silver, and brass, and in cutting of stones to set them, and in carving of wood," for the service of the tabernacle of Moses; and it is also written that God "filled them with wisdom of heart, to work all manner of work of the engraver, and with knowledge of all manner of workmanship of the cunning workman" (Exodus xxxi. 1—6).

The process of engraving is of ancient origin, and is one in which the fine arts and the workman's skill are equally brought into operation. The making of images, some of which existed in the time of Abraham, was a work of great antiquity, though they consisted merely of rude outlines on flat surfaces. This may claim to be the nearest approach to engraving of which we have any knowledge. In the middle ages, *niello* engraving held an im-important place among metal-workers; it consisted in making fine incisures on works of gold, silver, copper, &c., and filling them with a black enamel, and was called working in *niello*—a process which had a very important effect. This invention is ascribed to a native of Florence, who was deservedly celebrated for his genius and skill in the art, at the period of which we speak—the fifteenth century. To the same artist, whose name was Maso Finiguerra, is given the credit of having employed copper plates for engraving from which impressions were subsequently taken; and he also tried printing from engraved metal plates in this way.

Immediately the discovery became known in Italy, other goldsmiths and artists followed Finiguerra in his new handicraft, and the art of engraving was soon extensively practised. Throughout the sixteenth century it was considerably improved, and the skill of such artists as Botticelli, Marc Antonio Raimondi, and Benvenuto Cellini, the celebrated Italian goldsmith (who was called the prince of gold-workers), did much to raise the fame of the Italian engravers to a high standing, and to bring the art to a greater pitch of public appreciation than it had ever attained before. At first it was usual in Italy, Germany, and elsewhere, for the same person to prepare the design and afterwards engrave it; but afterwards, when the art became more mechanical, the two branches of it were divided: and, strange to say, that method has been somewhat extensively practised down to the present day.

It would be interesting enough to inquire into the history of the art, and dwell upon the progress that has been made down to our own time; but our present observations being limited, we shall avoid a lengthened description and come at once to the period of its introduction into England for commercial purposes; this will carry us about one hundred years back; and we wish it to be borne in mind, that the engraving of writing was the only branch of the art that had arrived at anything approaching excellence up to that period of time. This is fully proved by numerous specimens of mediæval work to be seen at the present day.

A great and powerful impulse was given in England to the art of wood-engraving by Thomas Bewick, who led the way to that success which has since crowned the efforts of its followers in our own country. To William Hogarth is due the credit of being the founder of the modern English school of painting; but our present mission being unconnected with that art, as such, we shall now proceed to point out its application to the useful arts, especially to gold jewellery. The honour is also given to Hogarth of being the founder of the present school of gold-engravers; but it was left to others to develop the art, and to them is due the present exalted position of the craft—principally to one Draper, a London apprentice, who was long familiarly known as the "father of engravers." One of the great aims of Draper was to make those who were under his tuition more skilful, if possible, than himself, a characteristic rarely found in the modern school of practical goldsmiths; but then we will not say how far the workmen themselves are to blame in the matter.

The trade is much indebted to Draper for improved methods of sharpening the gravers; and various other introductions of his have considerably aided the workman by simplifying the appliances, thus rendering the art more simple and its effects more beautiful.

For more than one hundred years engraving has been more or less practised for trading purposes in England. Notwithstanding this, however, it is by no means common to meet with a first-class workman; for, to reach this point, he must be an artist as well as a mechanic. This is not perhaps imperatively necessary to the ordinary practice of the art; but, as the embellishments produced on works of jewellery by the graver are added for purposes both artistic and ornamental, there is ample scope for the display of a considerable amount of knowledge as well as skill in the execution of his task. It will at once therefore be perceived that the engraver, to become a high-class workman, should not only have a natural ability for design, and a tolerably correct idea of the different periods and styles of ornamentation, but must also be possessed of great taste and judgment, as well as a delicacy of touch and acquired patience, to ensure reputation and success.

The process, or *modus operandi*, of the engraver

is as follows:—The workman, for the most part, uses only the ordinary *burin* or lozenge-shaped graver invented by Draper, together with several small gouges and needles for scooping out hollows or making very fine tracery, a sharp-edged scraper similar to a small three-square file sharpened at the point, for removing the burr raised by the graver, and a Turkey-stone upon which he sharpens his tools. He also uses a kind of cement, in which he secures the work previous to its manipulation, consisting of a mixture of Burgundy pitch, plaster-of-Paris, resin, and beeswax in the following proportions:—

Burgundy pitch	4 parts
Resin	4 "
Plaster-of-Paris	2 "
Beeswax	2 "

Place these articles in an earthen pipkin, or other suitable vessel, and melt carefully, stirring the mixture well until thoroughly incorporated; then pour into a vessel of cold water already provided; when the mass is cool enough to touch with the hands, it should be pressed, rolled, and kneaded together, in order to discharge the water contained therein. Should it turn out brittle, return it to the pipkin, and add more beeswax; put it through the same process as before, and work it well together, for the more it is worked the better it will be for use. When the proper degree of elasticity has been obtained, it is then ready for use, and any surplus mixture may be placed aside for a future time. In common engraving a portion of this cement is fixed upon various-sized blocks of wood, to which it strongly adheres by heat. The article to be manipulated upon is affixed to one of these, and embodied in the cement; and when properly set, the block is fastened in the vice, and the engraver performs the task allotted to him.

Best work is engraved in a somewhat different manner. The article is secured to a little stand, which moves upon a ball placed in a leathern socket, and fastened to a handle or other suitable piece of wood; the ball having a double rotatory action, the workman is enabled to bring it into any required position.

The engraver has only the eye to guide him in the various devices of his art, and as the result depends upon the skill of the operator, that eye should be a pretty correct one. Good light is very necessary in engraving; gaslight being extremely tedious and trying, globes, filled with water, are used, which, being placed between the workman and the gas-jet, steady the light, and throw it more clearly upon the work.

The articles are taken from the cement by gently heating them. The cement adhering to them may be removed by spirits of turpentine, or by heating and boiling out; but most jewellers object to the latter, their reason being, that it destroys the sharpness and brightness of the engraving; whether so or not, it is usually done in preparing for the chemical process of colouring. The brightness may, however, be preserved by a good coating of borax to the engraved parts.

Chasing.

Chasing, like engraving, to be performed well, requires considerable knowledge and practice; unlike engraving, however, the ornamental devices produced upon the surface of the work are all raised or embossed, and are effected in the following manner :—

The method of the chaser for one kind of work, is to go over the article with suitable tools, consisting of various-shaped punches, a large quantity being kept in readiness, of different sizes and patterns. These, on being applied to the surface of it in proper order, and tapped with the hammer, produce a slightly-raised figure, corresponding with that of the punch. If these punches have well-executed designs upon them, their impressions will be strikingly sharp and clear. Chasing is resorted to a great deal for solid work, and when effectually done it gives it a very artistic appearance; when applied to gold chains of this description, they look rich and beautiful. Much of the work of chasing on common or cheap articles of jewellery, such as scrolls, leaves, &c., is in imitation of engraving. The chaser, in order to give life and effect to the design he has in hand, should have a real artistic taste and feeling, as it is generally to his judgment that the matter is left. In performing his task, he takes a kind of wooden bowl, and fills it with cement; this is then fitted into a suitable leathern socket, and placed upon a strongly-fixed table, by which means his beautiful manipulations are performed with interesting effect.

There is another kind of chasing, the work produced being almost a facsimile of stamping by the press, but utterly devoid of the roundness which it produces: the hammer and the punch imparting a crispness and sharpness of design, if skilfully treated, not to be equalled by any other method.

Chasing appears to have been known to the old masters, for Benvenuto Cellini is said to have practised the art with wonderful skill and precision. A design may be rendered more distinct after the pattern has been greatly brought out in relief, by simply matting the ground. This plan was adopted by Cellini, and performed by him as follows:—A highly-hardened piece of steel was taken and broken through with one sharp blow of the hammer, when, if the break was even, and the texture or grain regular in the composition of the steel, an effective matting-punch was at once produced. This matting-tool appears to have been greatly used by the mediæval gold-workers in their processes of art-manufacture.

Articles of jewellery which have passed through the various branches of workmanship connected with the "making department" satisfactorily, are next transferred to the hands of the "electro-gilder," who deposits upon their surface a very thin film of pure gold, by means of electricity. Electro-gilding being a distinct branch of business, and usually carried on in premises apart from those of the manufacturing goldsmith, we shall for the present refrain from going into the subject, at least so far as concerns the general details of the process; being an entirely separate art, it requires different treatment. However, we may just explain the process in a few words. A solution of cyanide of gold is prepared in cyanide of potassium, and heated either in an enamelled saucepan, or stoneware jar, placed inside a pan containing water. The gold solution should not be allowed to boil, acting best at about 160° Fahr. To produce this heat the outer solution, when it is employed, must be boiling. The galvanic battery is next brought into requisition, and when ready for use, an "anode," consisting of a plate of pure gold, is fastened to the end of the wire issuing from the carbon or other negative element of the battery, and dipping into the preparation; the articles to be gilt are hung on the wire issuing from the zinc of the battery, and upon immersion in the solution, a film of pure gold will be almost instantaneously deposited upon them. The articles should be scrupulously clean, otherwise the operation will not take effect, and the solution becomes spoiled.

CHAPTER X.

Solders and Soldering.—Hard Solder.

PROPERLY speaking, solder is employed for the purpose of uniting the edges or surfaces of metals less fusible than itself, by means of heat; it may, therefore, be justly defined as a metallic cement used to unite different substances together. In connection with jewellery the pieces of material and the solders which join them together should agree as nearly as practicable in hardness and fusibility; for it is always the safest plan to employ the hardest solder, which the material in course of manufacture will possibly bear. This is nowhere more apparent than in the manufacture of gold chains, *particularly those of the curb pattern.* There are many varieties of gold solders, of different degrees of softness and hardness; which qualities are produced by the addition of the more fusible metal, silver, in variable proportions to the gold itself. It is customary with most jewellers to prepare their solders from the alloy of gold to which they are afterwards to be applied, many having secret methods proportioning them.

Coloured gold solders may be made by taking one part of fine silver to four, five, or six parts of alloyed gold, according to the quality and the degree of hardness required. These should not be made too poor in quality, for if they are, they will not colour properly. The more common forms of solder have been amply discussed in another part of this volume, together with their mode of application to the goldsmith's work. Great cleanliness is required both in regard to the solder and the surfaces of the work which are to be united together; otherwise, however excellent the solder may be, no junction can take place. For the use of those who prefer making their solders from unadulterated materials, we have compiled the following table, having fine gold as their basis:—

Coloured Solders.

Description.	Fine Gold.	Fine Silver.	Copper.
Best solder . .	12½ parts	4½ parts	3 parts
Medium solder .	10 ,,	6 ,,	4 ,,
Common solder .	8½ ,,	6½ ,,	5 ,,

These solders may be rolled flat and cut with

the shears or press into "pallions;" or if preferred, filed into dust, their suitability being adapted to either process. Throughout the whole of this treatise we have purposely omitted mentioning anything concerning the uses and applications of "soft solder," a term which has no reference to either the softer or harder solders of the same material of which we have been speaking; but to a totally different solder altogether, commonly called in the jewellery trade "soft tommy." Perhaps it would have been more correct, and we should have been better understood, if we had defined the former solders, of a more fusible nature, as "easy" in order to distinguish them. The time has, however, now arrived when we should say something concerning this "soft tommy."

Soft Solder.

It is called *soft* partly because it is used to unite much harder substances than itself, and partly because it can be applied to finished work without changing its colour, the melting point being so very low compared with the others of which we have previously spoken. It is largely employed by country jewellers and watchmakers; but in the manufactory it is almost scorned, and is one of the greatest drawbacks and troubles practical workmen have to encounter in dealing with *job-repairs;* it so adheres to the gold when once applied, that it is with the greatest difficulty it can be eradicated; and then sometimes it is even at the expense of the gold itself, into which it penetrates so deeply, that the slightest application of heat causes the gold to become perishable. Coloured articles cannot be re-coloured with this solder on them, neither can articles of jewellery be "*hard-soldered*" without its previous entire removal. And to do this is a very difficult task indeed, inasmuch as there are no methods known as yet, in the trade, whereby it can be removed effectually from the different qualities of gold. To supply this desideratum, we have long set ourselves the task, and we have now succeeded in introducing a plan into the trade, which will act as an effectual destruction of the evil; by this method, which we shall explain hereafter, soft solder can easily be removed from any quality of gold, silver, &c.

The composition of soft solder, and the exciting liquid employed in its application, have a prior claim on our attention, as we believe such information to be interesting and useful. The following is the best for all purposes connected with the jewellery trade, care being taken to procure the materials as pure as possible; if this is omitted it is liable to be bad; take—

Pure grain tin	. .	2 parts
Pure lead	. . .	1 „

In melting this composition, caution must be exercised so as not to overheat it; the process may be conveniently performed in an iron ladle, instead of the common crucible hitherto employed in preparing the other solders; and, in order to keep the mixture as near the same proportions as possible, the lead, which has a higher fusing point than tin, should first be melted, and the tin afterwards added; first heating it by holding it over the ladle (or other vessel employed in the operation) previous to its introduction, so as not to chill the lead. Lead fuses at a temperature of about 612° Fahr., and tin at a temperature of about 442° Fahr. When the two metals have become properly incorporated, the facility of which can be increased by gently stirring, the mixture must be withdrawn from the fire and poured either into a small ingot for rolling them flat, or cast into strips by pouring along the grooves of an old grate; for this latter purpose, it should not be poured from the ladle until it is beginning to cool a little. This may easily be ascertained by taking a piece of paper and dipping it into the heated mass, when, if it does not ignite, the mixture is in a proper state for casting. Dross, and other organic matter upon the surface, may be kept back from mixing with the solder, by the timely application of a piece of wood, held with the left hand to the mouth of the ladle. Even in this operation good solder can only be produced by careful attention to these principles. In soft-soldering, an entirely different stimulant to that employed in hard-soldering has to be used; this we shall designate as—

Soft-soldering Fluid.

This fluid is well known to all jewellers, but it bears various names in the different workshops, such as "monkey," "fake," &c.; its true chemical name, however, is chloride of zinc, and it is composed of a mixture of hydrochloric acid (spirits of salts) and metallic zinc, in the following proportions:—

Spirits of salts	2 parts
Metallic zinc	1 "

This solution is employed to dissolve or prevent oxidation of the surface of the joints about to be united, and it also acts as a stimulus to the flow of the solder; of course the joints should be quite free from dirt or grease, otherwise it cannot perform its proper functions. One of the best ways of preparing it, is to procure an earthen pipkin, and put into it two and a half ounces of spirits of salts and one ounce of metallic zinc in small pieces. The action of the acid upon the zinc at first will be energetic; the latter will become dissolved, with an evolution of hydrogen gas. When the zinc has dissolved, or the effervescence has partially ceased, the temperature may conveniently be increased by placing the pipkin with its contents upon a sheet of iron over a gas-jet; the extra half-ounce of spirits of salts will allow for loss by evaporation when this plan has to be resorted to. Sometimes it will be found necessary, especially when the acid is not good, to increase its temperature in order to effect its thorough saturation, for the more neutral the mixture the better it acts. The solution may be allowed to settle when sufficiently acted upon, and the supernatant liquor poured from the sediment into a bottle ready for use. This mixture or preparation will keep any length of time in a corked bottle. When this is employed in soft-soldering iron or steel, the addition to it of a small portion of powdered sal-ammoniac is a great improvement; a quarter of an ounce to the proportion of solution given above, will form a very good mixture; a tougher and more durable joint is produced by it; in cutting up small links by means of steel cutters, we have found its use a wonderful acquisition.

Dissolving Soft Solder.

Generally speaking, old work, which has to be repaired, re-gilt, or coloured, contains soft solder, the result of being mended by inexperienced persons; all this must be removed or destroyed before the articles can be properly repaired. It is a general belief among workmen that annealing and boiling out will destroy it, but it really has a contrary effect, the heat thus given tending only the more closely to amalgamate the solder with the gold. We have often tried to remove the solder after the annealing process by scraping and filing, and have always found that it had penetrated so deeply into the gold, that it would be utterly impossible to eradicate it by any such means. One of the common methods of treating this class of solder in the workshop, is to remove whatever you can by means of the scraper (which consists of a three-square file sharpened at the point), and then to place the article in tolerably strong muriatic acid for some time. Nitric acid is a much quicker way, but it cannot be safely applied to articles of inferior qualities of gold, as the acid would act upon the alloy of which they are partly composed; but for coloured gold it may be used with advantage and safety. From a long practical experience in the matter of soft solder, we have arrived at the conclusion that there is no better way of treating it than that which we are about to point out. Before, however, describing our hitherto secret method of treatment, it is desirable that we should explain (for the benefit of those workmen who are continually meeting with this kind of solder in their daily work, much to their annoyance) another system for its removal; one, we believe, solely practised by ourselves in Birmingham, for we have never yet met with a person who knew anything about it. The solvent employed was a mixture of muriatic acid and crocus (jeweller's polishing material), and prepared as follows: To eight ounces of muriatic acid add one ounce of crocus, and well shake it, in order that it may become perfectly mixed; of this mixture take one ounce, and add to it four ounces of hot water, place it in a pipkin, and keep up the heat by means of a gas-jet; put the articles containing the soft solder into it, and soon the desired result will be achieved.

But the plan most to be recommended, because the best of all we have been enabled to bring to bear upon this subject, is one which occupied us a long time, both in its consideration and accomplishment, and may therefore be safely applied to all classes of work, irrespective of quality. It can be adopted in the case of silver goods if desired, and that without any injurious effect whatever, whilst the time it takes to do the work is reduced to the minimum.

The destruction of the solder under this plan is effected as follows. Take—

Proto-sulphate of iron	2 ozs.
Nitrate of potassa	1 ,,
Water	10 ,,
	13 ozs.

Reduce the proto-sulphate of iron (green copperas) and nitrate of potassa (saltpetre) to a fine powder, then add these ingredients to the water, and boil the preparation in a cast-iron saucepan for some time; afterwards allow the liquid to cool, and in doing so it will shoot into fine crystals; if any of the liquid should remain uncrystallised, pour it from the crystals and again heat it, when, on cooling a second time, it will all have become crystallised. The crystallised salt should then be taken and dissolved in muriatic acid (spirits of salts), in the proportion of one ounce of salt to eight ounces of acid. Now take of the latter preparation one ounce, and add it to four ounces of boiling water in a pipkin, keeping up the heat by the means already stated. In a short space of time the most obstinate cases of soft solder will be cleanly and entirely removed, and without the work changing colour, if these instructions are properly carried out in preparing the mixture, &c.

CHAPTER XI.

Various Processes of Colouring and Finishing.—Dry-Colouring.

BEFORE entering upon an examination of this process, by which the surface of alloyed gold is changed into a rich and beautiful yellow colour; presenting, in goldsmith's work, a strikingly characteristic and most pleasing appearance, we desire to express the hope that we are not laying ourselves open to the charge of betraying trade secrets, our aim simply being to render a service which will prove useful to jewellers generally, as well as to manufacturers and workmen, by endeavouring (from a practical point of view) to explain in detail the real nature of a process little understood, and one which enriches and puts a finish upon their work.

Colouring, to the goldsmith, is strictly a trade term, and means, the giving of colour to an article after every other process of workmanship has been completed, and it is restricted by him to this particular process, which is one entirely chemical in its nature; its effect is to give to gold of inferior standard all the appearance of fine gold itself. This appearance is not an imaginary one, nor is it a mere superficial coating of the surface with gold of a higher quality, similar to gilding; but a peculiar and exact process of removing the base or inferior metal from gold articles, and leaving a film of gold behind of a deep rich colour, which no other process can equally effect. The simple fact is that gold-colouring is an effective process for refining the whole surface.

It is now about sixty years since coloured gold was first introduced into the English market, in its manufactured state as an article of commerce. At that time, and previously, the English gold-workers were "bright-workers" only. The goldsmith's work of that period had a red-looking appearance, very similar to the now well-known *Albion gold* in point of colour; the finish produced then was differently effected from that of the present day, being due solely to polishing; and upon the artificer in that branch, depended the beauty and excellence of finish which the work possessed. Articles of this description which are met with in the present day, are designated as articles made with the old red gold.

It has been said that the goldsmith who, by submitting his work to a chemical preparation, first produced a colour never before obtained by any process, was a Frenchman. Since the introduction of the art as a French invention, it has seen many changes,—both English and German,—not only in the mode of its application and the shades of colour produced, but also in the qualities of the gold operated upon.

There are two methods of colouring gold, called respectively the *dry colouring* and the *wet colouring;* the materials employed are nearly the same in all cases: they are—

1 part of salt
1 part of alum
2 parts of saltpetre

Dry-colouring cannot be performed upon gold inferior to 18-carats. We shall give several processes for wet-colouring, with their respective qualities of gold, as arranged and practised by ourselves. But we now proceed to the details of the process of dry-colouring, and shall give our information in a methodical manner, in order to be the more plain and intelligible, and shall describe the various operations generally employed, upon each of which depends failure or success. Among those that take precedence will be found the—

Original Process of Dry-Colouring.

This process for colouring superior articles of gold has been extensively practised by goldsmiths; it is not so complicated as many, and therefore may be performed with less skill. This is decidedly the original one; it requires the following materials:—

Nitrate of potassa . .	8 ozs.
Common salt . . .	4 "
Alum	4 "
	16 ozs.

The mixture should be reduced to powder and placed in a colour-pot, or common earthen pipkin, and allowed to dissolve slowly; this should be done over a fire that can easily be regulated, a gas furnace being the best for the purpose. The pot need only be large enough to give the work full play without allowing it to touch the bottom or sides, which would mark the articles dipped. It should be sufficiently filled with colour, so that when it rises it would come to the top. While dissolving, the mixture should be well stirred with an iron stirrer; it will then rise, and the work must at once be suspended in it by means of fine silver or platinum wire, and kept in continual motion until the liquid is about to sink in the pot, when the work must be taken out and at once immersed in clean muriatic acid pickle, which will remove the adhering colour. The colour in the pot will rise again after the withdrawal of the work, and of this opportunity advantage must be taken for a fresh dip. For plain work, generally two of these dips will be sufficient, but for hollow work three will be necessary. No description can give the exact time or explain the incidents connected with colouring; sometimes it will be produced as quickly again as others, and this knowledge can be acquired only by actual practice.

In this process there is not so much danger of spoiling the work as in the subsequent ones we shall refer to, for so intense a heat not being required, it can safely be left in the mixture for longer periods. Moreover, if preferred, the quenching directly after the stated periods of withdrawing the work from the colour, may be dispensed with altogether. The articles may be removed occasionally to ascertain if the mixture has operated sufficiently, and when this is made evident, they should be allowed to cool gradually, and afterwards immersed in perfectly clean sulphuric acid pickle, which will remove the adhering flux. After this is done, the articles must be rinsed in a weak solution of soda or potassa, then washed in hot soda and water, and finally rinsed well in clean bòiling water and placed in clean warm boxwood sawdust to dry. Articles coloured by this process may be burnished if deemed necessary; but the above mode of permanently finishing seems to have been formerly practised and to have found favour with many.

London Process of Dry-Colouring.

This process of colouring is far superior in point of richness to wet-colouring; it cannot, however, be employed for gold of inferior qualities. The new standard of 18-carats can be subjected to the action of the mixture successfully, and this is about its utmost limit. It is performed in the following manner. Take—

Nitrate of potassa	8 ozs.
Common salt	4 „
Alum	4 „
	16 ozs.

Reduce these to a fine powder in a wedgwood-ware mortar, and well mix together; then take a blacklead or iron-colour pot, about four inches high, which place in the fire upon a forge, or in a gas-furnace, and make red-hot. This may soon be done if placed upon the forge, by blowing with the forge-bellows; then put the above mixture into the pot, and thoroughly well fuse, stirring it with a thin iron rod. The heat given cannot be too strong, but it must be very carefully watched, and advantage taken of the proper opportunity for the immersion of the work. When the mixture is properly fused it will begin to assume a brown-yellow flame; when this yellow flame presents itself, the preparation is quite ready for the reception of the work, which must be suspended in bunches upon fine platinum wire and dipped into the mixture for a few seconds only, when it must be instantly withdrawn and plunged into boiling nitric acid pickle; if the exact colour required is not then produced, another dip, and sometimes a third may be necessary (especially in hollow work), to give the articles a fine rich appearance. The quenching in nitric acid removes any colour that may adhere to the work; but unless it is dried each time between the subsequent dips, the colour will fly about. This is caused by the articles being immersed wet, and the scald or burn from the mixture is particularly prominent. The drying out between each dip is not only tedious, but if minute portions of sawdust are left in the interstices of the work, the result of a second immersion would be little black patches upon the surface of the articles, considerably impairing their colour. In performing this latter process, it is advisable to wear an old glove to save the hand during manipulation. In colouring in this way it is always imperative that the operation should be quick, whereas in wet-colouring time is required. The gold lost by this method is very trifling, and it is therefore altogether unnecessary to preserve separately the spent colouring-mixture and dipping-acids; they may be thrown into the waste water-tub, or, if otherwise desired, into the floor-sweep. We shall have occasion hereafter to speak of another method of dry-colouring which we have successfully employed, so will now proceed to explain the modes of

Preparing the Work.

Before submitting the work to the action of the colouring preparation just described, it should be very carefully examined, in order to detect and eradicate marks or scratches; and this part of the process should not be overlooked, as it is of great importance in dry-colouring; in fact, the work cannot be too highly polished. This process has been already amply explained. Afterwards the work will require to be well washed out in a hot solution of soda, soap, and water, and dried in clean boxwood sawdust. According to one of the methods of preparation, it is then taken and covered with a layer of borax, which is best used for this purpose by taking it in the form of powder sufficient to complete the operation, and making it into a thick paste with water. The work may then either be dipped into this mixture or brushed over with it, and heated upon a clean fire until it turns nearly black, when it may be placed aside to cool; then boiled in clean diluted sulphuric acid pickle; rinsed well in clean water, and finally dried as before.

A very excellent plan, and one we have found to answer better in preparing the work for dry-colouring than the above, is to well buff it upon a soft piece of felt, such as is used by lappers in putting that exquisite finish upon *bright* gold chains. This must be done after the washing out subsequent to the polishing. When a high degree of brightness is produced by this means, it will require to be again washed out; for perfect cleanliness is of the utmost importance in carrying out this process, as well as the minor ones. Everything prepared in this manner takes an exceedingly high and bright colour, and is characterised by its general richness. Old work, or work to be re-coloured, must be annealed before the process of polishing, and carefully all stones, &c., removed to avoid injury to them, in any of the operations attendant upon this or any similar proceeding. The following are the different modes of

Finishing the Work.

After the proper colour has been obtained and the work removed from the nitric acid dipping solution, it should be rinsed in a very weak solution of potassa made hot; in order to neutralise the acid upon it, which otherwise might be the means of the colour becoming inferior after a time. It is then again rinsed in boiling water, and dried in clean warm boxwood sawdust, which should be as fine as possible, and which must on no account whatever be allowed to char or burn, or the beauty of the colour will be impaired. A camel-hair pencil is a tolerably good instrument for removing traces of sawdust from articles so finished; and it is of the utmost importance that the work should not be marked or scratched during the processes of colouring and finishing. This kind of finishing is much admired by many, although burnishing is greatly preferred by others. This is done by rubbing the whole surface with tools suitable for the different classes of goods, which comprise various-shaped steel and agate burnishers; when any of these best suited to the work, are dipped in a solution of weak ale, or soap and water, repeatedly, and applied skilfully to all the surfaces of the work, a fine rich and brilliant colour will be the result.

New Process of Dry-Colouring.

Superior articles of gold as regards quality, may be made to assume a beautiful deep colour, possessing all the appearance of fine gold itself, by immersing them for a few seconds in the following mixture, which must, however, be carefully prepared. To effect this, take—

Sal-ammoniac . .	4 ozs.
Saltpetre . . .	4 "
Borax	4 "
	12 ozs.

Reduce them all to a fine powder and well mix together; the preparation may then be treated exactly as those before recommended, with the exception that dilute sulphuric acid should be employed for dipping, instead of nitric or muriatic. For dry-colouring the solder used for the articles must be good; and the mixture of alloy of which they consist should have a preponderance of copper, the proportion of two parts copper to one part silver being a very convenient and useful amalgam to employ.

Some gold-colourers perfer simply to anneal, and boil the work in aquafortis pickle only, in preparing it for colouring. No doubt this is a good plan, but it produces a dead appearance; the main object to be attained is thorough cleanliness, and this to a considerable extent depends upon the intricacy or simplicity of the work in hand. The simplicity of the modes of preparation which we have described are preferable, especially the one of buffing the work previous to its immersion in the colour-pot; as thorough cleanliness is first obtained, and a subsequent brightness imparted, which is not lost in the colour produced upon the work. We have invariably found a richness of colour to result, unattainable by any other means; and we know further that it is always practised by an eminent London firm of goldsmiths. The brighter and cleaner the work, before submitting to this process of dry-colouring, the richer and more beautiful will be the colour effected by the chemical manipulation of this important art of the goldsmith.

Wet-Colouring.

In dealing with the, comparatively speaking, minor process—which, however, is much more extensively employed—commonly known in the trade as "wet-colouring," it will be best to inform the reader concerning the first, or theoretical principles, and then their useful application to this beautiful art, so as to render the information more perfect as regards practical utility.

Formerly it was an established principle, that to every ounce of work to be coloured there should be one pound of colour, composed of the following ingredients:—

4 ozs. of salt
4 ozs. of alum
8 ozs. of saltpetre.

Here it is evident that there was much misconception prevailing, the main supposition being that the amount of colour required should be strictly in proportion to the amount of work *in weight*, and corresponding with the proportions we have given. Now this idea is erroneous. It is not in proportion to the weight of work that the colour should be taken, but to the amount of surface presented to the action of the colouring mixture. For example, half-a-dozen solid gold chains might weigh as much as a dozen hollow ones, and yet the solid ones can be more effectually coloured in half the mixture in the same time, because of the difference of surface in the two "batches" of work, and the quicker action of the colour on plain surfaces. Therefore, the above rule is clearly wrong in practice.

Formerly, before the common qualities of gold articles were chemically treated for the purpose of imparting a fine rich colour to them, the processes employed were French. The original process of wet-colouring could not be used for a lower standard of gold than 16-carats, but now any quality above 12-carats can be coloured, and we have actually coloured 11-*carat gold;* the process, however, is a very delicate and skilful one, and one that could not be adopted from a monetary point of view. Since the adoption of this beautiful French art, numerous improvements have been brought to bear upon the subject, both from English and German workmen, and we may now almost consider that it has arrived at the point of maturity and perfection. It has extended gradually in the direction of the lower qualities until the supposed utmost limit has been reached; and in that direction the aims and successes of our own workmen have not been behind those of the foreigner. There are various methods employed by different firms, almost every one having a special mode of mixing, and thus a particular shade of colour is given tc the manufactures of each, according to taste or instructions; and the distinctive feature introduced is then considered a speciality of manufacture of the firm practising it.

On the first introduction of this art it was imagined that the presence of fine gold suspended in the colouring mixture would facilitate its action; accordingly, plates of that material were suspended with the work, in the colour, and the workmen were sometimes charged by their employers to give the articles an extra dip or two into it, in order to increase the richness by a thicker deposit of pure gold. By others 18-carat gold wire was always used to sustain the work whilst colouring by the wet process. Happily for the trade, all these conflicting ideas are dead and gone.

The ingredients employed in wet-colouring are all powerful agents in the dissolution of the baser alloy upon the surface of gold articles submitted to their action, and while dissolving this they have also a weaker action upon the gold itself; therefore this colouring should not be carried too far. The correctness of these remarks is fully borne out by the proportion in weight lost in colouring, being greater in proportion as the quality becomes lower. We believe that by very skilful management it is quite possible to utilise a portion of the dissolving gold again; for we have ourselves coloured the commoner qualities with a loss of only three grains to the ounce. This we have done repeatedly, and our opinion is to some extent corroborated by the quickness of colouring produced by the application of old colour, and the small percentage of loss sustained from the work. And further, if this old colour is taken after having been several times employed, the amount of gold recoverable will be found to be very small indeed. To show that the gold dissolving from the surface of the work operated upon has an inclination to deposit a percentage of itself upon the same work again, we may mention that we have deposited a thick coating of fine gold upon the platinum wire with which we suspended the work whilst colouring. This is the result, no doubt, of some chemical phenomenon of which we cannot properly explain the cause; but when we witness the beautiful colour, clear and quite smooth within itself, produced upon very common qualities, we cannot but surmise that something of this sort must be really going on during the action of the colour upon the work; otherwise these low qualities must appear very frost-bitten, and present quite an irregular surface.

Having now laid down the general principles of the process, we shall at once proceed to details, taking the methods as they have been introduced into the trade since the commencement of the art in this country.

French Process of Wet-Colouring.

Among the many methods for giving colour to gold at the earliest period, for commercial purposes, was the following, which was decidedly the original wet process, introduced into England from France. The work should be annealed on a clear fire, boiled out in aquafortis pickle, and suspended in bunches upon fine silver or platinum wire; a quantity of boiling water should be provided before commencing the operation. When this is done, take—

Nitrate of potassa . .	16 ozs.
Common salt . . .	8 „
Alum	8 „
	32 ozs.

Reduce the above ingredients to a fine powder in a mortar, and well mix them together; then place the mixture in a good-sized pipkin or crucible, to which add sufficient hot water until it has the consistency of a thick paste; it should be heated very slowly, and must be well stirred with a wooden spoon, when it will soon boil up. The work must then be immersed and left suspended for several minutes, when it should be withdrawn and plunged into a portion of the boiling water, which will remove the colour and show the progress of the operation. If the mixture should, during the time occupied in colouring, show a tendency to boil dry, an occasional spoonful of hot water must be added to thin it, but this should not by any means be added while the work is suspended in it. The colour should be permitted to boil very slowly and steadily, and the work should not be allowed to remain in it too long at one time—six minutes at the most, and that only at the commencement; the subsequent dips should be more frequent, and the colour thinned during the process. The latter, however, can be properly regulated only by practice, the best of teachers. On the introduction of the work it will become nearly black, and at each successive immersion it will be lighter, until the well-known colour of fine gold is attained. The work should, in all cases, be allowed to remain in the colour certainly not longer than twenty minutes; the time must be regulated according to the shade of colour required; and the nature of the alloy acting more quickly when the proportion of copper is greater than that of silver, this should especially be the case, when the above mixture is employed.

When the operation is completed, the surface of the work will be perfectly uniform, though dull, but it may be made brilliant by burnishing or scratching. Previous to every dip the work should be well rinsed in fresh boiling water, and at the conclusion it should be swilled in the same manner, and dried in boxwood sawdust. Scratching coloured work is a delicate operation, and requires care. It is done by the application of a fine brass wire brush and a solution of weak ale. Large plain surfaces should be very carefully scratched, but never crossways; if this is allowed to be done, little marks will be visible, and the beauty of workmanship and finish considerably impaired. This method should not be employed for a lower standard than 16-carats. Ten ounces of solid work with plain surfaces, and five ounces of hollow, can be effectually coloured in the above mixture. The average loss in this process will exceed one pennyweight per ounce.

London Process of Wet-Colouring.

Gold alloys of not less than 15 carats in quality may be made to assume the appearance of very fine gold of a beautiful straw colour, by boiling in the following preparation for a short time. Take—

Nitrate of potassa	15 ozs.
Common salt	7 ,,
Alum	7 ,,
Spirits of salts	1 ,,
	30 ozs.

Reduce the above salts as in the preceding case to a fine powder; then take a large blacklead colour-pot about eight inches high, and seven inches across the top, No. 16 size of Doulton's make; put about two spoonfuls of water at the bottom; then add the saltpetre, alum, and salt; place on the fire and very slowly dissolve and boil up, stirring well with a wooden spoon. Take the work, which has been well prepared by annealing and boiling out in aquafortis pickle, and suspended upon fine platinum wire; put it into the mixture for five minutes, and at the expiration of that time withdraw and rinse well in clean boiling water, then add the spirits of salts to the mixture in the pot; when it again boils up, put the work in for four minutes longer, and again rinse in fresh boiling water. Now add one spoonful of water to the mixture, and when it boils up again put in the work for three minutes, and again rinse. Next add two spoonfuls of water to the mixture in the pot; when it boils put the work in for two minutes, and again rinse. Lastly, thin the colour with about three spoonfuls of water, and when it boils up again, put in the work for one minute longer, well rinse in plenty of clean boiling water; the work is then done, and of a beautiful colour. Finish as usual.

This process is recommended when it is required that the colour should wear well; it will also produce a beautiful colour if properly attended to, and these instructions are carefully carried out. It was regularly practised in London by most goldsmiths for a number of years with great success. It should not, however, be used for a lower standard of gold than 15 carats. The proportions given will colour ten ounces of solid gold chains, and about five ounces of jeweller's work, which latter is generally of a bulky nature having large surfaces. The solder used upon the work must be very good to be nicely coloured by this process. Some goldsmiths have strongly recommended the employment of common salts for plunging the work into, after the last dip in colouring, as a means of neutralising the effects of any acid likely to be retained upon the articles. Others have advised the use of soda and potash solutions as substitutes for ale, in scratch-brushing. We may remark that we have tried these things, as well as several others we could mention tending in the same direction, but cannot say that we ever derived any great advantage from the use of them. The loss by this process of colouring will average about one pennyweight per ounce of work submitted to the action of the mixture. Time occupied in colouring, fifteen minutes.

Gold-workers are exposed to several pernicious vapours in the exercise of their trade, by far the worst being that which arises during the process of wet-colouring; from the action of the spirits of salts upon the work and the other ingredients. The effluvia arising therefrom, in badly-constructed workrooms, produces great distress to the operator, affecting the head, the stomach, and the whole nervous system. When the above symptoms present themselves, a good drink of new milk will counteract the evil, and act as a complete antidote to the mischievous effects of the poisonous and other noxious vapours, taken into the stomach during the performance of any of these processes.

Birmingham Process of Wet-Colouring.

Some time after the introduction of the art into this country, attention began to be directed to the application of the process to qualities inferior to those already named; and it was found that by the addition of small quantities of spirits of salts to the ingredients already in use it was possible to adapt it; and in attempting this experiment Birmingham was not backward, for it was one of the first towns which successfully accomplished it. Of the following ingredients take—

Nitrate of potassa . .	14 ozs.
Common salt . .	7 "
Alum . . .	7 "
Spirits of salts . .	2 "
	30 ozs.

Pound them all fine and mix well together; then take a blacklead colour-pot about eight inches high and seven inches across the mouth, and put the mixture (acid excepted) into it, which must dissolve very gradually. It should on no account be hurried or forced, for if it burns the colour will be spoiled, and consequently unfit for the work. As the heat increases the whole will begin to dissolve; then stir well with a wooden spoon, and, when the colour boils up, add the spirits of salts (muriatic acid), when the mixture will sink; stir it again, when it will soon boil up. Immediately take the work which has been properly prepared for the purpose, and fastened in bunches with fine silver or platinum wire, and immerse it in the colour for four minutes, keeping it well on the move all the time, so that all parts may be acted upon alike; this must be done in such a manner as to prevent scratches and marks, by its touching the bottom or sides of the pot. At the end of the above time, take out the work and rinse it well in quite clean boiling water, of which a copious supply should be provided. Next place it in the colour for a minute and a half; remove it again, and rinse well in fresh hot water. Now add two ounces of hot water to the preparation in the pot, when it will sink but soon rise again. When this takes place put in the work for one minute; it must then be withdrawn, and rinsed in fresh hot water. It will by this time begin to show the right colour, if all things have gone on properly. Lastly, dip the work in the mixture again for half a minute longer, finally rinsing for the last time in two vessels of fresh hot water, and then it should possess a very beautiful colour.

This colouring mixture should be used in proportion to the amount of surface the articles present to its action. The proportions given will be amply sufficient to colour effectually ten ounces of gold chains with plain surfaces, or five ounces of jeweller's work; and, if skilfully managed during

I

the operation, it will never prove a failure. This method will colour gold alloys very richly and evenly, if not below 14 carats; it may therefore be used advantageously to such as are not inferior to this quality. The average loss in taking all kinds of work will be about one pennyweight for every ounce submitted to its action.

Nevertheless in wet-colouring it sometimes happens, even under the most skilful management, that the colour burns, which gives the work a dead-brown appearance; if also the colour-pot has not been properly cleansed after a previous operation this effect will also be produced; so that in this process everything should be kept quite clean and free from grease or iron of any kind, as these are most injurious to the production of the fine, rich results which are sought for.

Preparing the Work.

There are several methods, as we have already remarked, of preparing the work for wet-colouring; each operator adopting the one which suits him best, and appears to claim an advantage over the others. We do not intend to assert that there is any particular advantage likely to accrue from the adoption of any particular process in the preparation of the work. The main principles are, thorough polishing (though this need not be so much the case as for dry-colouring, but still it is of great importance) and cleanliness, the latter element being very essential in the production of a good colour. The operator cannot be too careful in enforcing these two conditions.

Some persons prefer to colour from the black anneal; others to boil for a time in nitric acid pickle; others again, after the work has been well annealed, boil out in sulphuric acid pickle, and afterwards in clean water. In adopting any of these plans, the method is that, after the work has been well polished by means of the finest materials, and washed out, it must be placed upon an iron or copper pan and heated to redness upon a clear fire, the latter proceeding being of importance. If it appears greasy in the interstices, and it is desired to colour it black, it should be boiled out and again annealed; it may then be placed aside to cool, and afterwards suspended upon the wires usually employed for this purpose. In the work of re-colouring articles, it is by far the best plan to anneal them. Where this can be done, boil them out, and again anneal them, which process is easily performed. It is an economical plan to re-colour this description of goods in old colour, which should always be preserved for the purpose. If this appears dry or nearly so, when put into the pot, add one ounce of acid and one ounce of water; if tolerably liquid, make no addition whatever, for, in some instances, and especially where the alloys contain a great proportion of copper, the weaker the preparation the better and brighter is the colour produced upon the work.

Finishing the Work.

After the process of wet-colouring it is absolutely necessary that the work should go through another operation, that of "scratching;" which consists of submitting it to the revolving action of a circular brush of fine brass wire, mounted upon a lathe, after the manner of the round hair brushes used in polishing, and upon which a solution of weak ale is allowed to run from a small barrel with a tap to it. This removes any dull colour that may be upon the work, and gives it a perfectly bright and uniform surface. Frosting is effected by keeping the points of the wires of the brush quite straight, and running the lathe very fast, just letting the ends touch the surface of the work; to do this accurately requires great practice. After this process has been performed, the work must be well rinsed in either hot or cold water, and finally dried in warm boxwood sawdust, which must not be allowed to burn or char in any way: if so the colour of the work will be much damaged, and part of the beauty destroyed. A soft brush will remove all traces of sawdust from the interstices of the articles which have passed through this operation.

German Process of Wet-Colouring.

The German process of colouring gold articles can be applied to that metal of a still inferior standard; and if carefully operated upon, even 12-carat gold may be made to assume a beautiful rich yellow, possessing all the appearance of fine gold, by immersion in the following chemical preparation until the desired colour has been obtained. It consists in some cases of a reduction of the salts usually employed, the abolition of the alum altogether, whilst a double proportion of spirits of salts (muriatic acid) is added to supply the place. A very good mixture, to which we have just referred, is prepared as follows, one which is especially recommended for large work. Take—

Nitrate of potassa . .	14 ozs.
Common salt . .	7 ,,
Muriatic acid . .	5 ,,
	26 ozs.

Reduce the above salts to a fine powder in a mortar, keeping them perfectly clean all the time; well mix them together; then take a blacklead colour-pot about seven inches high and six inches across the top, place it on the fire and well dry; when this is done put into it the colouring-salts, stirring them well with a wooden spoon; when thoroughly dried fine and hot, add the muriatic acid (spirits of salts); the colour will then soon boil up. Now take the work which has been previously prepared quite clean and free from grease, and also suspended upon fine silver or platinum wire, and place it in the preparation for three minutes, keeping it slightly on the move during this period, when it must be withdrawn and instantly plunged into a vessel of clean boiling water, and then into a second vessel of the same. Next add two ounces of hot water to the colour, and when it boils up, again place the work in the mixture for one minute longer; rinse in fresh boiling water as before stated. It will then be done, and of a fine colour if all things have been carefully attended to; dry in clean boxwood sawdust as usual. The work must be well and carefully scratched in weak ale, which liquid is perhaps the best for all practical purposes, or burnished with a proper burnishing-chain if desired; we much prefer the latter, because of the very rich colour it produces. After the work has been well rinsed in clean water subsequent to these operations and dried as before pointed out, it is then ready for the transactions of the commercial world.

The drying of the salts at the commencement is to remove the water taken up during their crystallisation, which operates injuriously where so large a proportion of muriatic acid is employed. A colouring is given to jeweller's work by this process in a much quicker time than could possibly be done by any of the preceding ones, but it is nevertheless much more difficult to perform. It takes considerable practice to become a good colourer; for, if not very skilfully treated, the large proportion of muriatic acid has a tendency to rot the work, as well as to reduce it to a honeycombed state, which latter condition would render it quite unsaleable. The time occupied by this process is four minutes, and the loss occasioned thereby will average about eighteen grains per ounce of the work under manipulation.

The Birmingham process occupies about seven minutes, with a greater proportion of loss of material. Gold alloys to be effectually coloured by the German process should contain rather more silver than has been recommended for the others of which we have treated; because by this process a clean, deep, and smooth colour cannot be produced under any other circumstances. The work would otherwise be frosted or sweated; and a very inferior colour would be the result, if these or similar instructions were not carried out.

It is well to avoid as much as possible the introduction of wet articles into the colour without previously shaking the surplus water from them. Neither should the colour be thinned until the articles submitted to its action begin to show in an unmistakable manner the appearance of gold; for if this should be done, they are sure to come from the colour-pot in a very rough state. This appearance of the work in the German process has successively baffled the skill and ingenuity of several gold-colourers of the old school in this country; and we have often smiled at the arguments in favour of the addition of water when the colour of the work could not be properly effected in the given time, but came out black, which was probably due to the weakness of the acid employed, as it is liable to lose its strength if the mouth of the bottle be not sufficiently secured. The addition of water at such a time as this would certainly be fatal to the excellence of the finish; the proper remedy would be an increase of muriatic acid to the colouring mixture, an extra dip into which would soon produce the desired colour. This should always be done before the weakening or *watering* process commences.

Articles of the commoner qualities, to be effectually treated by this process, must not under any considerations whatever (as we have previously remarked) contain too much copper; for this is the cause of many failures. Under other circumstances, where a large proportion of copper is employed, this weakening process seems to facilitate the object to be achieved; and where a much smaller proportion of muriatic acid is mixed with the other ingredients its addition is both practicable and advantageous. By the addition of water to the German mixture before the colour has been brought up, upon a second immersion of the work a violent attack is made upon it, which, instead of producing colour, acts as a solvent on the metals; and so powerful is this, that a few minutes' immersion would result, if the articles were thin, in their utter destruction.

In concluding our observations on gold-colouring we have simply to remark that the whole process is nothing less than an abstraction of the baser alloy from the surface, which leaves the gold behind with

I 3

a full, rich colour; its effect being to add richness to the colour given to the surface of gold articles of inferior standards, and being nearly perfect in its resemblance to fine gold itself.

Lapping.

This is a distinct process of finishing jewellery-work. It is not much resorted to in coloured work, and when it is employed, it is sometimes performed before the articles are coloured, and sometimes after, according to choice. It is distinguished from scratching, by the evenness of surface, and the lustre, it leaves upon the parts to which it has been applied; and this can be ascertained by an examination of the work after this operation. It is principally confined to bright gold chains and ear-rings, a class of jewellery to which its adaptation is most suitable, as it enhances the beauty of their appearance very much. The lapper produces the plain and diamond-shaped surfaces by the rotary action of the lapidary's wheel, which consists of a specially-prepared composition disc, secured in a lathe vertically upon a horizontal spindle. This has a shoulder in the middle, against which the disc of metal is firmly held by a nut and screw from the other side. This lap or disc weighs about five pounds, and is made of a mixture of two parts purè grain tin to one part of pure lead; to which, for edge-laps, may be judiciously added one pennyweight of fine copper to every pound of the mixture. To effect a complete amalgamation of the component parts, the lead, being the least fusible metal, should be first melted and the tin afterwards added, first well heating it, to prevent too sudden a chill of the lead. If necessary to add the copper, it should be melted separately, and added to the other ingredients when in the liquid state, and be well stirred. Care should be exercised in the casting, in order to prevent waste.

The lap having been properly adjusted by skimming, it is then "headed in," a process performed by the application of flour emery, by means of a brush, to the right-hand side of the lap, and pressed in with a hard flint stone. In heading-in a lap, the emery is used in the wet state. This done, the gold-cutter, as he is familiarly called, takes his work, and submits it to the revolving lap or disc; but before doing so, he submits it to a preparation he has by the side of him, which is used for protecting the gilding or surfaces not subjected to his particular work. He dips the articles into a liquid mixture of gum arabic, two parts, and gamboge, one part; they are then well dried, but must not be overheated; this has a tendency to protect the gilding whilst under the manipulative skill of the gold-cutter. This gum or cement is soluble in hot water; consequently, in washing out, it parts from the gold, and leaves a colour upon the work. The lapping process is a curious one, and it is truly marvellous to see the skilful and practised workman turning the links of gold chains between his thumb and finger with great dexterity and accuracy; and while to all appearance it seems as if they are being presented in a haphazard fashion to the lap, the most perfect-shaped diamonds are being produced. This is called faceting.

Square-lapping is now extensively practised; it adds a sharpness and lustre to the work not equalled by any other means. The gold taken from articles during the process of lapping remains —the greater portion of it, at least—upon the lap. The emery cuts and retains the gold upon it; this, however, is prevented from interfering with the process, by wiping the side of the lap with a tow of cotton waste, damped with oil. This cotton waste must be strictly preserved, and subjected to a special mode of treatment for the recovery of the metal.

CHAPTER XII.

Collecting and Refining Waste Gold.

In wet-colouring, the waste water in which the work has been rinsed, as well as the exhausted colouring-salts, should be carefully preserved, by pouring them into a large stoneware jar kept for the purpose, as they all contain gold; and without such precautions, where a large manufacturing trade is being done, the loss in the course of a year would be very great. All the gold can be recovered from these waste waters by a very simple and at the same time effective process, entailing little or no expense, such as the following method. Take—

Proto-sulphate of iron	2 ozs.
Boiling water about	16 ,,
	18 ozs.

Mix together, and when the salt is all dissolved add it to the solution in the jar, and stir it well; the gold will then begin to precipitate; this must be repeated each time after colouring, and as the jar becomes full a little more proto-sulphate of iron (copperas) must be added, and the contents well stirred. If this produces no effect upon the solution, the gold has all been precipitated. It should then be allowed to settle, when the supernatant water may be decanted or poured away; but care should be taken not to disturb the precipitate, which consists of a dark spongy mass at the bottom. The sediment must then be well washed several times with hot water to free it from the acid; thoroughly dried in an iron pan or ladle, and afterwards melted with a quantity of dry carbonate of potash and common salt, with a proportionate part of common bottle glass, in a crucible. The ingredients may be prepared as follows. Take—

Prepared sediment . .	8 ozs.
Carbonate of potash .	4 "
Common salt . . .	2 "
Common bottle glass .	2 "
	16 ozs.

Reduce all the ingredients to a fine powder, and well mix them together; great heat will be required in the fusion of the mixture, in order to effect the complete reduction of the gold; to assist which, a small portion of saltpetre may be occasionally added to the contents in the pot; but this must be done with care. Sal-enixon, or sandiver, may be used in the reduction of the above mixture, if preferred, to refine it more thoroughly, as either will draw the iron or other impurities into the flux, leaving the button of gold at the bottom of the crucible.

Collection and Treatment of Jeweller's Lemel.

Having comprehensively described the art processes, mechanical and chemical, comprised in the business of a goldsmith, we shall now proceed to explain with some amount of detail the economical processes of a jeweller's establishment. The practice of economy, strictly enforced, is the only true safeguard of the goldsmith against misfortune. His trade reminds us somewhat of the professional money-changer, who exchanges 19*s.* 11½*d.* for a sovereign. The goldsmith or jeweller, however, has not only bad debts to guard against, but also the serious item of waste of material. For in all the various processes through which the precious metal has to pass; with every touch of the file, of the lapidary's wheel, and each application of the polishing mixture, every revolution of the drill, and stroke of the various tools employed, as well as each time the work is annealed and boiled out, minute portions of gold according to the quality of the alloy are detached. Waste therefore is one of the chief features to be seriously considered and avoided in every jewellery establishment.

To begin, we shall say a word or two about the economy of jeweller's *lemel*, which consists of the very small particles of gold-dust removed from the various articles under process of manufacture by means of the file, turning-tool, graver, &c. It is almost impossible to keep this lemel or gold-dust free from organic matter and impurity; and the consequence of this is fully apparent in the loss occasioned in its collection, although it is always done separately and with care.

Workmen have the gold weighed out to them, each one being responsible for his own portion; and the operatives employed in its manufacture have to account for, and weigh up to within a grain of, the quantity given out to them; always deducting therefrom the usual allowance for waste or loss in working, which commonly amounts to six grains to the ounce, in the making department. This allowance constitutes or forms another kind of waste, of which we intend to speak hereafter. For the scrap, dust, and refuse of every kind, is carefully swept up from the floor of the workshop twice a day, sifted and well searched for the purpose of detecting any small portions of gold which may be visible to the naked eye. When this is done, the refuse which remains is scrupulously taken care of and sold to the refiner who will give the most for it.

Lemel is subjected to various kinds of treatment in the different workshops of this country, everyone claiming to employ the best method for its recovery. There is, however, a great deal yet to be learnt before the economical processes (as we call them) belonging to the jewellers' trade, have attained perfection; at least, so far as some houses are concerned. In some establishments the workmen are allowed to weigh-in their lemel in a most dirty state, that is, containing a considerable amount of organic matter; the usual allowance for loss in working being granted, it operates injuriously against the economy of the business arrangements. Such conditions are certainly in favour of the workmen, but they encourage a tendency to exercise less care than is right for the property and welfare of their employers.

There are, however, better methods than these, which may be put into operation without inconvenience, and should commence in the first instance with the workmen. By the adoption of the following plan, the operation commonly attendant upon the employer or his manager (such as sifting and examining the lemel for the detection of iron and steel filings, organic matter, &c.) should be performed by the workmen before weighing it into the warehouse, where their responsibility ceases. This may be very simply performed by providing an iron ladle, and the lemel should then be treated as follows:—Sift it well through a fine sieve to separate the small portions of gold from the dust, letting the lemel fall on to a clean sheet of paper provided for the purpose; this should then be carefully put into the iron ladle, and heated until all the organic matter is entirely destroyed. When the burnt lemel has sufficiently cooled, put the magnet through it in order to collect and remove whatever iron or steel filings may be contained therein. This should be a part of the responsible duties of each workman, and ought to be strictly enforced. The scrap should be always separated from the lemel. Its treatment has been already spoken of.

There are two methods in use for the collection of the lemel; the first is performed in the following manner. Take—

MIXING FOR THE CRUCIBLE.

Lemel or gold-dust .	12 ozs.
Carbonate of potassa .	2 ,,
Common salt . .	1 ,,
	15 ozs.

Well mix the lemel with the salts, and then place the preparation in a skittle-pot, after which place a layer of common salt on it, and transfer it to the furnace. A greater proportion of the mixture should not be put into the crucible than will fill it to within one inch of the top, to be safe, as it rises in the furnace and may overflow. When the fire is at its height, the heat must be continued for half an hour longer; the pot, at the expiration of that time, must be carefully withdrawn, and placed aside to cool, when it may be broken at the bottom with a hammer, and the gold will then be found in a button. A little nitrate of potassa (saltpetre) may be added occasionally when it is in a state of fusion, in order to refine the mass more thoroughly; but the saltpetre must be added with very great care; for if too much be put in, and organic matter be still present, it will rise above the top of the melting-pot, and carry some portion of the precious metal with it. This may be prevented, however, by the timely application of a little extra dry common salt, in powder, and, if added at the proper moment, no evil consequences will result. The button of gold, which will consist of an alloy of gold, silver, and copper, may again be melted with a little potash, borax, or charcoal as flux, and poured into an ingot-mould; it may then again be worked up, if of proper quality after assay (there is no advantage in this), or granulated and refined as may be desired.

The reducing, or collecting salts should be used in proportion to the lemel sought to be recovered, and in about the quantities we have given. We have used sal-enixon instead of the saltpetre as the refining agent, and prefer it for many reasons; first, it is considerably cheaper and answers quite as well—perhaps better; and, in the second place, it keeps the flux and lemel towards the bottom of the crucible, which the saltpetre does not.

Another good plan, and one which has found great favour with some manufacturers, is to put the lemel in an ordinary melting-pot, with a very little flux, such as carbonate of potash or soda; and when it is well melted the crucible must be withdrawn and the contents poured into a casting-mould. The lemel bar may at once be sent to the refiners for sale, or may be exchanged for new gold. By adopting this plan goldsmiths are not subjected to so much loss through having had an indifferent working gold, as no lemel will be in these bars. Lemel is the principal cause of bad gold, the unworkable qualities of which are to be adjudged more from the presence of this, than any other reason.

Recovering Jewellers' Waste.

The sediment which accumulates in the scratch-brush and polishing-boxes, lappers' cotton waste, and all other waste of a similar description, should be carefully collected and thoroughly burnt in a closed iron pan, or other suitable vessel. This process will considerably reduce the bulk of it, and also destroy any organic matter that may be present. The burning must be cautiously effected, to prevent the light particles of gold from going with the draught up the chimney; and for this same reason, it is advisable to employ for such purposes a strong iron pan with a lid to it. When the burning has been carried far enough—which, with a steady fire, will occupy a whole night for each panful of waste, refuse, &c.—and the operation is finally completed, the remaining ash must be put through a fine sieve; the refuse which remains in the sieve should be pounded, and again sifted, when the waste is what is called *good*, and is then ready for the refiner's test.

If it is desired to collect the gold from the above (and sometimes such is the case), the following plan should be resorted to. Take—

Polishings, &c. . .	8 ozs.
Carbonate of potash. .	4 "
Common salt . . .	2 "
Sal-enixon . . .	1 "
	15 ozs.

The above salts should be reduced to powder, and well mixed with the polishings, in the proportion stated. The substance to be operated upon in this case being of a much drier and lighter nature than lemel, a greater proportion of salts is necessary, in order to bring down the gold into a button. After being carefully prepared, place the mixture in a crucible, called in the trade a "skittle-pot" (from its resemblance to a skittle), and treat as has been recommended for collecting lemel only, with this difference—as the mixture sinks towards the bottom of the pot in this process, more of the mixture of polishings must be added from time to time, until the crucible has received as much as it will conveniently hold. When perfectly fused a very few crystals of saltpetre must be added occasionally during the operation, as a quicker fusion is obtained by imparting moisture or liquidness to the preparation. The action of the saltpetre on the mixture must at first be closely watched, and if it is at all likely to overflow, a small quantity of dried common salt (which should always be provided in case of emergency) should at once be thrown in, as it has a great tendency to force the flux downwards. If sufficient saltpetre has been added to the fused mass it will remove from the gold whatever iron, steel, zinc, and even brass and copper, may be present; leaving the gold in a button at the bottom of the crucible, which should subsequently be broken at the base for its recovery, after standing a sufficient time for cooling. Sandiver, bichloride of mercury, brown potash, and sal-enixon are all useful fluxes, having a tendency to destroy the impurities in precipitates of this kind.

It is never worth while to collect the gold from the polishings, lappings, &c., in the manner just described, only simply for the sake of experiment. It is unprofitable to the manufacturing goldsmith, considering the cost of materials, firing, and workmen's time in effecting it. The safest and most economical plan is to sell all such waste containing gold, to the refiner, after a test has been made (the quantity required for that purpose being two ounces) in the same manner as for floor-sweep; the full value is then sure to be realised.

Some persons in the trade have strongly recommended mixing this class of waste with the ordinary floor-sweep — a system to which we strongly object, because this description of waste is generally very rich in gold; and it would be a difficult task to incorporate it properly with so large a quantity as the ordinary sweep usually consists of, so as to realise its utmost value. Hence we say that a part of its value would be lost to the manufacturing jeweller and goldsmith; and we venture to say that we are not expressing idle or theoretical opinions, for we have had considerable experience, and paid more than ordinary attention to this point, with a view to economise and reduce the waste to which jewellers are subjected. We must, therefore, contend, in the interests of the trade, that there should be three separate and distinct processes of treatment for the recovery of gold from this waste, refuse, &c.

The first should have reference to lappers' cotton waste, and the sediment which accumulates in the polishings and scratching-boxes, with all other waste of a similar description.

The second should relate to the wash-hand

waters, old pickling solutions, spent colouring mixture, and rinsing waters (for we prefer these going into the general waste-water tub), together with the washing and swilling waters, employed in the establishment for every purpose, and of every possible description.

The third should comprise the general sweep—that is, the sweepings from the floors of the different workshops in the manufactory, the old worn-out crucibles, the ashes and cinders from the various fires employed, and the dirt and refuse of every conceivable kind which is at all worth preserving. The dross from the fluxes employed in melting should be separately preserved. This may again be put through the fire when a sufficient quantity has been collected, and a compact little lump of gold will invariably be the result. If preferred, instead of troubling with the latter process, it may be sold to the refiner separately. The waste products of manufacturing jewellers are usually collected and treated in this manner quarterly or half-yearly.

Refining Lemel.

This branch of the art, which is more chemical than otherwise, is not practised by gold-workers on a large scale, for manufacturing or commercial purposes; neither would there be any advan-

K

tage by its adoption from a pecuniary point of view, for it would entail a considerable outlay of capital for the apparatus which is indispensable to the operation; without yielding any appreciable return, and would probably be only so much capital unnecessarily sunk in the business. Besides, the refiner and assayer, whose special business it is, and who has every appliance at his command, can do it so much better and cheaper, that manufacturers have, for this reason also, never introduced it as a practical part of their trade.

To those unacquainted with the process of separating gold from the other metals with which it might be alloyed, the following information will be useful:—

The lemel must first be collected in the usual way, according to the principles already laid down. To separate the alloy from the gold, the composition will have to be submitted to the action of nitric acid; but as the alloy of gold consists probably of such proportions that the nitric acid cannot effectually do its work (too great a proportion of gold resists the influence of nitric acid), therefore it will be necessary to re-melt the bar of lemel gold, and to add to it, if of 9-carat quality, one-half of its weight of silver, a little potash or charcoal being used as a flux. When the mixture is properly incorporated, to effect which it should be well stirred, it is poured from some height into a deep vessel of water, being briskly stirred in a circular direction during the operation. The *granulation* of the gold can be performed skilfully, by the operator standing upon a stool and carefully pouring the molten metal into a vessel beneath. The alloy of gold will then be found at the bottom of the water in small grains, which must be carefully collected in order to avoid waste. However, a little is almost sure to happen, even with the greatest care. These grains are then taken and placed in a suitable German flask, which should be quite free from lead, and treated with nitric acid in the following manner. Take—

Alloy of gold . . .	1 oz.
Nitric acid . . .	1 ,,
Water	2 ,,

This mixture should be allowed to stand for several hours. Towards the end of the operation it will be necessary to raise its temperature, in order to promote the requisite chemical action. All the ingredients, except the gold, will become dissolved, and the latter will be in the form of a dark-brown powder at the bottom of the glass. It will be advisable, in order to effect the entire

K 2

removal of the baser alloys, to pour the solution of nitric acid, containing the silver, copper, &c., into another vessel, for subsequent treatment. Fresh nitric acid should now be added to the gold and heat applied, in order to remove any percentage of base alloy, which would be the means of making the gold brittle. When the acid is found to have no action of any kind upon the gold, it must be again poured off, and the gold well washed with hot water, to remove any trace of alloy that may be discovered in its interstices. At this stage the gold is pure, or at all events sufficiently pure for every practical purpose, requiring now only to be melted with borax or potash.

Unless every particle of alloy is removed from the gold, it is very likely to be brittle when it comes to be worked up again; for that reason, if for no other, it is better to entrust it to the practical refiner, for, as we have already said, it never pays the working jeweller to do it himself. Even refiners' best gold from the lemel bar never works up like the refined native gold.

Gold collected from the other waste material of jewellers may be treated in this manner if preferred.

To Recover Gold from the Waste Waters of the Jeweller.

There are various methods in operation among jewellers for the recovery of the gold from their waste waters, &c., a few of which we think it necessary to describe.

The old plan of dealing with these waste waters was very unsatisfactory in a pecuniary sense. It consisted merely of a moderately-sized tub for the collection of liquid substances of every kind employed in the manufactory; this tub was fitted with a wooden tap about one-third from the bottom; precisely under this was placed a circular framework of wood, of sieve-like form, with a rather closely-fabricated piece of felt or flannel attached loosely to the rim, so constructed as to form a cavity in the centre for the collection of the liquid, as it issued slowly from the tap immediately above it. This, after filtering through the above apparatus, was allowed to run away, no more notice whatever being taken of it.

Now this liquid carried along with it a considerable portion of gold, as we shall show presently. But before doing so, we desire first to allude to improvements subsequently effected, or rather, presumed improvements; of which the following is one of several which found much favour some years ago, when jewellers began to pay *special* attention to the economy of their establishments, with the view of reducing the working loss to the lowest extent possible, compatible with safe working. This loss was considered excessive, in proportion to the quantity of manufactured articles produced out of a given quantity of material; and a comparison of weights showed such to have been actually the case. To economise, therefore, the following method of treatment was strongly recommended at the time, and was supposed to deal effectually with the liquid substances used in the different stages of manufacture, both chemical and mechanical.

Several large tubs were to be provided differing in sizes, and placed in a row, each succeeding one to be smaller than the preceding. In each of these tubs taps were to be fitted, which could be turned at any time. First of all the water would have to be conveyed by lead piping, from the several workshops connected with the manufactory, into the largest tub; when this had become full, the tap could be turned on and all the surplus water carried over into the next, and so on, until the last in the row was reached; and in this, a piping in place of the tap must be firmly secured, to convey the whole of the liquid, after its passage through the row of tubs, into a large tank of deal sawdust as a final protection to the whole process. The latter part could be conveniently performed by placing the sawdust in the yard or some out-building belonging to the premises, where the surplus water might drain away. It was supposed that by this means the whole of the gold would be recovered, on the ground that the passage of the water through the tubs would be so checked, and so slow, that the small particles of gold would all sink to the bottom, and thus be eventually saved.

Unfortunately such could not be the case. In the jewellers' pickles and other waste liquids, there are minute pieces of gold, which no amount of filtering, or passing through a series of tubs of stagnant water can possibly recover, unless some chemical ingredient be added thereto, which has the power of reducing the gold to its metallic state. For it should be understood that the dissolved gold (and there is a considerable quantity in the waste waters of jewellers) passes through the filter as freely as the liquid itself. Therefore, unless this is acted upon chemically, no hope can possibly be entertained of its ultimate recovery by the jeweller.

But the best method of all for collecting the gold from these waters, is to provide three large tubs of different sizes, placing them in a row; into the largest or first tub is put the exhausted pickling solutions, the water in which the workpeople have washed their hands, that in which the work has been washed out, the exhausted colouring-salts and rinsings, and the swilling waters of every description. Into this tub is fitted a tap level with the top of the second, and one in the second level with the top of the third, to allow the liquid to run from one to the other in rotation. A quantity of proto-sulphate of iron (green copperas) is dissolved in boiling water and added occasionally to each of the three tubs, more especially the largest, which is the *final* receptacle for all the used-up liquids. The proto-sulphate of iron precipitates the dissolved gold held in solution to a metallic state, and so purifies and clears it, that by the time it leaves the last tub every particle of gold will have become precipitated, and the water appear perfectly clear; so clear in fact that it cannot be distinguished from clean spring water.

The sediment at the bottom of the tubs, after the clear water has been withdrawn from them (which is best done with a syphon), may be well mixed with deal sawdust in order to dry up the remaining liquid, and afterwards well burnt and sifted as fine as possible. Instead of taps (which are liable to become corroded or destroyed) being employed for the conveyance of the water into the various tubs, stout glass syphons may be successfully used, and are more economical, the different chemical agents in the liquid having no action on them, while they have upon the others. It is a very good plan when these syphons are used to allow the water to run, as it leaves the last tub, upon a filter placed on a cane-bottomed sieve; the very clearest water then only can run away. By such a method the sediment in the tubs is in no danger of being disturbed. It may, instead of being mixed with the sawdust, be placed on several of these filters, and the moisture being gradually withdrawn, the substance remains well dried, and can afterwards be reduced to powder.

If the proto-sulphate of iron be added judiciously and at the proper times, such precautions as subsequent filtering, &c., will not be necessary; for every particle of gold will be precipitated in a manner so truly effective, that no further attention will be required. We have had several trials made by refiners and assayers, of the waste waters, after the above chemical has been added, and their investigations have always resulted in not a particle of

K 3

gold visible to the naked eye being found in the samples.

The gold may be collected into a button by the means which have been already described, using sandiver as one of the principal refining agents; it does not, however, pay, and it would be far better to abandon any attempt at it. It may be put into the ordinary floor-sweep if preferred, or kept separate and a trial made by the refiners; the latter plan is much the better one, where a large manufacturing trade is being done.

Oxalic acid will also precipitate gold from its solution, but it is considerably dearer than the salt of iron we have recommended; but if it be desired to precipitate it without the addition of another metal, then this acid may be used with advantage.

Jewellers' Sweep.

Jewellers' sweep constitutes the whole of the sweepings from the floors of the workshops in the manufactory, which should in a well-regulated place be swept twice a day, and the refuse preserved and carefully sorted every morning with the view of gathering up the small particles of gold visible to the naked eye, which have been dropped during the work of the day. After this has been done, and the gold removed, the sweepings must be well burnt, and as much of the organic matter destroyed as possible. They must then be well pounded in a large cast-iron mortar, and preserved for the refiner. This latter plan may be dispensed with, if found inconvenient in the working department of the establishment; the whole refuse should then be sent periodically to a grinding-mill where steam power is employed, where a large quantity of sweep can be reduced to powder in a very short time. It should of course be previously well burnt, to facilitate the action of the rollers upon the material. The old melting-pots of every description, and the burnt cinders and ashes from the furnace and muffles, should also be collected with the sweep; in fact, everything at all worth preserving should be taken care of and sold to the refiner; for it is the attention given these matters in the course of production that constitutes the greatest amount of success in the manufacture of goldsmith's work. In concluding our subject, we shall give some valuable tables of alloys and solders, prepared and used by ourselves, together with other information which will be equally useful to the trade.

CHAPTER XIII.

Tables of Specific Gravities, Alloys, &c.

THE specific gravities of the various metals and their alloys, as given in this work, have all been calculated arithmetically. Perhaps the more correct method would be, to do so by means of the hydrostatic balance. This consists of an ordinary balance, of which the pans are suspended by strings of unequal length. The shorter pan has a hook attached to its under side, to which the substance should be suspended by a hair or filament of silk. In ascertaining the specific gravity of any material by these means, it is necessary to find out first its weight, when weighed in air, and secondly to learn how much that weight is reduced by weighing in water. The second weight thus obtained is deducted from the first, and then the specific gravity required is at once obtained by dividing the first weight, or weight in air, by this difference. To conduct this operation with nicety requires great care, and a very delicate balance must be employed in the test, in order to arrive at strictly accurate results. The water in such cases is commonly preferred at a temperature of 60° Fahr. The following example will render our meaning tolerably clear, and convey a better idea of the process. Presuming that the substance in question is a sovereign, it would be represented as follows :—

A sovereign weighs 123·27 grains in air.
A sovereign weighs 116·67 grains in water.

$$123{\cdot}27 - 116{\cdot}67 = 6{\cdot}60$$
$$123{\cdot}27 \div 6{\cdot}60 = 18{\cdot}67$$

The specific gravity therefore of a sovereign, which consists of 22-carat gold, is 18·67, and closely approximates to our calculated tables. The specific gravity of bodies may be conveniently ascertained by either of these means.

Different Qualities of Gold reduced to various Standards, so as to suit the several COLOURING PROCESSES mentioned underneath.

Composition of a Sovereign.

	oz.	dwts.	grs.
Fine gold, per oz.	0	18	8
Refined copper	0	1	16
	1	0	0

22-carat reduced to 18-carat, cost 64*s*. 6*d*. per oz.

	oz.	dwts.	grs.
4 sovereigns	1	0	12
Fine silver	0	2	0
Swedish copper	0	2	12
	1	5	0

Suitable for the dry-colouring process.

18-carat reduced to 16-carat, cost 58*s*. per oz.

	oz.	dwts.	grs.
18-carat scrap	1	0	0
Fine silver	0	0	5
Swedish copper	0	2	7
	1	2	12

Suitable for the French colouring process.

18-carat reduced to 15-carat, cost 54*s*. 6*d*. per oz.

	oz.	dwts.	grs.
18-carat scrap	1	0	0
Fine silver	0	0	18
Swedish copper	0	3	6
	1	4	0

Suitable for the London colouring process.

18-carat reduced to 14-carat, cost 51*s*. per oz.

	oz.	dwts.	grs.
18-carat scrap	1	0	0
Fine silver	0	1	4
Swedish copper	0	4	14
	1	5	18

Suitable for the Birmingham colouring process.

18-carat reduced to 13-carat, cost 47*s*. 6*d*. per oz.

	oz.	dwts.	grs.
18-carat scrap	1	0	0
Fine silver	0	1	18
Swedish copper	0	6	0
	1	7	18

Suitable for the German colouring process.

18-carat reduced to 12½-carat, cost 45*s.* 6*d.* per oz.

	oz.	dwts.	grs.
18-carat scrap	1	0	0
Fine silver	0	2	0
Swedish copper	0	7	0
	1	9	0

Can be coloured by the German process only.

22-carat reduced to 16-carat, cost 58*s.* per oz.

	oz.	dwts.	grs.
4 sovereigns	1	0	12
Fine silver	0	2	6
Swedish copper	0	5	6
	1	8	0

Suitable for the French colouring process.

16-carat reduced to 15-carat, cost 54*s.* 6*d.* per oz.

	oz.	dwts.	grs.
16-carat scrap	1	0	0
Fine silver	0	0	12
Swedish copper	0	0	21
	1	1	9

Suitable for the London colouring process

16-carat reduced to 14-carat, cost 51*s.* per oz.

	oz.	dwts.	grs.
16-carat scrap	1	0	0
Fine silver	0	0	21
Swedish copper	0	2	3
	1	3	0

Suitable for the Birmingham colouring process.

16-carat reduced to 13-carat, cost 47*s.* 6*d.* per oz.

	oz.	dwts.	grs.
16-carat scrap	1	0	0
Fine silver	0	1	3
Swedish copper	0	3	12
	1	4	15

Suitable for the German colouring process.

16-carat reduced to 12½-carat, cost 45*s.* 6*d.* per oz.

	oz.	dwts.	grs
16-carat scrap	1	0	0
Fine silver	0	1	12
Swedish copper	0	4	6
	1	5	18

Can be coloured by the German process only.

22-carat reduced to 15-carat, cost 54*s*. 6*d*. per oz.

	oz.	dwts.	grs.
4 sovereigns	1	0	12
Fine silver	0	3	0
Swedish copper	0	6	12
	1	10	0

Suitable for the London colouring process.

15-carat reduced to 14-carat, cost 51*s*. per oz.

	oz.	dwts.	grs.
15-carat scrap	1	0	0
Fine silver	0	0	4
Swedish copper	0	1	8
	1	1	12

Suitable for the Birmingham colouring process.

15-carat reduced to 13-carat, cost 47*s*. 6*d*. per oz.

	oz.	dwts.	grs.
15-carat scrap	1	0	0
Fine silver	0	0	21
Swedish copper	0	2	6
	1	3	3

Suitable for the German colouring process.

15-carat reduced to 12½-carat, cost 45*s*. 6*d*. per oz.

	oz.	dwts.	grs.
15-carat scrap	1	0	0
Fine silver	0	1	0
Swedish copper	0	3	0
	1	4	0

Can be coloured by the German process only.

22-carat reduced to 14-carat, cost 51*s*. per oz.

	oz.	dwts.	grs.
4 sovereigns	1	0	12
Fine silver	0	3	18
Swedish copper	0	7	18
	1	12	0

Suitable for the Birmingham colouring process.

14-carat reduced to 13-carat, cost 47*s*. 6*d*. per oz.

	oz.	dwts.	grs.
14-carat scrap	1	0	0
Fine silver	0	0	9
Swedish copper	0	1	6
	1	1	15

Suitable for the German colouring process.

14-carat reduced to 12½-carat, cost 45*s.* 6*d.* per oz.

	oz.	dwts.	grs.
14-carat scrap	1	0	0
Fine silver	0	0	15
Swedish copper	0	1	21
	1	2	12

Can be coloured by the German process only.

22-carat reduced to 13-carat, cost 47*s.* 6*d.* per oz.

	oz.	dwts.	grs.
4 sovereigns	1	0	12
Fine silver	0	4	12
Swedish copper	0	9	12
	1	14	12

Suitable for the German colouring process.

13-carat reduced to 12½-carat, cost 45*s.* 6*d.* per oz.

	oz.	dwts.	grs.
13-carat scrap	1	0	0
Fine silver	0	0	3
Swedish copper	0	0	21
	1		0

Can be coloured by the German process only.

Wet-coloured solder from 13-carat gold.

	oz.	dwts.	grs.
13-carat scrap	1	0	0
Fine silver	0	3	12
Composition	0	0	12
	1	4	0

Colours well by the German process.

Table showing the Chief Places for the Manufacture of Jewellery in the different parts of the World.

Countries.	Principal Cities or Towns.
England	London and Birmingham.
France	Paris, Lyons, Bordeaux, and Rouen.
Germany.	Frankfort, Pforzheim, and Carlsruhe.
Austria	Prague, Vienna, and Hungary.
America	Newark, Philadelphia, and Providence.
Australia	Melbourne and Sydney.

Reducing Standard Gold to various Qualities.
Table for Mixing.

Qualities.	Standard Gold.	Mixture of Alloy.
22 carats.	22 parts.	None.
21 „	21 „	1 part.
20 „	20 „	2 „
19 „	19 „	3 „
18 „	18 „	4 „
17 „	17 „	5 „
16 „	16 „	6 „
15 „	15 „	7 „
14 „	14 „	8 „
13 „	13 „	9 „
12 „	12 „	10 „
11 „	11 „	11 „
10 „	10 „	12 „
9 „	9 „	13 „
8 „	8 „	14 „
7 „	7 „	15 „

Reducing Fine Gold to various Qualities.
Table for Mixing.

Qualities.	Fine Gold.	Mixture of Alloy.
24 carats.	24 parts.	None.
23 „	23 „	1 part.
22 „	22 „	2 „
21 „	21 „	3 „
20 „	20 „	4 „
19 „	19 „	5 „
18 „	18 „	6 „
17 „	17 „	7 „
16 „	16 „	8 „
15 „	15 „	9 „
14 „	14 „	10 „
13 „	13 „	11 „
12 „	12 „	12 „
11 „	11 „	13 „
10 „	10 „	14 „
9 „	9 „	15 „
8 „	8 „	16 „
7 „	7 „	17 „

Table showing the Proportion of Alloy to be added to One ounce of Standard Gold in making the following Qualities.

Qualities.	Standard Gold.			Alloy to be added.			Total.		
Carats.	oz.	dwts.	grs.	oz.	dwts.	grs.	oz.	dwts.	grs.
21	1	0	0	0	0	23	1	0	23
20	1	0	0	0	2	0	1	2	0
19	1	0	0	0	3	4	1	3	4
18	1	0	0	0	4	10	1	4	10
17	1	0	0	0	5	21	1	5	21
16	1	0	0	0	7	12	1	7	12
15	1	0	0	0	9	8	1	9	8
14	1	0	0	0	11	10	1	11	10
13	1	0	0	0	13	20	1	13	20
12	1	0	0	0	16	16	1	16	16
11	1	0	0	1	0	0	2	0	0
10	1	0	0	1	4	0	2	4	0
9	1	0	0	1	8	21	2	8	21
8	1	0	0	1	15	0	2	15	0
7	1	0	0	2	2	20	3	2	20

Table showing the Proportion of Alloy to be added to One ounce of Fine Gold in making the following Qualities.

Qualities.	Fine Gold.			Alloy to be added.			Total.		
Carats.	oz.	dwts.	grs.	oz.	dwts.	grs.	oz.	dwts.	grs.
23	1	0	0	0	0	20	1	0	20
22	1	0	0	0	1	18	1	1	18
21	1	0	0	0	2	20	1	2	20
20	1	0	0	0	4	0	1	4	0
19	1	0	0	0	5	6	1	5	6
18	1	0	0	0	6	16	1	6	16
17	1	0	0	0	8	5	1	8	5
16	1	0	0	0	10	0	1	10	0
15	1	0	0	0	12	0	1	12	0
14	1	0	0	0	14	6	1	14	6
13	1	0	0	0	16	22	1	16	22
12	1	0	0	1	0	0	2	0	0
11	1	0	0	1	3	15	2	3	15
10	1	0	0	1	8	0	2	8	0
9	1	0	0	1	13	8	2	13	8
8	1	0	0	2	0	0	3	0	0
7	1	0	0	2	8	12	3	8	12

Table showing the amount of Silver to be added to the undermentioned Qualities in the Refining of Gold Alloys.

Qualities.	Amount of gold alloy.			Silver to be added.		
	oz.	dwts.	grs.	oz.	dwts.	grs.
22 carats.	1	0	0	2	13	8
20 ,,	1	0	0	2	6	16
18 ,,	1	0	0	2	0	0
16 ,,	1	0	0	1	13	8
15 ,,	1	0	0	1	10	0
14 ,,	1	0	0	1	6	16
13 ,,	1	0	0	1	3	8
12 ,,	1	0	0	1	0	0
11 ,,	1	0	0	0	16	16
10 ,,	1	0	0	0	13	8
9 ,,	1	0	0	0	10	0
8 ,,	1	0	0	0	6	16
7 ,,	1	0	0	0	3	8
6 ,,	1	0	0			

Table showing the relative Value of different Qualities.

Qualities.			£	s.	d	
23-carat	gold	is worth	4	2	6	per ounce.
22	,,	,,	3	19	0	,,
21	,,	,,	3	15	6	,,
20	,,	,,	3	12	0	,,
19	,,	,,	3	8	6	,,
18	,,	,,	3	5	0	,,
17	,,	,,	3	1	6	,,
16	,,	,,	2	18	0	,,
15	,,	,,	2	14	6	,,
14	,,	,,	2	11	0	,,
13	,,	,,	2	7	6	,,
12	,,	,,	2	4	0	,,
11	,,	,,	2	0	6	,,
10	,,	,,	1	17	0	,,
9	,,	,,	1	13	6	,,
8	,,	,,	1	10	0	,,
7	,,	,,	1	6	6	,,

TABLE OF COLOURED GOLD ALLOYS SUITABLE FOR THE FOLLOWING PROCESSES.

Description.	Fine Gold.			Fine Silver.			Swedish Copper.			Total.			Qualities.
	oz.	dwts.	grs.	oz.	dwts.	grs.	oz.	dwts.	grs.	oz.	dwts.	grs.	
Dry Colouring . . .	1	0	0	0	2	6	0	4	10	1	6	16	18-carat.
French Colouring . .	1	0	0	0	2	12	0	7	12	1	10	0	16-carat.
London Colouring . .	1	0	0	0	3	6	0	8	18	1	12	0	15-carat.
Birmingham Colouring .	1	0	0	0	4	0	0	10	6	1	14	6	14-carat.
German Colouring . .	1	0	0	0	4	18	0	12	6	1	17	0	13-carat.

TABLE OF COLOURED GOLD SOLDERS, SUITABLE FOR THE FOLLOWING PROCESSES.

Description.	Fine Gold.			Fine Silver.			Copper or Compo.			Total.			Value per oz.		
	oz.	dwts.	grs.	oz.	dwts.	grs.	oz.	dwts.	grs.	oz.	dwts.	grs.	£	s.	d.
Dry Colouring . . .	1	0	0	0	6	0	0	4	0	1	10	0	2	18	0
French Colouring . .	1	0	0	0	8	0	0	7	0	1	15	0	2	10	0
London Colouring . .	1	0	0	0	11	0	0	9	0	2	0	0	2	5	0
Birmingham Colouring .	1	0	0	0	12	12	0	10	0	2	2	12	2	2	6
German Colouring . .	1	0	0	0	13	0	0	12	0	2	5	0	2	0	0
Best Bright	1	0	0	1	1	0	1	0	0	3	1	0	1	10	0

Table of the Duty on Gold at 17s. per oz., as charged at the Assay Office.

dwts.		£	s.	d.	ozs.		£	s.	d.
1	. .	0	0	10	1	. .	0	17	0
2	. .	0	1	8	2	. .	1	14	0
3	. .	0	2	7	3	. .	2	11	0
4	. .	0	3	5	4	. .	3	8	0
5	. .	0	4	3	5	. .	4	5	0
6	. .	0	5	1	6	. .	5	2	0
7	. .	0	5	11	7	. .	5	19	0
8	. .	0	6	10	8	. .	6	16	0
9	. .	0	7	8	9	. .	7	13	0
10	. .	0	8	6	10	. .	8	10	0
11	. .	0	9	4	11	. .	9	7	0
12	. .	0	10	2	12	. .	10	4	0
13	. .	0	11	1	13	. .	11	1	0
14	. .	0	11	11	14	. .	11	18	0
15	. .	0	12	9	15	. .	12	15	0
16	. .	0	13	7	16	. .	13	12	0
17	. .	0	14	5	17	. .	14	9	0
18	. .	0	15	4	18	. .	15	6	0
19	. .	0	16	2	19	. .	16	3	0
Under 12 grs. nothing.					20	. .	17	0	0

Table showing the Proportion of Alloy to be added to Wet-coloured Scrap, containing 10 dwts. 12 grs. of fine Gold per oz., in order to make the regular 9-carat quality, containing 7 dwts. of fine Gold per oz.

$$20\cdot \times 12{\cdot}6 = 252{\cdot}0$$
$$20\cdot \times 8{\cdot}4 = 168{\cdot}0$$
$$252{\cdot}0 - 168{\cdot}0 = 84{\cdot}0$$
$$84{\cdot}0 \div 8{\cdot}4 = 10 \text{ dwts. of alloy.}$$

$$20 \times 12\tfrac{12}{20} = 252$$
$$20 \times 8\tfrac{8}{20} = 168$$
$$252 - 168 = 84$$
$$84 \div 8\tfrac{8}{20} = 10 \text{ dwts. of alloy.}$$

If 10 dwts. 12 grs. = 252 grs, 7 dwts. = 168 grs

$$20 \times 252 = 5{,}040$$
$$20 \times 168 = 3{,}360$$
$$5{,}040 - 3{,}360 = 1{,}680$$
$$1{,}680 \div 168 = 10 \text{ dwts. of alloy.}$$

Assayers' Weight.

A carat is not an absolute weight as regards gold, but is merely the twenty-fourth part of a unit; whether that unit constitutes pound, ounce, pennyweight, or grain. The carat is used by goldsmiths to denote the purity of gold, and is divided into four grains, and each grain into four quarters; and these again into as many subdivisions as may be necessary. The assay weight of gold being a pound, the carat would be represented as follows:—

	dwts.	grs.
Assay carat of a pound	10	0
Assay grain of a pound	2	12
Assay quarter-grain of a pound . . .	0	15
Assay carat of an ounce	0	20
Assay grain of an ounce	0	5
Assay quarter-grain of an ounce . .	0	1¼

According to the table here given, the assay quarter-grain is in reality one and a quarter-grain troy weight.

ASSAYERS' REPORT.

1,000th parts.	Fine gold in lb. troy.			No. of carats.	
Parts of fine gold.	ozs.	dwts.	grs.	carats.	grs.
1,000	12	0	0	24	0
959	11	10	0	23	0
916	11	0	0	22	0
834	10	0	0	20	0
750	9	0	0	18	0
709	8	10	0	17	0
667	8	0	0	16	0
625	7	10	0	15	0
584	7	0	0	14	0
542	6	10	0	13	0
521	6	5	0	12	2
500	6	0	0	12	0
458	5	10	0	11	0
417	5	0	0	10	0
375	4	10	0	9	0
354	4	5	0	8	2

CHAPTER XIV.

Useful Hints.—Lemel.

KEEP all filings, dust, and turnings as free from emery-cloth, and all other organic matter, as possible.

Hand-Washing.

In the manufacture of goldsmiths' work, it should be a compulsory rule of the establishment where it is conducted, that no one leaves the place without washing his hands, at dinner-time and at night.

Gold-Cutters.

It is a good plan to give to each lapper about two ounces of cotton waste daily, and to see that it is returned with the finished work every night at the conclusion of the day's work. A large box should be specially provided, well lined with sheet lead or zinc, for its reception.

Workpeople's Aprons.

The aprons and towels used by the workpeople

in all branches of the trade, should be washed at the manufactory; accommodation for which should be provided; and the water so used carefully saved for subsequent treatment, by pouring into the general waste-water tub. By adopting this method a considerable quantity of gold otherwise taken off the premises, is recoverable in the course of a year, the means being simple and effectual.

Shop Floors.

If the shop floors are well covered with sheet iron, the joints soldered together, and the edges turned up round the ends and sides of the various workshops, it will prevent any of the gold from finding its way into the woodwork of the flooring, and thus effect a great saving. Sheet zinc may be employed instead of the iron if preferred, but it is more liable to wear through. To prevent this it should be covered with perforated iron gratings; the latter also help to prevent anything from being carried out of the shops which is likely to adhere to the bottoms of the boots of the workpeople, by rubbing it off and collecting it in the holes of the gratings, thus rendering its recovery certain. Care must be taken when sheet zinc is employed with the pickle, so as not to spill it on the zinc floor, or it would soon be destroyed. A great saving is effected by the application of a process like this, where gold is manufactured into commercial wares.

Testing Gold.

A solution for testing whether an article is made of gold or base metal may be made as follows :—

Nitric acid . . .	2 ounces.
Water . . .	4 drachms.
Muriatic acid . .	1 scruple.

Well mix them together and keep ready for use in a stoppered glass bottle. In testing the purity of gold by means of this mixture, it is sufficient to merely touch the object with the stopper (which should have a long dropper dipping into the mixture) and closely watch the action of the acid upon the article in question. If it produces no effect, which is the case with gold, it does not always prove that the article is genuine; it may be thickly gilt, or plated with gold; therefore, to be sure, where any doubt exists, it is advisable to rub a file over some part of the surface, and then apply the acid to *that part*; if base metal the fraud will at once be detected. Any quality of gold above 9-carat, we may safely say, will stand this test.

Inferior qualities may be ascertained by the acid boiling more or less green, and this is the case with common gold. Common qualities, if alloyed with much silver, will partially stand this test; but then the colour is considerably paler, and this will act as a guide as to their real nature.

Conclusion.

In conclusion, permit us to say, that the information afforded in these pages in connection with this very interesting branch of art and industry is thoroughly practical, and highly trustworthy in a commercial sense. We trust, therefore, that the trade will be generally benefited by coming into possession of valuable knowledge acquired only by many years of close study and personal attention devoted to the subject.

Conclusion.

APPENDIX.

Results of Experiments and Researches.
Details of Modern Processes.

(1.) In melting gold it has been recommended to employ small lumps of charcoal as flux. There is no possible advantage in such a method or manner of treatment, for the use of flux at all is to prevent the molten metal from becoming oxidised on the surface, which it does when heated in the presence of a current of air. Now the object of employing flux is not so much to assist in promoting the fusion of the component parts of the several alloys as it is to prevent the oxidation taking place; hence, we repeat, to prevent *which* effectually the surface of the gold and alloy in the pot, when it reaches the molten state at least, must be absolutely secured against currents of air, and especially those which are to be found in all jewellers' melting furnaces; and if such precautions are not regarded, oxidation, loss of metal, and bad workable gold is the general result. Now, what is oxidation? It is the operation of converting any metallic substance into an oxide, and oxide in chemistry means a compound of oxygen and a base, and not being in an acid state may be called metallic rust. The oxygen being an electro-negative element, constituting the vital part of the atmosphere, attacks the copper

L 3

first, which is the weaker element of alloy, and brings it under its influence, and so forms what is called the *base* in conformity with chemical science. To put it plainer, we should say the action of the air upon molten metal without a protective coating destroys its homogeneousness. Altogether we do not wish to be understood to convey the meaning that a slight oxidation of the surface of molten gold renders every part of the bar unworkable, as that to a great extent depends on the pouring of the mass into the ingot mould. If the oxide, which appears like a scum on the surface, is prevented from going into the ingot mould with the liquid mass, then the gold may be perfectly workable; but assuming this to be very generally the case, a great loss of material has taken place, and a remnant left behind which might as well have been in the bar of gold, and which would have been had oxidation been prevented at an earlier stage of the process. When this oxide—or nature-destroyed gold—runs into the ingot mould, it either appears upon the end of the bar of metal in a corrugated mass, or, on the other hand, it forms what to all appearance seems like little circular discs of unmelted metal, the unmelted portion forming semi-detached scales which subsequently roll into the gold and destroy its smoothness and clearness. Now all this may be prevented by using the purest vegetable charcoal as flux, and well stirring the melted alloy before pouring. The flux is best added on the verge of commencing fusion, as oxidation takes place very rapidly at this stage of the operation of melting jewellers' alloys, unless a suitable covering is given to the surface to keep away the air, which is the promoter of oxidation.

(2.) Sometimes ingots of gold turn out of the mould with a serrated edge or edges; this is due to sundry causes, which may also be avoided by the acquisition of a proper knowledge of all the general details connected with a process so uncertain in its action; for there are very few jewellers indeed who have not experienced some trouble and annoyance in this special part of their trade. We have met with these obstacles in our business, and we can therefore speak of them with that amount of *real practical* knowledge so absolutely essential to the production of a treatise like this, which only aims at the dissemination of really useful practical information to the gold-working trade. The causes which lead to these serrated edges will be here explained, and as a matter of necessity the best remedies will be given, together with such other information which is likely to be of service in the preparing of perfect bars of alloyed gold. Imperfect bars of gold usually roll with a more extended jaggered edge as the process proceeds, and consequently causes a great deal of waste in the trimming of the edges when used in sheet gold, and when in wire the outside strips break into short pieces of a few inches in length in the slitting of them. One of the causes of these imperfect bars is through the badly mitring of the ingot mould; it may admit the air, which always causes serrated edges, spitting and loss of metal. Again, the ingot mould may *even be* mitred properly, and yet not throw out a perfect bar of metal. This may be owing to a little grit getting between the parts which should meet securely together, so evenly, in fact, as to render the mould perfectly air-tight. Occasionally new ingot moulds warp when heated. The remedy in such cases would be a re-grinding of the surfaces which meet each other, or otherwise a thick coating of whitening made into a paste with water and applied to the parts which admit the air. Again, when the ingot is not sufficiently well heated, defects in the casting will also appear; it is the same when the heat given has been too great. The right heat may be ascertained by throwing a few drops of water on the mould, when, if it rather quickly boils off, it may be used with every advantage and safety. Finally, the heat must be much greater than can be borne by the hand.

(3.) New ingot moulds should be well greased before using, to prevent the gold adhering to them. It is much better and safer to close them up and pour in a solution of salt and water, and let it remain for a day or two before using them; this causes oxidation—or rust of the surfaces—and is an excellent preventive to the gold sticking, which is sometimes found to be so obstinate as to cause chipping of the mould, thus rendering it useless for further operations.

(4.) In badly prepared moulds a porosity is given to the gold in the casting, apart from other considerations, and it is clearly discernible before the rolling process takes place. The inexperienced may detect this porosity readily enough, when once having seen a bar of its kind, by the unevenness of surface, which is sunken in, in places upon the upper side, and exhibiting numerous small cracks and blow-holes, all caused by a current of air meeting the molten metal as it is poured and proceeds down the mould prepared for its reception. When gold and its alloys are imperfectly fused a long point is generally left adhering to the end of the bar, and these porous irregularities show themselves also in the form of a scaly and unsmooth surface, and produce altogether very inferior castings. The remedy for this will be a remelting with a far greater addition of heat.

(5.) The alloys of gold should not be over-heated, and ought to be poured almost immediately after complete fusion has taken place; the latter may be easily ascertained by stirring with an iron rod, previously heated to just redness; the time of pouring, that is, when the fused mass is ready, is generally arrived at by the touch, it having more of a watery touch, and not at all cloggy, like it has when not properly fused. The ingot moulds should be rather slanting and not quite straight, the former being more convenient to pour into; and also it prevents spitting into the face of the operator when that irregularity takes place. Gold should certainly be stirred, and especially in Hall-marked qualities, in order to produce a perfect mixture, which would assay evenly. This information is given in answer to several questions we have received from correspondents wishing to be practically advised upon the subjects of these remarks.

(6.) *Blue gold* is very difficult to prepare at all times; it has, however, a very pleasing effect when used in conjunction with other shades of coloured gold in the formation of artistic work, so that a few remarks upon its treatment may be of some service to that class of art-workers who are striving to promote "art and taste in design" as opposed to the "cheap and the vulgar." Blue gold is a mixture of iron and gold. The formula for 18 carat is as follows:—

BLUE GOLD.

	oz.	dwts.	grs.
Gold, fine . . .	0	15	0
Iron Charcoal . . .	0	5	0
	1	0	0

This alloy will cost about 64s. per ounce, and is of a light blue colour. The colour is shown to advantage in the finish by well polishing the parts composed of it, and then pecking it up with the engraving or chasing tool. No colouring should be allowed to take place with this gold, but where it is unavoidable the colour must be subsequently removed by the usual mechanical means, or the proper shade of colour would not be given to this alloy of gold. The preparation of the mixture being the most important point with which we are now concerned, calls for a few detailed remarks upon it. It is best prepared in the mixture by dipping iron wire not too thick into the molten gold, which should be well covered with charcoal flux—and this is one of the most important points of its preparation—to prevent oxidation. The iron used, of which charcoal is by far the best in producing homogeneous alloys with gold, should be quite clean and free from oxide before adding it to the gold. It may be cleansed by dipping for a very short time in weak sulphuric acid pickle and afterwards well rinsed and dried; or, secondly, well emery-clothed until it has become perfectly bright. The right quantity of iron should then be added to the gold in the crucible at the proper moment, little by little, until the specified quality of lower alloy required has been reached. The alloy is then to be cast, hammered well down the narrow edges, annealed, again hammered, and again annealed, in order to make it tough. It is quite as well to hammer the bar upon the broad or flat surface, after the first few hammerings have taken place on the edges, to render it the more easily workable in subsequent stages. The ingot mould may advantageously be heated somewhat hotter for this alloy of gold. Gold and iron easily combine in almost any proportion, providing the heat given to cause fusion has been great enough; gold facilitates the fusion of iron, hence it is that the iron should always be made an addition to the fused gold in preparing its composition.

(7.) An alloy of *pale yellow colour* may be made by a small addition of iron to pure gold, say in the proportion of 1-12th of iron to 11-12ths of gold, forming 22 carat gold. The formula constituting one ounce of the mixture would be as follows:—

PALE YELLOW GOLD.

	oz.	dwts.	grs.
Gold, fine . . .	0	18	8
Iron Charcoal . . .	0	1	16
	1	0	0

This alloy costs about 78s. 3d. per ounce before it is put into the melting pot, the latter, of course, increasing the cost a little in accordance to the success of the operation. Iron becomes rapidly oxidised in contact with the air, therefore it is of the greatest importance that a good protective coating should always be secured for the surface of the fused mass in the crucible.

(8.) Another alloy employed in jewellery is to be found occasionally alloyed with iron. It is called *grey gold*. It has a greyish yellow appearance, and is used for leaves and other ornaments. The following is the 20 carat formula :—

GREY GOLD.

	oz.	dwts.	grs.
Gold, fine	0	16	16
Iron Charcoal	0	3	8
	1	0	0

This alloy costs about 71s. 3d. per ounce; and the same remarks and treatment apply to this alloy as to the others named, the details of which having been given when describing them, it will be unnecessary for a further comprehensive description here.

(9.) Formerly the bath employed for imparting the colour of fine gold to jewellery consisted chiefly of the following ingredients: an alkaline nitrate, such as a nitrate of potash or soda and common salt, to which was added some acid sulphate, like alum, or ferric oxide, in order to produce a dilute *aqua regia*. Dr. Wagner, a German, attempted to substitute the latter in place of the former, but without success. He is stated, however, to have accomplished his object by using a solution composed as follows:—

Bromine	1 gramme.
Calcic Bromide	25 grammes.
Water	1 litre.

Sometimes in place of the calcic bromide he used 30 grammes of potassic bromide. The articles are reported to be left in the solution from three to five minutes, then removed and rinsed in the usual way with clean water, and afterwards drawn through a solution of sodic hyposulphite. This recipe is said to accomplish all the purposes which it was intended it should do. Now, our experience has been different, and we unhesitatingly say no such successful results can be achieved by its employment as those stated. No; not even with the best quality of gold jewellers employ in their businesses. We have submitted all the higher qualities of gold to the action of the above mixture without achieving any good commercial success. 18-carat gold cannot be made to present a fine rich colour when treated with it, not so fine, in fact, as it can with dilute sulphuric acid alone; in short, such recipes are not only utterly worthless and misleading to the trade, but they go through the various scientific journals without the fraud being detected, and, consequently, eventually come to be looked upon as established facts. The mixture may be employed for the purpose of removing tarnish from newly-coloured gold goods, which may have become tarnished in stock, but for any other purpose we cannot recommend its employment.

(10.) The following mixture is even better than the above for renovating tarnished goods; it can be used in the following proportions:—

Bicarbonate of Soda	2 oz.
Chloride of Lime	1 „
Common Salt	1 „
Water	16 „
	20 oz.

Well mix together and apply with a soft brush. A very small quantity of solution is sufficient for effecting the desired purpose, and it may be used either cold or in a lukewarm state. Plain articles may be brightened equal to new by putting a spot or two of the liquid upon them from the stopper of the bottle and lightly brushing over the surfaces with fine tissue paper until sufficiently dried off to accomplish the object intended.

(11.) In colouring by the French process without acid, some years ago, we substituted sulphuric acid for the alum, as formerly employed therein, and found it an advantage with some alloys of gold, when the quality was good. The process was rendered much quicker, and the surface of the work presented a much brighter appearance, than when alum was used. Any quality over 14 carats could be coloured by it. This colouring solution was quick in its action, and, if not employed too strong, was not so liable to rot the work as was the more extended process of alum colouring, for alum is a very penetrating salt, and often caused the work to appear overdone. The following were the proportions of ingredients we used when substituting sulphuric acid for alum :—

Saltpetre	8 oz.
Salt	4 „
Sulphuric Acid	1 „
Water	3 „
	16 oz.

The sulphuric acid if added to the other chemicals when they had dissolved in the colour-pot caused effervescence and escape of gas, which was not altogether agreeable and pleasant to the operator in charge of the process. To dispense with which, and render the process more readily accomplished, we mixed together the sulphuric acid and the water in their gelid state, then poured the mixture into the colour-pot, and afterwards added the salts in as fine a powder as was possible. Next, we placed the pot upon the fire and allowed the contents to boil. The work to be coloured was then taken and put into the boiling mixture in bunches in the usual way, and allowed to remain therein, with gentle agitation, for *four minutes*, when it was withdrawn, and well rinsed in boiling water. The colour was then slightly thinned with hot water, and on its again boiling the work was again put in for *two minutes*, and again well rinsed. At this stage the colour required to be further thinned and boiled up, when the work was for the third time put in again for *one minute longer*, and, finally, rinsed as before. It was then ready for finishing by the scratch brush or burnisher, whichever preferred. Jewellers' work treated by this recipe in the manner described receives a fine and bright colour if the quality is 14 carats and upwards. Seven minutes is the time in all the work should be in the colour-pot, and the above quantity of solution will be sufficient to colour 10 oz. of solid gold chains or rings and about 5 oz. of hollow work; but this will to a great extent depend upon the amount of surface, as all must be conveniently covered in the pot to produce an even and reguline surface.

(12.) In precipitating gold in the waste waters of jewellers, care should be taken not to add too much of the precipitating salt—copperas—as if too much is added to a given bulk of solution it will cause the re-dissolving of the precipitating gold, which then passes off with the water as it is drawn away and is lost. Of late an unusual quantity of light hollow work has been made, that is, work drawn on iron wire, and before the work can be finished this iron wire has to be dissolved from the interior of it. Now, we have found in adding the liquid and the residuum from the process to the general waste waters, that it caused too much of the sulphate of iron to be added to properly effect the purpose intended, viz., the precipitation of the gold. The effect of this increased volume of sulphuric acid and the sulphate of oxide of iron combined was the re-dissolving of the gold precipitate, causing it to be held in the solution as at first, and as the supernatant water was finally drawn off the sediment it very naturally passed away with it. The truth of this assertion may readily be verified by taking a small quantity of the solution from the bulk and largely diluting it with water; when, on the addition to it of a few drops of a very pure solution of proto-sulphate of iron, it produces turbidness, the gold cannot have been effectually precipitated in the first instance; or, on the other hand, the redissolution of the precipitate must have taken place as indicated. The best way to treat the spent liquid from the iron dissolving, which contains sulphuric acid not decomposed and sulphate of oxide of iron, is to keep a special receptacle formed of stoneware for receiving and preserving it; no hindrance or disadvantage will thereby accrue to the gold-worker in causing a departure from the usual waste-water treatment of his establishment, which otherwise would have to be, or a consequent loss of gold would be annually taking place.

(13.) It is not generally known in the gold-workers' trade that common washing soda quickly dissolves, in conjunction with hot water, the hard cake of sulphate of iron which forms in the dissolving vessel, when the liquid becomes saturated with it, which it does if attention be not constantly directed thereto. The plan adopted in some gold-working establishments, where crystallisation is found to have taken place, is to put into the vessel some water, and then place it upon the gas jet and heat it until the whole is completely dissolved again. This method takes a long time to do, and therefore causes a great waste of time, which may be utilised to greater advantage. If the crystallised mass, after the remaining uncrystallised liquid is poured from the surface, be treated as follows, complete liquefaction will almost immediately take effect :—Take about one ounce of the soda above named, either in powder or the lump will do for the purpose, and put it into the vessel containing the substance to be operated upon, then add a small quantity of boiling water, when great effervescence will instantaneously commence; this may be increased, and dissolution of the incrustated mass assisted by taking the pipkin—which is the best vessel that can be employed—with the right hand and briskly moving it in a circular direction, thus causing greater agitation of the liquid with increased action of the salt, and the breaking up of the refractory mass into the liquid state, at which stage it should be poured off, and a fresh addition of the sodic salt and boiling water should be made, when the crystallisation of the iron salt is found to be hard and large in quantity, which will very often be found to be the case where there are unlimited proportions of iron to be dissolved, when the liquid employed for the latter purpose has been strong, and its removal from the pipkin has not been effected at the proper time.

(14.) A simple test for distinguishing steel tools from iron ones, which have the same polish and workmanship alike, as if all were steel, consists as follows, and when it is wanted to make the distinction quickly, place a spot of dilute nitric acid upon the tool, and if the tool remains pretty clear, or at the most only shows a whitish mark, then the characteristics named prove it to be iron; but if it shows a dark mark where touched by the acid it is steel. The acid testing solution may be of the strength of one of acid to four of water. The marks can be rubbed off by repolishing the part affected.

(15.) A mild test for ascertaining the quality of some of the various alloys of gold is prepared in the manner here stated, and applied to a clean or filed part of the article to be tested:—Nitric acid 8 drachms; water 4 drachms. Keep the preparation in a small glass phial with a long stopper dipping into the acid, which is most convenient for conveying the liquor from the phial to the work to be tested. This test will have no effect with the higher alloys of gold, like the one given in the earlier part of this work, but it is a more simple and ready test for the lower qualities, causing very slight discolouration in alloys of 8 or 9 carats if properly alloyed. It will be found, therefore, more suitable for the general jeweller, when these qualities are brought under his special notice. The nitric acid employed should be of the greatest chemical purity.

(16.) A very useful gold colour for ordinary work is composed of the undermentioned formula. There should be a fair amount of silver in the alloy composing the work, for producing a bright, smooth surface:—

Nitrate of Potash	8 oz.
Common Salt	4 ,,
Muriatic Acid	4 ,,
	16 oz.

Take a black-lead colour-pot, large enough to prevent the colour boiling over when it reaches that point, place it on the fire and make hot, then put in the powdered salts, stirring them all the time until fine and hot. The acid is then to be added, and the heat increased until the boiling point is attained. The work is next put in and allowed to remain with gentle agitation for 3 *minutes*, when it is withdrawn and rinsed in boiling water to which a spot or two of muriatic acid has been added. Now thin the colour with 1 oz. of muriatic acid and 1 oz. of water, and boil it up again. Finally, put in the work for 1 *minute longer*, then well rinse as before in fresh hot water, scratch-brush, and dry in sawdust, and the colouring is completed with a capital effect, if properly manipulated from the commencement of the process. This solution will colour 46s. gold and upwards with every satisfaction.

(17.) We have often tried to colour gold in an entire liquid solution after the style of the electro-gilding process, and ultimately hope to be commercially successful in the endeavour. In the meantime, however, we have succeeded with some alloys of gold in colouring with the following chemicals. The solution employed would be a dilute *aqua-regia*, and it was the nearest approach to good gold colouring we could arrive at after some months of experimenting. The aqua-regia was prepared on a much more dilute scale than that of the true aqua-regia. It consisted as follows :—

Hydrochloric Acid, chemincally pure .	8 oz.
Nitric Acid, chemically pure	1 ,,

These were intimately well mixed and put into a stoppered bottle for use. When we desired to colour, we used to take 4 oz. of the liquid arising from the old process of colouring, or from this when sufficient had accumulated, to 1 oz. of the above prepared mixture. The solution was then boiled and the work dipped in for a period of from one to three minutes, according to the depth of shade required upon the work. Nitrate of potash (saltpetre) may be substituted for the nitric acid in preparing the above formula, and in colouring with some alloys we have found it an advantage. To 8 oz. of muriatic acid 2 oz. of saltpetre would be required in making the aqua-regia. The muriatic acid should be gently heated until the saltpetre is dissolved, then placed aside to cool, and afterwards bottled securely. When required for use in colouring, well shake the mixture in the bottle, and take of the same proportions as previously stated. Good recipe for good gold. Colour deep.

(18.) Another colouring mixture we have found to answer in experimenting in that direction, viz.—

Hydrochloric Acid . . .	6 parts.
Nitric Acid	1 ,,
Chloride of Ammonia . .	1 ,,
Biborate of Soda . . .	1 ,,
Water	1 ,,
	10 parts.

This solution was used repeatedly as old colour; and when it was desired to revive the strength of it a little, the same proportion of dilute aqua-regia was added when colouring, as named in the previous recipe.

M

(19.) To dissolve copper from gold articles, take 2 oz. of proto-sulphate of iron and dissolve it in half a pint of water, then add to it in powder 2 oz. of nitrate of potash, boil the mixture for some time, and afterwards pour it into a shallow vessel to cool and crystallize, then to every ounce of the crystallized salt add 8 oz. of muriatic acid, and preserve in a bottle for use. 2 oz. of the above preparation should be mixed with 2 oz. of boiling water as the right proportion to use in dissolving copper, or 1 oz. of nitric acid may be used to 4 oz. of boiling water as a substitute.

(20.) Tarnished gold may be renovated and the oxide removed from new or soiled work by applying warm spirits of wine with a soft brush or flannel, when its brilliancy will be restored again.

(21.) High quality gold articles, when their colour has deterioriated, can be restored to their primitive beauty by the application of the following mixture. It is thus composed:—

Sesquioxide of Iron . . .	3 oz.
Calcined Borax	2 ,,
Chloride of Ammonia . . .	1 ,,
Water to form paste . . .	2 ,,
	8 oz.

Well mix the powdered ingredients together until a thick and even paste has been formed, then take the work and either dip it into the mixture or otherwise brush it over with it, care being taken to see that it is well covered with the colour. The articles to be brightened are then taken and placed upon a copper pan, and heated over a clear fire until all hissing sound has ceased and the articles have received a moderate amount of heat, when they are withdrawn, placed aside to cool, and afterwards boiled out in weak muriatic acid to dissolve the colouring salts adhering to the surface. Well rinsing, scratching, and drying completes the process. This produces a fine and high colour to rich gold if the alloy is of a deep hue. It may be used for restoring the colour to repaired places of gold chains, which have had to be mended after the colour has been given to them, and when it is not safe or economical to put them through the acid process again. After the soldering has been completed, take a little of the above composition prepared as stated and apply it to the soldered parts, then heat the parts only very gently with the gas jet by means of the mouth blow-pipe, allow to cool, then by dissolving the adhering flux by the means before stated, and slightly scratch-brushing the places that have been re-coloured, rinsing and drying the work completely restores the evenness of surface.

(22.) Another mixture that may be used in the same manner. It consists of the following chemicals :—

Sesquioxide of Iron	3 oz.
Acetate of Copper	3 ,,
Calcined Borax	1 ,,
Water to form paste . . .	2 ,,
	9 oz.

The acetate of copper should be well dried before

using to free it from the vinegar, or it will probably corrode the work. In this recipe the sesquioxide of iron should be the red, whereas in the other it may be the yellow. The treatment is exactly the same as that in the one just described.

(23.) As it is difficult to procure, at the time when most wanted, alloys for solders that are the most suitable and advantageous for the various kinds of work without no little inconvenience in effecting a proper composition, we here append a list suitable for all the qualities of coloured gold work as manufactured by jewellers and goldsmiths :—

"Gold Solder to cost 58s. per oz. suitable for 18-carat work."

	oz.	dwts.	grs.
Gold, fine . . .	1	0	0
Silver, fine . . .	0	6	0
Copper wire . . .	0	4	0
	1	10	0

Or 3 dwts. of copper and 1 dwt. of compo. instead of all copper.

"Gold Solder to cost 53s. 6d. per oz. suitable for 18-carat work."

	oz.	dwts.	grs.
Gold, fine . . .	1	0	0
Silver, fine . . .	0	7	0
Copper wire . . .	0	5	12
	1	12	12

Or 4 dwts. of copper and 1½ dwts. of compo. instead of all copper.

"Gold Solder to cost 50s. per oz. suitable for 16-carat work."

	oz.	dwts.	grs.
Gold, fine . . .	1	0	0
Silver, fine . . .	0	8	0
Copper wire . . .	0	7	0
	1	15	0

Or 5 dwts. of copper and 2 dwts. of compo. instead of all copper.

"Gold Solder to cost 44*s.* per oz. suitable for 15-carat work."

	oz.	dwts.	grs.
Gold, fine . . .	1	0	0
Silver, fine . . .	0	10	0
Copper wire . . .	0	10	0
	2	0	0

Or 7½ dwts. of copper and 2½ dwts. of compo. instead of all copper.

"Gold Solder to cost 40s. per oz. suitable for 14-carat work."

	oz.	dwts.	grs.
Gold, fine . . .	1	0	0
Silver, fine . . .	0	12	12
Copper wire . . .	0	12	12
	2	5	0

Or 9½ dwts. of copper and 3 dwts. of compo. instead of all copper.

M 2

"Gold Solder to cost 37s. 6d. per oz. suitable for any coloured work."

	oz.	dwts.	grs.
Gold, fine . . .	1	0	0
Silver, fine . . .	0	15	0
Copper wire . . .	0	12	12
	2	7	12

Or $9\frac{1}{2}$ dwts. of copper and 3 dwts. of compo. instead of all copper.

(24.) Since so much iron has been used in the trade of late, in the preparation of light hollow work, a few words in reference to the treatment of lemel, or filings arising therefrom, will be most welcome to that circle of the trade. The iron which the lemel contains can never all be got out with the magnet; in the melting of it we have experienced a difficulty in effecting a clear and perfect collection, such as did not present itself in lemel free from iron. We, however, reduced the process to the same simplicity as the former one, by using the following flux in the following manner.

Take—

Lemel	20 oz.
Potash	1 "
Salt	1 "
Sandever	1 "
Saltpetre	1 "
	24 oz.

Well mix the lemel with half of each of the two former salts and put it into a sufficiently large clay crucible to prevent boiling over when it rises. Put the remaining half of the potash and salt on the top and press it down a little, then place the crucible in a good wind furnace well surrounded with coke, and give it a great heat; when the mass has become liquid through the penetration of the former salts add a portion of the sandever and saltpetre, but only in portions at a time, otherwise the contents of the crucible may rise and pass a part of it away by flowing over the top, and this is to be guarded against. When the whole of the sandever and saltpetre has been added in this way continue the heat for half an hour or so; the crucible should then be withdrawn, allowed to cool, and subsequently broken to recover the lump of gold, &c. The button of gold is then weighed, the difference from its former weight noted, and a final melting in a plumbago pot with a little charcoal flux, and pouring into an ingot mould, would complete the process. The bar of metal is then quite ready for the assay to be taken in order to ascertain the quality of it.

(25.) 18-carat gold articles, and upwards, made from *bright alloys*, can be made to present a beautiful bright mirror-looking appearance by well polishing all over, inside and out, with pumice and emery, then with oil and rottenstone, and finally finishing upon the buff with a little rouge of the best quality and a touch or two of grease. Work high in quality finished in this manner requires no gilding or colouring to put a superior surface to it; and when it is well washed out with soap in a hot solution of potash or soda it looks very beautiful and rich. The bright alloy for 18 carats is composed as follows:—

	oz.	dwts.	grs.
Gold, fine . . .	0	15	3
Silver, fine . . .	0	2	21
Copper wire . . .	0	2	0
	1	0	0

Add 2 grs. of copper per oz. for loss in melting.

This alloy is for Hall-marking, and the three grains extra of fine gold in the alloy is an allowance for the gold never being bought quite pure, and to enable it to pass the Hall in safety. The two grains of copper added for melting loss we have found to be an advantage, since it keeps the alloy more uniform as to its original weight, and the cost per ounce is more certain and regular, whilst its safety in passing the Hall is more than guaranteed by its adoption.

(26.) When coloured gold work intended for colouring has, by accident in mistaking the solder, become soldered with silver solder, which renders it unfit for the process, it can be prepared for it again by placing the work in tolerably strong nitric acid of good commercial quality and free from muriatic acid, as the latter would cause the mixture to be decomposed, with liberation of chlorine and dissolution of the gold. This is therefore to be avoided, in order to prevent the complete destruction of the work when seeking only for the removal of the inferior solder which has been inadvertently applied to its connections. The nitric acid solution, if chemically pure acid is employed, will entirely free the work from all traces of this solder, as the acid will break it up and dissolve it without injuring the articles operated upon in any way. After the solder has been removed and the work taken from the solution of acid, it should be rinsed, annealed, and boiled out in dilute sulphuric acid—commonly called oil of vitriol—before resoldering again with the proper solder. The nitric acid solution should be of a good strength, although not too strong; a good mixture consists of one of acid to four of water. This is a convenient strength for effecting the above purpose; it should be used hot, and the necessary degree of heat can be kept up to the point required by means of the gas jet.

(27.) Designs of gold articles as now made for the market are of such a delicate make and construction, some of them, that they have to be supported underneath in the process of manufacture with iron wire; charcoal is the best for the purpose, and should be the only kind used, because any other is very difficult to remove. At the finish of the work this iron has to be removed by dissolving in some acid with which it has great chemical attraction. Sulphuric acid is the best for this purpose; it is sold under the name of oil of vitriol, at a cost of three-halfpence per lb. To dissolve the iron from the work, take a stoneware jar or pipkin large enough for the work in hand, put the work into it, and add sufficient boiling water to well cover the work; the pipkin must not be filled with water, for when the acid is added it will boil over and carry all the liquid away without its being properly utilised. In putting the acid to the water great care should be taken to prevent its flying about, as the scald or burn will destroy everything it comes in contact with. The proper way to add it to the boiling water would be as follows:—Take an ordinary copper boiling-out pan, and firstly put into that receptacle the oil of vitriol, and then take hold of the mouthpiece with a long pair of tongs, and very gradually pour the contents into the pipkin holding the work and the boiling water. When this is done, place the pipkin with its contents in a water bath or upon a sand bath, but if these conveniences are not at hand put it upon a sheet of iron with a gas light underneath, which will keep the mixture at a regular temperature. After the expiration of one hour the liquid will require to be poured off, and another addition of hot water and oil of vitriol, as before, made to the work. This should be kept in action a little longer, when a third one is made, and which generally completes the process if all things have been favourable. The strength of solution which acts best is this: to every 8 oz. of boiling water take 1 oz. of oil of vitriol; that would be 5 oz. of oil of vitriol to the quart of boiling water. These proportions refer to when the solution is kept hot by means of the gas jet, and not when the dissolution is allowed to proceed without its action being increased by the aid of applied heat. In the latter case, the dissolving mixture may wisely be used a little stronger. By this process a large quantity of iron may be dissolved without affecting the gold in the least degree. Three hours, with proper attention bestowed upon it, is ample time for removing the iron from a batch of work containing it.

(28.) A dead pale lemon colour can be given to 18-carat plain work when the alloy is right by carrying out the following instructions. The work requires to be well polished in order to present a nice surface, after which process it is washed in hot soda water and dried; it is then annealed by placing over a clear fire upon a copper pan. The annealing oxidises the surface of the work, and thereby renders it the more attackable by the acid employed in the subsequent process. When the work has cooled from the annealing, it is suspended upon a wire and then dipped into boiling dilute nitric acid, free from muriatic acid, when the articles will present a fine rich lemon colour.

(29.) Most jewellers, at some time or other of their experience, may have met with accidents in the melting and pouring of their alloys. Such, for instance, as a pot cracking, the spilling or the upsetting of a portion of the metal from the crucible into the fire. The following mode of recovery of lost metal we have found the best and most practical in the workshop with the ordinary appliances usually at the command of jewellers and goldworkers. Collect the whole of the burnt coke, ashes, and other refuse used in the melting operation, and first of all well wash it several times with water to remove the dust and other extraneous matter; the sediment left behind is then well dried and pounded as fine as possible in a cast-iron mortar; it is afterwards put through a sieve as fine as is convenient to prevent the small particles of gold from going through the meshes with the powdered dust. The gold is now picked at this stage from the refuse in the sieve; and if there be any solid particles of refuse still unpounded it is put through the process again. It is very seldom that the whole of the gold can be collected when once spilled into the fire, but the major portion of it can be recovered by these means. The other goes into the sweep to be treated by the refiner.

(30.) In carrying out any of these suggestions it is important that the chemicals employed for the purpose should be of the best quality, if not chemically pure, when complete success and good commercial results are desired to be achieved by the adoption of any of the various processes described in this work.

INDEX.

N

O

THE END.

WEALE'S RUDIMENTARY SCIENTIFIC SERIES.

*** The volumes of this Series are freely Illustrated with Woodcuts, or otherwise, where requisite. Throughout the following List it must be understood that the books are bound in limp cloth, unless otherwise stated; *but the volumes marked with a ‡ may also be had strongly bound in cloth boards for 6d. extra.*

N.B.—In ordering from this List it is recommended, as a means of facilitating business and obviating error, to quote the numbers affixed to the volumes, as well as the titles and prices.

CIVIL ENGINEERING, SURVEYING, ETC.

No.

31. *WELLS AND WELL-SINKING.* By JOHN GEO. SWINDELL, A.R.I.B.A., and G. R. BURNELL, C.E. Revised Edition. With a New Appendix on the Qualities of Water. Illustrated. 2s.

35. *THE BLASTING AND QUARRYING OF STONE*, for Building and other Purposes. With Remarks on the Blowing up of Bridges. By Gen. Sir JOHN BURGOYNE, Bart., K.C.B. Illustrated. 1s. 6d.

43. *TUBULAR, AND OTHER IRON GIRDER BRIDGES*, particularly describing the Britannia and Conway Tubular Bridges. By G. DRYSDALE DEMPSEY, C.E. Fourth Edition. 2s.

44. *FOUNDATIONS AND CONCRETE WORKS*, with Practical Remarks on Footings, Sand, Concrete, Béton, Pile-driving, Caissons, and Cofferdams, &c. By E. DOBSON. Fifth Edition. 1s. 6d.

60. *LAND AND ENGINEERING SURVEYING.* By T. BAKER, C.E. New Edition, revised by EDWARD NUGENT, C.E. 2s.‡

80*. *EMBANKING LANDS FROM THE SEA.* With examples and Particulars of actual Embankments, &c. By J. WIGGINS, F.G.S. 2s.

81. *WATER WORKS*, for the Supply of Cities and Towns. With a Description of the Principal Geological Formations of England as influencing Supplies of Water; and Details of Engines and Pumping Machinery for raising Water. By SAMUEL HUGHES, F.G.S., C.E. New Edition. 4s.‡

118. *CIVIL ENGINEERING IN NORTH AMERICA*, a Sketch of. By DAVID STEVENSON, F.R.S.E., &c. Plates and Diagrams. 3s.

167. *IRON BRIDGES, GIRDERS, ROOFS, AND OTHER WORKS.* By FRANCIS CAMPIN, C.E. 2s. 6d.‡

197. *ROADS AND STREETS (THE CONSTRUCTION OF).* By HENRY LAW, C.E., revised and enlarged by D. K. CLARK, C.E., including pavements of Stone, Wood, Asphalte, &c. 4s. 6d.‡

203. *SANITARY WORK IN THE SMALLER TOWNS AND IN VILLAGES.* By C. SLAGG, A.M.I.C.E. Revised Edition. 3s.‡

212. *GAS-WORKS, THEIR CONSTRUCTION AND ARRANGEMENT*; and the Manufacture and Distribution of Coal Gas. Originally written by SAMUEL HUGHES, C.E. Re-written and enlarged by WILLIAM RICHARDS, C.E. Seventh Edition, with important additions. 5s. 6d.‡

213. *PIONEER ENGINEERING.* A Treatise on the Engineering Operations connected with the Settlement of Waste Lands in New Countries. By EDWARD DOBSON, Assoc. Inst. C.E. 4s. 6d.‡

216. *MATERIALS AND CONSTRUCTION*; A Theoretical and Practical Treatise on the Strains, Designing, and Erection of Works of Construction. By FRANCIS CAMPIN, C.E. Second Edition, revised. 3s.‡

219. *CIVIL ENGINEERING.* By HENRY LAW, M.Inst. C.E. Including HYDRAULIC ENGINEERING by GEO. R. BURNELL, M.Inst. C.E. Seventh Edition, revised, with large additions by D. KINNEAR CLARK, M.Inst. C.E. 6s. 6d., Cloth boards, 7s. 6d.

☞ *The ‡ indicates that these vols. may be had strongly bound at 6d. extra.*

LONDON: CROSBY LOCKWOOD AND CO.,

MECHANICAL ENGINEERING, ETC.

33. *CRANES*, the Construction of, and other Machinery for Raising Heavy Bodies. By JOSEPH GLYNN, F.R.S. Illustrated. 1s. 6d.

34. *THE STEAM ENGINE*. By Dr. LARDNER. Illustrated. 1s. 6d.

59. *STEAM BOILERS:* their Construction and Management. By R. ARMSTRONG, C.E. Illustrated. 1s. 6d.

82. *THE POWER OF WATER*, as applied to drive Flour Mills, and to give motion to Turbines, &c. By JOSEPH GLYNN, F.R.S. 2s.‡

98. *PRACTICAL MECHANISM*, the Elements of; and Machine Tools. By T. BAKER, C.E. With Additions by J. NASMYTH, C.E. 2s. ‡

139. *THE STEAM ENGINE*, a Treatise on the Mathematical Theory of, with Rules and Examples for Practical Men. By T. BAKER, C.E. 1s. 6d.

164. *MODERN WORKSHOP PRACTICE*, as applied to Marine, Land, and Locomotive Engines, Floating Docks, Dredging Machines, Bridges, Cranes, Ship-building, &c., &c. By J. G. WINTON. Illustrated. 3s.‡

165. *IRON AND HEAT*, exhibiting the Principles concerned in the Construction of Iron Beams, Pillars, and Bridge Girders, and the Action of Heat in the Smelting Furnace. By J. ARMOUR, C.E. 2s. 6d.‡

166. *POWER IN MOTION:* Horse-Power, Toothed-Wheel Gearing, Long and Short Driving Bands, and Angular Forces. By J. ARMOUR, 2s. 6d.‡

171. *THE WORKMAN'S MANUAL OF ENGINEERING* DRAWING. By J. MAXTON. 5th Edn. With 7 Plates and 350 Cuts. 3s. 6d.‡

190. *STEAM AND THE STEAM ENGINE*, Stationary and Portable. By JOHN SEWELL and D. K. CLARK, M.I.C.E. 3s. 6d.‡

200. *FUEL*, its Combustion and Economy. By C. W. WILLIAMS; With Recent Practice in the Combustion and Economy of Fuel—Coal, Coke, Wood, Peat, Petroleum, &c.—by D. K. CLARK, M.I.C.E. 3s. 6d.‡

202. *LOCOMOTIVE ENGINES*. By G. D. DEMPSEY, C.E.; with large additions by D. KINNEAR CLARK, M.I.C.E. 3s.‡

211. *THE BOILERMAKER'S ASSISTANT* in Drawing, Templating, and Calculating Boiler and Tank Work. By JOHN COURTNEY, Practical Boiler Maker. Edited by D. K. CLARK, C.E. 100 Illustrations. 2s.

217. *SEWING MACHINERY:* Its Construction, History, &c., with full Technical Directions for Adjusting, &c. By J. W. URQUHART, C.E. 2s.‡

223. *MECHANICAL ENGINEERING*. Comprising Metallurgy, Moulding, Casting, Forging, Tools, Workshop Machinery, Manufacture of the Steam Engine, &c. By FRANCIS CAMPIN, C.E. 2s. 6d.‡

236. *DETAILS OF MACHINERY*. Comprising Instructions for the Execution of various Works in Iron. By FRANCIS CAMPIN, C.E. 3s.‡

237. *THE SMITHY AND FORGE;* including the Farrier's Art and Coach Smithing. By W. J. E. CRANE. Illustrated. 2s. 6d.‡

238. *THE SHEET-METAL WORKER'S GUIDE;* a Practical Handbook for Tinsmiths, Coppersmiths, Zincworkers, &c. With 94 Diagrams and Working Patterns. By W. J. E. CRANE. 1s. 6d.

251. *STEAM AND MACHINERY MANAGEMENT:* with Hints on Construction and Selection. By M. POWIS BALE, M.I.M.E. 2s. 6d.‡

254. *THE BOILERMAKER'S READY-RECKONER*. With Examples of Practical Geometry and Templating. By JOHN COURTNEY. Edited by D. K. CLARK, M.Inst.C.E. 4s., limp; 5s., half-bound.

255. *LOCOMOTIVE ENGINE-DRIVING*. A Practical Manual for Engineers in charge of Locomotive Engines. By MICHAEL REYNOLDS, M.S.E. Seventh Edition. 3s. 6d., limp; 4s. 6d. cloth boards. [*Just published.*

256. *STATIONARY ENGINE-DRIVING*. A Practical Manual for Engineers in charge of Stationary Engines. By MICHAEL REYNOLDS, M.S.E. Third Edition. 3s. 6d. limp; 4s. 6d. cloth boards. [*Just published.*

☞ *The ‡ indicates that these vols. may be had strongly bound at 6d. extra.*

MINING, METALLURGY, ETC.

4. *MINERALOGY*, Rudiments of; a concise View of the General Properties of Minerals. By A. RAMSAY, F.G.S., F.R.G.S., &c. Third Edition, revised and enlarged. Illustrated. 3s. 6d.‡ [*Just published.*

117. *SUBTERRANEOUS SURVEYING*, Elementary and Practical Treatise on, with and without the Magnetic Needle. By THOMAS FENWICK, Surveyor of Mines, and THOMAS BAKER, C.E. Illustrated. 2s. 6d.‡

133. *METALLURGY OF COPPER*; an Introduction to the Methods of Seeking, Mining, and Assaying Copper, and Manufacturing its Alloys. By ROBERT H. LAMBORN, Ph.D. Woodcuts. 2s. 6d.‡

135. *ELECTRO-METALLURGY*; Practically Treated. By ALEXANDER WATT, F.R.S.S.A. Eighth Edition, revised, with additional Matter and Illustrations, including the most recent Processes. 3s.‡

172. *MINING TOOLS*, Manual of. For the Use of Mine Managers, Agents, Students, &c. By WILLIAM MORGANS. 2s. 6d.‡

72*. *MINING TOOLS, ATLAS* of Engravings to Illustrate the above, containing 235 Illustrations, drawn to Scale. 4to. 4s. 6d.; cloth boards, 6s.

176. *METALLURGY OF IRON.* Containing History of Iron Manufacture, Methods of Assay, and Analyses of Iron Ores, Processes of Manufacture of Iron and Steel, &c. By H. BAUERMAN, F.G.S. Fifth Edition, revised and enlarged. 5s.‡

180. *COAL AND COAL MINING.* By WARINGTON W. SMYTH, M.A., F.R.S. Sixth Edition, revised. 3s. 6d.‡ [*Just published.*

195. *THE MINERAL SURVEYOR AND VALUER'S COMPLETE GUIDE*, with new Traverse Tables, and Descriptions of Improved Instruments; also the Correct Principles of Laying out and Valuing Mineral Properties. By WILLIAM LINTERN, Mining and Civil Engineer. 3s. 6d.‡

214. *SLATE AND SLATE QUARRYING*, Scientific, Practical, and Commercial. By D. C. DAVIES, F.G.S., Mining Engineer, &c. 3s.‡

220. *MAGNETIC SURVEYING, AND ANGULAR SURVEYING*, with Records of the Peculiarities of Needle Disturbances. Compiled from the Results of carefully made Experiments. By W. LINTERN. 2s.

ARCHITECTURE, BUILDING, ETC.

16. *ARCHITECTURE—ORDERS*—The Orders and their Æsthetic Principles. By W. H. LEEDS. Illustrated. 1s. 6d.

17. *ARCHITECTURE—STYLES*—The History and Description of the Styles of Architecture of Various Countries, from the Earliest to the Present Period. By T. TALBOT BURY, F.R.I.B.A., &c. Illustrated. 2s.
*** ORDERS AND STYLES OF ARCHITECTURE, *in One Vol.*, 3s. 6d.

18. *ARCHITECTURE—DESIGN*—The Principles of Design in Architecture, as deducible from Nature and exemplified in the Works of the Greek and Gothic Architects. By E. L. GARBETT, Architect. Illustrated. 2s.6d.

*** *The three preceding Works, in One handsome Vol., half bound, entitled* "MODERN ARCHITECTURE," *price* 6s.

22. *THE ART OF BUILDING*, Rudiments of. General Principles of Construction, Materials used in Building, Strength and Use of Materials, Working Drawings, Specifications, and Estimates. By E. DOBSON, 2s.‡

25. *MASONRY AND STONECUTTING*: Rudimentary Treatise on the Principles of Masonic Projection and their application to Construction. By EDWARD DOBSON, M.R.I.B.A., &c. 2s. 6d.‡

42. *COTTAGE BUILDING.* By C. BRUCE ALLEN, Architect. Ninth Edition, revised and enlarged. Numerous Illustrations. 1s. 6d.

45. *LIMES, CEMENTS, MORTARS, CONCRETES, MASTICS, PLASTERING*, &c. By G. R. BURNELL, C.E. Twelfth Edition. 1s. 6d.

☞ *The ‡ indicates that these vols. may be had strongly bound at 6d. extra.*

Architecture, Building, etc., *continued.*

57. *WARMING AND VENTILATION.* An Exposition of the General Principles as applied to Domestic and Public Buildings, Mines, Lighthouses, Ships, &c. By C. TOMLINSON, F.R.S., &c. Illustrated. 3s.

111. *ARCHES, PIERS, BUTTRESSES, &c.:* Experimental Essays on the Principles of Construction. By W. BLAND. Illustrated. 1s. 6d.

116. *THE ACOUSTICS OF PUBLIC BUILDINGS;* or, The Principles of the Science of Sound applied to the purposes of the Architect and Builder. By T. ROGER SMITH, M.R.I.B.A., Architect. Illustrated. 1s. 6d.

127. *ARCHITECTURAL MODELLING IN PAPER,* the Art of. By T. A. RICHARDSON, Architect. Illustrated. 1s. 6d.

128. *VITRUVIUS—THE ARCHITECTURE OF MARCUS VITRUVIUS POLLO.* In Ten Books. Translated from the Latin by JOSEPH GWILT, F.S.A., F.R.A.S. With 23 Plates. 5s.

130. *GRECIAN ARCHITECTURE,* An Inquiry into the Principles of Beauty in; with an Historical View of the Rise and Progress of the Art in Greece. By the EARL OF ABERDEEN. 1s.

*** *The two preceding Works in One handsome Vol., half bound, entitled* "ANCIENT ARCHITECTURE," *price* 6s.

132. *THE ERECTION OF DWELLING-HOUSES.* Illustrated by a Perspective View, Plans, Elevations, and Sections of a pair of Semi-detached Villas, with the Specification, Quantities, and Estimates, &c. By S. H. BROOKS. New Edition, with Plates. 2s. 6d.‡

156. *QUANTITIES AND MEASUREMENTS,* How to Calculate and Take them in Bricklayers', Masons', Plasterers', Plumbers', Painters', Paper-hangers', Gilders', Smiths', Carpenters', and Joiners' Work. By A. C. BEATON, Architect and Surveyor. New and Enlarged Edition. Illus. 1s. 6d.

175. *LOCKWOOD & CO.'S BUILDER'S AND CONTRACTOR'S* PRICE BOOK, containing the latest Prices of all kinds of Builders' Materials and Labour, and of all Trades connected with Building, &c., &c. Edited by F. T. W. MILLER, Architect. Published annually. 3s. 6d.; half bound, 4s.

182. *CARPENTRY AND JOINERY*—THE ELEMENTARY PRINCIPLES OF CARPENTRY. Chiefly composed from the Standard Work of THOMAS TREDGOLD, C.E. With Additions, Alterations, and Corrections from the Works of the most Recent Authorities, and a TREATISE ON JOINERY by E. WYNDHAM TARN, M.A. Fourth Edition, Revised and extended, with numerous Illustrations. 3s. 6d.‡ [*Just published.*

182*. *CARPENTRY AND JOINERY. ATLAS* of 35 Plates to accompany the above. With Descriptive Letterpress. 4to. 6s.; cloth, 7s. 6d.

185. *THE COMPLETE MEASURER;* the Measurement of Boards, Glass, &c.; Unequal-sided, Square-sided, Octagonal-sided, Round Timber and Stone, and Standing Timber, &c. By RICHARD HORTON. Fifth Edition. 4s.; strongly bound in leather, 5s.

187. *HINTS TO YOUNG ARCHITECTS.* By G. WIGHTWICK. New Edition. By G. H. GUILLAUME. Illustrated. 3s. 6d.‡

188. *HOUSE PAINTING, GRAINING, MARBLING, AND SIGN WRITING:* a Practical Manual of, with a Course of Elementary Drawing for House-Painters, Sign-Writers, &c., and a Collection of Useful Receipts. By ELLIS A. DAVIDSON. Fourth Edition. With Coloured Plates. 5s. cloth limp; 6s. cloth boards.

189. *THE RUDIMENTS OF PRACTICAL BRICKLAYING.* In Six Sections: General Principles; Arch Drawing, Cutting, and Setting; Pointing; Paving, Tiling, Materials; Slating and Plastering; Practical Geometry, Mensuration, &c. By ADAM HAMMOND. Fifth Edition. 1s. 6d.

191. *PLUMBING.* A Text-Book to the Practice of the Art or Craft of the Plumber. With Chapters upon House Drainage. Fourth Edition. With 330 Illustrations. By W. P. BUCHAN. 3s. 6d.‡

☞ *The ‡ indicates that these vols. may be had strongly bound at 6d. extra.*

Architecture, Building, etc., *continued.*

192. *THE TIMBER IMPORTER'S, TIMBER MERCHANT'S,* and BUILDER'S STANDARD GUIDE. By RICHARD E. GRANDY. Second Edition, Revised. 3s.‡

206. *A BOOK ON BUILDING, Civil and Ecclesiastical,* including CHURCH RESTORATION. With the Theory of Domes and the Great Pyramid, &c. By Sir EDMUND BECKETT, Bart., LL.D., Q.C., F.R.A.S. 4s. 6d.‡

226. *THE JOINTS MADE AND USED BY BUILDERS* in the Construction of various kinds of Engineering and Architectural Works. By WYVILL J. CHRISTY, Architect. With upwards of 160 Engravings on Wood. 3s.‡

228. *THE CONSTRUCTION OF ROOFS OF WOOD AND IRON* By E. WYNDHAM TARN, M.A., Architect. Second Edition, revised. 1s. 6d.

229. *ELEMENTARY DECORATION:* as applied to the Interior and Exterior Decoration of Dwelling-Houses, &c. By JAMES W. FACEY, Jun. Illustrated with Sixty-eight explanatory Engravings. 2s.

230. *HANDRAILING* (A Practical Treatise on). Showing New and Simple Methods for finding the Pitch of the Plank, Drawing the Moulds, Bevelling, Jointing-up, and Squaring the Wreath. By GEORGE COLLINGS. Illustrated with Plates and Diagrams. 1s. 6d.

247. *BUILDING ESTATES:* a Rudimentary Treatise on the Development, Sale, Purchase, and General Management of Building Land, including the Formation of Streets and Sewers, and the Requirements of Sanitary Authorities. By FOWLER MAITLAND, Surveyor. Illustrated. 2s.

248. *PORTLAND CEMENT FOR USERS.* By HENRY FAIJA, Assoc. M. Inst. C.E. Second Edition, corrected. Illustrated. 2s.

252. *BRICKWORK:* a Practical Treatise, embodying the General and Higher Principles of Bricklaying, Cutting and Setting, &c. By F. WALKER, Certificated by the Science and Art Department in Building Construction, Solid Geometry, &c. 1s. 6d.

253. *THE TIMBER MERCHANT'S, SAW-MILLER'S, AND* IMPORTER'S FREIGHT-BOOK AND ASSISTANT. By WM. RICHARDSON. With a Chapter on Speeds of Saw-Mill Machinery, &c. By M. POWIS BALE, A.M.Inst.C.E., and a London Price List for Timber and Deal Sawing, &c., 1884. 3s.‡ [*Just published.*

SHIPBUILDING, NAVIGATION, MARINE ENGINEERING, ETC.

51. *NAVAL ARCHITECTURE.* An Exposition of the Elementary Principles of the Science, and their Practical Application to Naval Construction. By J. PEAKE. Fifth Edition, with Plates and Diagrams. 3s. 6d.‡

53*. *SHIPS FOR OCEAN AND RIVER SERVICE,* Elementary and Practical Principles of the Construction of. By H. A. SOMMERFELDT, Surveyor of the Royal Norwegian Navy. With an Appendix. 1s. 6d.

53**. *AN ATLAS OF ENGRAVINGS* to Illustrate the above. Twelve large folding plates. Royal 4to, cloth. 7s. 6d.

54. *MASTING, MAST-MAKING, AND RIGGING OF SHIPS,* Rudimentary Treatise on. Also Tables of Spars, Rigging, Blocks; Chain, Wire, and Hemp Ropes, &c., relative to every class of vessels. By ROBERT KIPPING, N.A. Fifteenth Edition. Illustrated. 2s.‡

54*. *IRON SHIP-BUILDING.* With Practical Examples and Details for the Use of Ship Owners and Ship Builders. By JOHN GRANTHAM, Consulting Engineer and Naval Architect. 5th Edition, with Additions. 4s.

54**. *AN ATLAS OF FORTY PLATES* to Illustrate the above. Fifth Edition. 4to, boards. 38s.

55. *THE SAILOR'S SEA BOOK:* a Rudimentary Treatise on Navigation. By JAMES GREENWOOD, B.A. With numerous Woodcuts and Coloured Plates. New and enlarged edition. By W. H. ROSSER. 2s. 6d.‡

☞ *The ‡ indicates that these vols. may be had strongly bound at 6d. extra.*

Shipbuilding, Navigation, Marine Engineering, etc., *cont.*

83*bis*. *THE FORMS OF SHIPS AND BOATS:* Hints, Experimentally Derived, on some of the Principles regulating Shipbuilding. By W. BLAND. Seventh Edition, revised, with numerous Illustrations and Models. 1s. 6d.

99. *NAVIGATION AND NAUTICAL ASTRONOMY*, in Theory and Practice. By Prof. J. R. YOUNG. New Edition. 2s. 6d.

106. *SHIPS' ANCHORS*, a Treatise on. By G. COTSELL, N.A. 1s. 6d.

149. *SAILS AND SAIL-MAKING*, an Elementary Treatise on. With Draughting, and the Centre of Effort of the Sails. Also, Weights and Sizes of Ropes; Masting, Rigging, and Sails of Steam Vessels, &c., &c. Eleventh Edition. By ROBERT KIPPING, N.A., Sailmaker. Illustrated. 2s. 6d.‡

155. *THE ENGINEER'S GUIDE TO THE ROYAL AND* MERCANTILE NAVIES. By a PRACTICAL ENGINEER. Revised by D. F. M'CARTHY, late of the Ordnance Survey Office, Southampton. 3s.

55 & 204. *PRACTICAL NAVIGATION.* Consisting of The Sailor's Sea-Book. By JAMES GREENWOOD and W. H. ROSSER. Together with the requisite Mathematical and Nautical Tables for the Working of the Problems. By HENRY LAW, C.E., and Professor J. R. YOUNG. With numerous Wood Engravings and Coloured Plates. 7s. Strongly half-bound.

AGRICULTURE, GARDENING, ETC.

61*. *A COMPLETE READY RECKONER FOR THE ADMEA*-SUREMENT OF LAND, &c. By A. ARMAN. Second Edition, revised and extended by C. NORRIS, Surveyor, Valuer, &c. 2s.

131. *MILLER'S, MERCHANT'S, AND FARMER'S READY* RECKONER. With approximate values of Millstones, Millwork, &c. 1s.

140. *SOILS, MANURES, AND CROPS.* (Vol. 1. OUTLINES OF MODERN FARMING.) By R. SCOTT BURN. Woodcuts. 2s.

141. *FARMING & FARMING ECONOMY*, Notes, Historical and Practical, on. (Vol. 2. OUTLINES OF MODERN FARMING.) By R. SCOTT BURN. 3s.

142. *STOCK; CATTLE, SHEEP, AND HORSES.* (Vol. 3. OUTLINES OF MODERN FARMING.) By R. SCOTT BURN. Woodcuts. 2s. 6d.

145. *DAIRY, PIGS, AND POULTRY*, Management of the. By R. SCOTT BURN. With Notes on the Diseases of Stock. (Vol. 4. OUTLINES OF MODERN FARMING.) Woodcuts. 2s.

146. *UTILIZATION OF SEWAGE, IRRIGATION, AND* RECLAMATION OF WASTE LAND. (Vol. 5. OUTLINES OF MODERN FARMING.) By R. SCOTT BURN. Woodcuts. 2s. 6d.

**** *Nos. 140-1-2-5-6, in One Vol., handsomely half-bound, entitled* "OUTLINES OF MODERN FARMING." By ROBERT SCOTT BURN. *Price* 12s.

177. *FRUIT TREES*, The Scientific and Profitable Culture of. From the French of DU BREUIL. Revised by GEO. GLENNY. 187 Woodcuts. 3s. 6d.‡

198. *SHEEP; THE HISTORY, STRUCTURE, ECONOMY, AND* DISEASES OF. By W. C. SPOONER, M.R.V.C., &c. Fourth Edition, enlarged, including Specimens of New and Improved Breeds. 3s. 6d.‡

201. *KITCHEN GARDENING MADE EASY.* By GEORGE M. F. GLENNY. Illustrated. 1s. 6d.‡

207. *OUTLINES OF FARM MANAGEMENT, and the Organization of Farm Labour:* Treating of the General Work of the Farm; Field and Live Stock; Contract Work; Labour, &c. By R. SCOTT BURN. 2s. 6d.‡

208. *OUTLINES OF LANDED ESTATES MANAGEMENT:* Treating of the Varieties of Lands, Methods of Farming, Farm Buildings, Irrigation, Drainage, &c. By R. SCOTT BURN. 2s. 6d.‡

**** *Nos. 207 & 208 in One Vol., handsomely half-bound, entitled* "OUTLINES OF LANDED ESTATES AND FARM MANAGEMENT." By R. SCOTT BURN. *Price* 6s.

☞ *The ‡ indicates that these vols. may be had strongly bound at 6d. extra.*

Agriculture, Gardening, etc., *continued.*

209. *THE TREE PLANTER AND PLANT PROPAGATOR.* A Practical Manual on the Propagation of Forest Trees, Fruit Trees, Flowering Shrubs, Flowering Plants, &c. By SAMUEL WOOD. 2s.‡

210. *THE TREE PRUNER.* A Practical Manual on the Pruning of Fruit Trees, including also their Training and Renovation; also the Pruning of Shrubs, Climbers, and Flowering Plants. By SAMUEL WOOD. 2s.‡

*** *Nos.* 209 *&* 210 *in One Vol., handsomely half-bound, entitled* "THE TREE PLANTER, PROPAGATOR, AND PRUNER." By SAMUEL WOOD. *Price* 5*s.*

218. *THE HAY AND STRAW MEASURER:* Being New Tables for the Use of Auctioneers, Valuers, Farmers, Hay and Straw Dealers, &c. By JOHN STEELE. Fourth Edition. 2s.

222. *SUBURBAN FARMING.* The Laying-out and Cultivation of Farms, adapted to the Produce of Milk, Butter, and Cheese, Eggs, Poultry, and Pigs. By Prof. JOHN DONALDSON and R. SCOTT BURN. 3s. 6d.‡

231. *THE ART OF GRAFTING AND BUDDING.* By CHARLES BALTET. With Illustrations. 2s. 6d.‡

232. *COTTAGE GARDENING;* or, Flowers, Fruits, and Vegetables for Small Gardens. By E. HOBDAY. 1s. 6d.

233. *GARDEN RECEIPTS.* Edited by CHARLES W. QUIN. 1s. 6d.

234. *THE KITCHEN AND MARKET GARDEN.* Compiled by C. W. SHAW, Editor of "Gardening Illustrated." 3s.‡

239. *DRAINING AND EMBANKING.* A Practical Treatise, embodying the most recent experience in the Application of Improved Methods. By JOHN SCOTT, late Professor of Agriculture and Rural Economy at the Royal Agricultural College, Cirencester. With 68 Illustrations. 1s. 6d.

240. *IRRIGATION AND WATER SUPPLY.* A Treatise on Water Meadows, Sewage Irrigation, Warping, &c.; on the Construction of Wells, Ponds, and Reservoirs; and on Raising Water by Machinery for Agricultural and Domestic Purposes. By Prof. JOHN SCOTT. With 34 Illus. 1s. 6d.

241. *FARM ROADS, FENCES, AND GATES.* A Practical Treatise on the Roads, Tramways, and Waterways of the Farm; the Principles of Enclosures; and the different kinds of Fences, Gates, and Stiles. By Professor JOHN SCOTT. With 75 Illustrations. 1s. 6d.

242. *FARM BUILDINGS.* A Practical Treatise on the Buildings necessary for various kinds of Farms, their Arrangement and Construction, including Plans and Estimates. By Prof. JOHN SCOTT. With 105 Illus. 2s.

243. *BARN IMPLEMENTS AND MACHINES.* A Practical Treatise on the Application of Power to the Operations of Agriculture; and on various Machines used in the Threshing-barn, in the Stock-yard, and in the Dairy, &c. By Prof. J. SCOTT. With 123 Illustrations. 2s.

244. *FIELD IMPLEMENTS AND MACHINES.* A Practical Treatise on the Varieties now in use, with Principles and Details of Construction, their Points of Excellence, and Management. By Professor JOHN SCOTT. With 138 Illustrations. 2s.

245. *AGRICULTURAL SURVEYING.* A Practical Treatise on Land Surveying, Levelling, and Setting-out; and on Measuring and Estimating Quantities, Weights, and Values of Materials, Produce, Stock, &c. By Prof. JOHN SCOTT. With 62 Illustrations. 1s. 6d.

*** *Nos.* 239 *to* 245 *in One Vol., handsomely half-bound, entitled* "THE COMPLETE TEXT-BOOK OF FARM ENGINEERING." By Professor JOHN SCOTT. *Price* 12*s.*

250. *MEAT PRODUCTION.* A Manual for Producers, Distributors, &c. By JOHN EWART. 2s. 6d.‡

☞ *The ‡ indicates that these vols. may be had strongly bound at 6d. extra.*

MATHEMATICS, ARITHMETIC, ETC.

32. *MATHEMATICAL INSTRUMENTS*, a Treatise on; in which their Construction and the Methods of Testing, Adjusting, and Using them are concisely Explained. By J. F. HEATHER, M.A., of the Royal Military Academy, Woolwich. Original Edition, in 1 vol., Illustrated. 1s. 6d.

*** *In ordering the above, be careful to say, "Original Edition" (No. 32), to distinguish it from the Enlarged Edition in 3 vols. (Nos. 168-9-70.)*

76. *DESCRIPTIVE GEOMETRY*, an Elementary Treatise on; with a Theory of Shadows and of Perspective, extracted from the French of G. MONGE. To which is added, a description of the Principles and Practice of Isometrical Projection. By J. F. HEATHER, M.A. With 14 Plates. 2s.

178. *PRACTICAL PLANE GEOMETRY:* giving the Simplest Modes of Constructing Figures contained in one Plane and Geometrical Construction of the Ground. By J. F. HEATHER, M.A. With 215 Woodcuts. 2s.

83. *COMMERCIAL BOOK-KEEPING.* With Commercial Phrases and Forms in English, French, Italian, and German. By JAMES HADDON, M.A., Arithmetical Master of King's College School, London. 1s. 6d.

84. *ARITHMETIC*, a Rudimentary Treatise on: with full Explanations of its Theoretical Principles, and numerous Examples for Practice. By Professor J. R. YOUNG. Tenth Edition, corrected. 1s. 6d.

84*. A KEY to the above, containing Solutions in full to the Exercises, together with Comments, Explanations, and Improved Processes, for the Use of Teachers and Unassisted Learners. By J. R. YOUNG. 1s. 6d.

85. *EQUATIONAL ARITHMETIC*, applied to Questions of Interest, Annuities, Life Assurance, and General Commerce; with various Tables by which all Calculations may be greatly facilitated. By W. HIPSLEY. 2s.

86. *ALGEBRA*, the Elements of. By JAMES HADDON, M.A. With Appendix, containing miscellaneous Investigations, and a Collection of Problems in various parts of Algebra. 2s.

86*. A KEY AND COMPANION to the above Book, forming an extensive repository of Solved Examples and Problems in Illustration of the various Expedients necessary in Algebraical Operations. By J. R. YOUNG. 1s. 6d.

88. *EUCLID*, THE ELEMENTS OF: with many additional Propositions
89. and Explanatory Notes: to which is prefixed, an Introductory Essay on Logic. By HENRY LAW, C.E. 2s. 6d.‡

*** *Sold also separately, viz.:—*

88. EUCLID, The First Three Books. By HENRY LAW, C.E. 1s. 6d.
89. EUCLID, Books 4, 5, 6, 11, 12. By HENRY LAW, C.E. 1s. 6d.

90. *ANALYTICAL GEOMETRY AND CONIC SECTIONS*, By JAMES HANN. A New Edition, by Professor J. R. YOUNG. 2s.‡

91. *PLANE TRIGONOMETRY*, the Elements of. By JAMES HANN, formerly Mathematical Master of King's College, London. 1s. 6d.

92. *SPHERICAL TRIGONOMETRY*, the Elements of. By JAMES HANN. Revised by CHARLES H. DOWLING, C.E. 1s.

*** *Or with "The Elements of Plane Trigonometry," in One Volume, 2s. 6d.*

93. *MENSURATION AND MEASURING.* With the Mensuration and Levelling of Land for the Purposes of Modern Engineering. By T. BAKER, C.E. New Edition by E. NUGENT, C.E. Illustrated. 1s. 6d.

101. *DIFFERENTIAL CALCULUS*, Elements of the. By W. S. B. WOOLHOUSE, F.R.A.S., &c. 1s. 6d.

102. *INTEGRAL CALCULUS*, Rudimentary Treatise on the. By HOMERSHAM COX, B.A. Illustrated. 1s.

105. *MNEMONICAL LESSONS.*—GEOMETRY, ALGEBRA, AND TRIGONOMETRY, in Easy Mnemonical Lessons. By the Rev. THOMAS PENYNGTON KIRKMAN, M.A. 1s. 6d.

136. *ARITHMETIC*, Rudimentary, for the Use of Schools and Self-Instruction. By JAMES HADDON, M.A. Revised by A. ARMAN. 1s. 6d.

137. A KEY TO HADDON'S RUDIMENTARY ARITHMETIC. By A. ARMAN. 1s. 6d.

☞ *The ‡ indicates that these vols. may be had strongly bound at 6d. extra.*

Mathematics, Arithmetic, etc., *continued.*

168. *DRAWING AND MEASURING INSTRUMENTS.* Including—I. Instruments employed in Geometrical and Mechanical Drawing, and in the Construction, Copying, and Measurement of Maps and Plans. II. Instruments used for the purposes of Accurate Measurement, and for Arithmetical Computations. By J. F. HEATHER, M.A. Illustrated. 1s. 6d.

169. *OPTICAL INSTRUMENTS.* Including (more especially) Telescopes, Microscopes, and Apparatus for producing copies of Maps and Plans by Photography. By J. F. HEATHER, M.A. Illustrated. 1s. 6d.

170. *SURVEYING AND ASTRONOMICAL INSTRUMENTS.* Including—I. Instruments Used for Determining the Geometrical Features of a portion of Ground. II. Instruments Employed in Astronomical Observations. By J. F. HEATHER, M.A. Illustrated. 1s. 6d.

⁂ *The above three volumes form an enlargement of the Author's original work, "Mathematical Instruments."* (*See No. 32 in the Series.*)

168.
169.
170. } *MATHEMATICAL INSTRUMENTS.* By J. F. HEATHER, M.A. Enlarged Edition, for the most part entirely re-written. The 3 Parts as above, in One thick Volume. With numerous Illustrations. 4s. 6d.‡

158. *THE SLIDE RULE, AND HOW TO USE IT;* containing full, easy, and simple Instructions to perform all Business Calculations with unexampled rapidity and accuracy. By CHARLES HOARE, C.E. With a Slide Rule in tuck of cover. 2s. 6d.‡

196. *THEORY OF COMPOUND INTEREST AND ANNUITIES*; with Tables of Logarithms for the more Difficult Computations of Interest, Discount, Annuities, &c. By FÉDOR THOMAN. 4s.‡

199. *THE COMPENDIOUS CALCULATOR;* or, Easy and Concise Methods of Performing the various Arithmetical Operations required in Commercial and Business Transactions; together with Useful Tables. By D. O'GORMAN. Twenty-sixth Edition, carefully revised by C. NORRIS. 3s., cloth limp; 3s. 6d., strongly half-bound in leather.

204. *MATHEMATICAL TABLES,* for Trigonometrical, Astronomical, and Nautical Calculations; to which is prefixed a Treatise on Logarithms. By HENRY LAW, C.E. Together with a Series of Tables for Navigation and Nautical Astronomy. By Prof. J. R. YOUNG. New Edition. 4s.‡

204*. *LOGARITHMS.* With Mathematical Tables for Trigonometrical, Astronomical, and Nautical Calculations. By HENRY LAW, M.Inst.C.E. New and Revised Edition. (Forming part of the above Work). 3s.

221. *MEASURES, WEIGHTS, AND MONEYS OF ALL NATIONS,* and an Analysis of the Christian, Hebrew, and Mahometan Calendars. By W. S. B. WOOLHOUSE, F.R.A.S., F.S.S. Sixth Edition. 2s.‡

227. *MATHEMATICS AS APPLIED TO THE CONSTRUCTIVE ARTS.* Illustrating the various processes of Mathematical Investigation, by means of Arithmetical and Simple Algebraical Equations and Practical Examples. By FRANCIS CAMPIN, C.E. Second Edition. 3s.‡

PHYSICAL SCIENCE, NATURAL PHILOSOPHY, ETC.

1. *CHEMISTRY.* By Professor GEORGE FOWNES, F.R.S. With an Appendix on the Application of Chemistry to Agriculture. 1s.

2. *NATURAL PHILOSOPHY,* Introduction to the Study of. By C. TOMLINSON. Woodcuts. 1s. 6d.

6. *MECHANICS,* Rudimentary Treatise on. By CHARLES TOMLINSON. Illustrated. 1s. 6d.

7. *ELECTRICITY;* showing the General Principles of Electrical Science, and the purposes to which it has been applied. By Sir W. SNOW HARRIS, F.R.S., &c. With Additions by R. SABINE, C.E., F.S.A. 1s. 6d.

7*. *GALVANISM.* By Sir W. SNOW HARRIS. New Edition by ROBERT SABINE, C.E., F.S.A. 1s. 6d.

8. *MAGNETISM;* being a concise Exposition of the General Principles of Magnetical Science. By Sir W. SNOW HARRIS. New Edition, revised by H. M. NOAD, Ph.D. With 165 Woodcuts. 3s. 6d.‡

☞ *The ‡ indicates that these vols. may be had strongly bound at 6d. extra.*

Physical Science, Natural Philosophy, etc., *continued.*

11. *THE ELECTRIC TELEGRAPH;* its History and Progress; with Descriptions of some of the Apparatus. By R. SABINE, C.E., F.S.A. 3s.

12. *PNEUMATICS,* for the Use of Beginners. By CHARLES TOMLINSON. Illustrated. 1s. 6d.

72. *MANUAL OF THE MOLLUSCA;* a Treatise on Recent and Fossil Shells. By Dr. S. P. WOODWARD, A.L.S. Fourth Edition. With Appendix by RALPH TATE, A.L.S., F.G.S. With numerous Plates and 300 Woodcuts. 6s. 6d. Cloth boards, 7s. 6d.

96. *ASTRONOMY.* By the late Rev. ROBERT MAIN, M.A. Third Edition, by WILLIAM THYNNE LYNN, B.A., F.R.A.S. 2s.

97. *STATICS AND DYNAMICS,* the Principles and Practice of; embracing also a clear development of Hydrostatics, Hydrodynamics, and Central Forces. By T. BAKER, C.E. 1s. 6d.

138. *TELEGRAPH,* Handbook of the; a Guide to Candidates for Employment in the Telegraph Service. By R. BOND. Fourth Edition. Including Questions on Magnetism, Electricity, and Practical Telegraphy, by W. McGREGOR. 3s.‡

173. *PHYSICAL GEOLOGY,* partly based on Major-General PORTLOCK'S "Rudiments of Geology." By RALPH TATE, A.L.S., &c. Woodcuts. 2s.

174. *HISTORICAL GEOLOGY,* partly based on Major-General PORTLOCK'S "Rudiments." By RALPH TATE, A.L.S., &c. Woodcuts. 2s. 6d.

173 & 174. *RUDIMENTARY TREATISE ON GEOLOGY,* Physical and Historical. Partly based on Major-General PORTLOCK'S "Rudiments of Geology." By RALPH TATE, A.L.S., F.G.S., &c. In One Volume. 4s. 6d.‡

183 & 184. *ANIMAL PHYSICS,* Handbook of. By Dr. LARDNER, D.C.L., formerly Professor of Natural Philosophy and Astronomy in University College, Lond. With 520 Illustrations. In One Vol. 7s. 6d., cloth boards.

*** *Sold also in Two Parts, as follows:—*

183. ANIMAL PHYSICS. By Dr. LARDNER. Part I., Chapters I.—VII. 4s.
184. ANIMAL PHYSICS. By Dr. LARDNER. Part II., Chapters VIII.—XVIII. 3s.

FINE ARTS.

20. *PERSPECTIVE FOR BEGINNERS.* Adapted to Young Students and Amateurs in Architecture, Painting, &c. By GEORGE PYNE. 2s.

40 *GLASS STAINING, AND THE ART OF PAINTING ON GLASS.* From the German of Dr. GESSERT and EMANUEL OTTO FROMBERG. With an Appendix on THE ART OF ENAMELLING. 2s. 6d.

69. *MUSIC,* A Rudimentary and Practical Treatise on. With numerous Examples. By CHARLES CHILD SPENCER. 2s. 6d.

71. *PIANOFORTE,* The Art of Playing the. With numerous Exercises & Lessons from the Best Masters. By CHARLES CHILD SPENCER. 1s. 6d.

69-71. *MUSIC & THE PIANOFORTE.* In one vol. Half bound, 5s.

181. *PAINTING POPULARLY EXPLAINED,* including Fresco, Oil, Mosaic, Water Colour, Water-Glass, Tempera, Encaustic, Miniature, Painting on Ivory, Vellum, Pottery, Enamel, Glass, &c. With Historical Sketches of the Progress of the Art by THOMAS JOHN GULLICK, assisted by JOHN TIMBS, F.S.A. Fifth Edition, revised and enlarged. 5s.‡

186. *A GRAMMAR OF COLOURING,* applied to Decorative Painting and the Arts. By GEORGE FIELD. New Edition, enlarged and adapted to the Use of the Ornamental Painter and Designer. By ELLIS A. DAVIDSON. With two new Coloured Diagrams, &c. 3s.‡

246. *A DICTIONARY OF PAINTERS, AND HANDBOOK FOR* PICTURE AMATEURS; including Methods of Painting, Cleaning, Relining and Restoring, Schools of Painting, &c. With Notes on the Copyists and Imitators of each Master. By PHILIPPE DARYL. 2s. 6d.‡

☞ *The ‡ indicates that these vols. may be had strongly bound at 6d. extra.*

INDUSTRIAL AND USEFUL ARTS.

23. *BRICKS AND TILES*, Rudimentary Treatise on the Manufacture of. By E. DOBSON, M.R.I.B.A. Illustrated, 3s.‡

67. *CLOCKS, WATCHES, AND BELLS*, a Rudimentary Treatise on. By Sir EDMUND BECKETT, LL.D., Q.C. Seventh Edition, revised and enlarged. 4s. 6d. limp; 5s. 6d. cloth boards.

83**. *CONSTRUCTION OF DOOR LOCKS*. Compiled from the Papers of A. C. HOBBS, and Edited by CHARLES TOMLINSON, F.R.S. With Additions by ROBERT MALLET, M.I.C.E. Illus. 2s. 6d.

162. *THE BRASS FOUNDER'S MANUAL;* Instructions for Modelling, Pattern-Making, Moulding, Turning, Filing, Burnishing, Bronzing, &c. With copious Receipts, &c. By WALTER GRAHAM. 2s.‡

205. *THE ART OF LETTER PAINTING MADE EASY*. By J. G. BADENOCH. Illustrated with 12 full-page Engravings of Examples. 1s.

215. *THE GOLDSMITH'S HANDBOOK*, containing full Instructions for the Alloying and Working of Gold. By GEORGE E. GEE. 3s.‡

224. *COACH BUILDING*, A Practical Treatise, Historical and Descriptive. By J. W. BURGESS. 2s. 6d.‡

225. *THE SILVERSMITH'S HANDBOOK*, containing full Instructions for the Alloying and Working of Silver. By GEORGE E. GEE. 3s.‡

235. *PRACTICAL ORGAN BUILDING*. By W. E. DICKSON, M.A., Precentor of Ely Cathedral. Illustrated. 2s. 6d.‡

249. *THE HALL-MARKING OF JEWELLERY PRACTICALLY CONSIDERED*. By GEORGE E. GEE. 3s.‡

MISCELLANEOUS VOLUMES.

36. *A DICTIONARY OF TERMS used in ARCHITECTURE, BUILDING, ENGINEERING, MINING, METALLURGY, ARCHÆOLOGY, the FINE ARTS, &c.* By JOHN WEALE. Fifth Edition. Revised by ROBERT HUNT, F.R.S. Illustrated. 5s. limp; 6s. cloth boards.

50. *THE LAW OF CONTRACTS FOR WORKS AND SERVICES*. By DAVID GIBBONS. Third Edition, enlarged. 3s.‡

112. *MANUAL OF DOMESTIC MEDICINE*. By R. GOODING, B.A., M.D. Intended as a Family Guide in all Cases of Accident and Emergency. Third Edition. 2s.‡

112*. *MANAGEMENT OF HEALTH*. A Manual of Home and Personal Hygiene. By the Rev. JAMES BAIRD, B.A. 1s.

150. *LOGIC*, Pure and Applied. By S. H. EMMENS. 1s. 6d.

153. *SELECTIONS FROM LOCKE'S ESSAYS ON THE HUMAN UNDERSTANDING*. With Notes by S. H. EMMENS. 2s.

154. *GENERAL HINTS TO EMIGRANTS*. Notices of the various Fields for Emigration, Hints on Outfits, Useful Recipes, &c. 2s.

157. *THE EMIGRANT'S GUIDE TO NATAL*. By ROBERT JAMES MANN, F.R.A.S., F.M.S. Second Edition. Map. 2s.

193. *HANDBOOK OF FIELD FORTIFICATION*, intended for the Guidance of Officers Preparing for Promotion. By Major W. W. KNOLLYS, F.R.G.S. With 163 Woodcuts. 3s.‡

194. *THE HOUSE MANAGER:* Being a Guide to Housekeeping. Practical Cookery, Pickling and Preserving, Household Work, Dairy Management, the Table and Dessert, Cellarage of Wines, Home-brewing and Wine-making, the Boudoir and Dressing-room, Travelling, Stable Economy, Gardening Operations, &c. By AN OLD HOUSEKEEPER. 3s. 6d.‡

194. 112. & 112*. *HOUSE BOOK (The)*. Comprising:—I. THE HOUSE MANAGER. By an OLD HOUSEKEEPER. II. DOMESTIC MEDICINE. By RALPH GOODING, M.D. III. MANAGEMENT OF HEALTH. By JAMES BAIRD. In One Vol., strongly half-bound, 6s.

☞ *The ‡ indicates that these vols. may be had strongly bound at 6d. extra.*

EDUCATIONAL AND CLASSICAL SERIES.

HISTORY.

1. **England, Outlines of the History of;** more especially with reference to the Origin and Progress of the English Constitution. By WILLIAM DOUGLAS HAMILTON, F.S.A., of Her Majesty's Public Record Office. 4th Edition, revised. 5s.; cloth boards, 6s.

5. **Greece, Outlines of the History of;** in connection with the Rise of the Arts and Civilization in Europe. By W. DOUGLAS HAMILTON, of University College, London, and EDWARD LEVIEN, M.A., of Balliol College, Oxford. 2s. 6d.; cloth boards, 3s. 6d.

7. **Rome, Outlines of the History of:** from the Earliest Period to the Christian Era and the Commencement of the Decline of the Empire. By EDWARD LEVIEN, of Balliol College, Oxford. Map, 2s. 6d.; cl. bds. 3s. 6d.

9. **Chronology of History, Art, Literature, and Progress,** from the Creation of the World to the Conclusion of the Franco-German War. The Continuation by W. D. HAMILTON, F.S.A. 3s.; cloth boards, 3s. 6d.

50. **Dates and Events in English History,** for the use of Candidates in Public and Private Examinations. By the Rev. E. RAND. 1s.

ENGLISH LANGUAGE AND MISCELLANEOUS.

11. **Grammar of the English Tongue,** Spoken and Written. With an Introduction to the Study of Comparative Philology. By HYDE CLARKE, D.C.L. Fourth Edition. 1s. 6d.

11*. **Philology:** Handbook of the Comparative Philology of English, Anglo-Saxon, Frisian, Flemish or Dutch, Low or Platt Dutch, High Dutch or German, Danish, Swedish, Icelandic, Latin, Italian, French, Spanish, and Portuguese Tongues. By HYDE CLARKE, D.C.L. 1s.

12. **Dictionary of the English Language,** as Spoken and Written. Containing above 100,000 Words. By HYDE CLARKE, D.C.L. 3s. 6d.; cloth boards, 4s. 6d.; complete with the GRAMMAR, cloth bds., 5s. 6d.

48. **Composition and Punctuation,** familiarly Explained for those who have neglected the Study of Grammar. By JUSTIN BRENAN. 17th Edition. 1s. 6d.

49. **Derivative Spelling-Book:** Giving the Origin of Every Word from the Greek, Latin, Saxon, German, Teutonic, Dutch, French, Spanish, and other Languages; with their present Acceptation and Pronunciation. By J. ROWBOTHAM, F.R.A.S. Improved Edition. 1s. 6d.

51. **The Art of Extempore Speaking:** Hints for the Pulpit, the Senate, and the Bar. By M. BAUTAIN, Vicar-General and Professor at the Sorbonne. Translated from the French. 7th Edition, carefully corrected. 2s. 6d.

52. **Mining and Quarrying,** with the Sciences connected therewith. First Book of, for Schools. By J. H. COLLINS, F.G.S., Lecturer to the Miners' Association of Cornwall and Devon. 1s.

53. **Places and Facts in Political and Physical Geography,** for Candidates in Examinations. By the Rev. EDGAR RAND, B.A. 1s.

54. **Analytical Chemistry,** Qualitative and Quantitative, a Course of. To which is prefixed, a Brief Treatise upon Modern Chemical Nomenclature and Notation. By WM. W. PINK and GEORGE E. WEBSTER. 2s.

THE SCHOOL MANAGERS' SERIES OF READING BOOKS,

Edited by the Rev. A. R. GRANT, Rector of Hitcham, and Honorary Canon of Ely; formerly H.M. Inspector of Schools.

INTRODUCTORY PRIMER, 3d.

	s. d.		s. d.
FIRST STANDARD	0 6	FOURTH STANDARD	1 2
SECOND „	0 10	FIFTH „	1 6
THIRD „	1 0	SIXTH „	1 6

LESSONS FROM THE BIBLE. Part I. Old Testament. 1s.

LESSONS FROM THE BIBLE. Part II. New Testament, to which is added THE GEOGRAPHY OF THE BIBLE, for very young Children. By Rev. C. THORNTON FORSTER. 1s. 2d. *** Or the Two Parts in One Volume. 2s.

FRENCH.

24. **French Grammar.** With Complete and Concise Rules on the Genders of French Nouns. By G. L. STRAUSS, Ph.D. 1s. 6d.

25. **French-English Dictionary.** Comprising a large number of New Terms used in Engineering, Mining, &c. By ALFRED ELWES. 1s. 6d.

26. **English-French Dictionary.** By ALFRED ELWES. 2s.

25,26. **French Dictionary** (as above). Complete, in One Vol., 3s.; cloth boards, 3s. 6d. *** Or with the GRAMMAR, cloth boards, 4s. 6d.

47. **French and English Phrase Book:** containing Introductory Lessons, with Translations, several Vocabularies of Words, a Collection of suitable Phrases, and Easy Familiar Dialogues. 1s. 6d.

GERMAN.

39. **German Grammar.** Adapted for English Students, from Heyse's Theoretical and Practical Grammar, by Dr. G. L. STRAUSS. 1s. 6d.

40. **German Reader:** A Series of Extracts, carefully culled from the most approved Authors of Germany; with Notes, Philological and Explanatory. By G. L. STRAUSS, Ph.D. 1s.

41-43. **German Triglot Dictionary.** By N. E. S. A. HAMILTON. In Three Parts. Part I. German-French-English. Part II. English-German-French. Part III. French-German-English. 3s., or cloth boards, 4s.

41-43 & 39. **German Triglot Dictionary** (as above), together with German Grammar (No. 39), in One Volume, cloth boards, 5s.

ITALIAN.

27. **Italian Grammar,** arranged in Twenty Lessons, with a Course of Exercises. By ALFRED ELWES. 1s. 6d.

28. **Italian Triglot Dictionary,** wherein the Genders of all the Italian and French Nouns are carefully noted down. By ALFRED ELWES. Vol. 1. Italian-English-French. 2s. 6d.

30. **Italian Triglot Dictionary.** By A. ELWES. Vol. 2. English-French-Italian. 2s. 6d.

32. **Italian Triglot Dictionary.** By ALFRED ELWES. Vol. 3. French-Italian-English. 2s. 6d.

28,30, 32. **Italian Triglot Dictionary** (as above). In One Vol., 7s. 6d. Cloth boards.

SPANISH AND PORTUGUESE.

34. **Spanish Grammar,** in a Simple and Practical Form. With a Course of Exercises. By ALFRED ELWES. 1s. 6d.

35. **Spanish-English and English-Spanish Dictionary.** Including a large number of Technical Terms used in Mining, Engineering, &c., with the proper Accents and the Gender of every Noun. By ALFRED ELWES. 4s.; cloth boards, 5s. *** Or with the GRAMMAR, cloth boards, 6s.

55. **Portuguese Grammar,** in a Simple and Practical Form. With a Course of Exercises. By ALFRED ELWES. 1s. 6d.

56. **Portuguese-English and English-Portuguese Dictionary.** Including a large number of Technical Terms used in Mining, Engineering, &c., with the proper Accents and the Gender of every Noun. By ALFRED ELWES. 5s.; cloth boards, 6s. *** Or with the GRAMMAR, cloth boards, 7s. [*Just published.*

HEBREW.

46*. **Hebrew Grammar.** By Dr. BRESSLAU. 1s. 6d.

44. **Hebrew and English Dictionary,** Biblical and Rabbinical; containing the Hebrew and Chaldee Roots of the Old Testament Post-Rabbinical Writings. By Dr. BRESSLAU. 6s.

46. **English and Hebrew Dictionary.** By Dr. BRESSLAU. 3s.

44,46. 46*. **Hebrew Dictionary** (as above), in Two Vols., complete, with the GRAMMAR, cloth boards, 12s.

LATIN.

19. **Latin Grammar.** Containing the Inflections and Elementary Principles of Translation and Construction. By the Rev. THOMAS GOODWIN, M.A., Head Master of the Greenwich Proprietary School. 1s.

20. **Latin-English Dictionary.** By the Rev. THOMAS GOODWIN, M.A. 2s.

22. **English-Latin Dictionary;** together with an Appendix of French and Italian Words which have their origin from the Latin. By the Rev. THOMAS GOODWIN, M.A. 1s. 6d.

20,22. **Latin Dictionary** (as above). Complete in One Vol., 3s. 6d. cloth boards, 4s. 6d. *** Or with the GRAMMAR, cloth boards, 5s. 6d.

LATIN CLASSICS. With Explanatory Notes in English.

1. **Latin Delectus.** Containing Extracts from Classical Authors, with Genealogical Vocabularies and Explanatory Notes, by H. YOUNG. 1s. 6d.

2. **Cæsaris** Commentarii de Bello Gallico. Notes, and a Geographical Register for the Use of Schools, by H. YOUNG. 2s.

3. **Cornelius Nepos.** With Notes. By H. YOUNG. 1s.

4. **Virgilii** Maronis Bucolica et Georgica. With Notes on the Bucolics by W. RUSHTON, M.A., and on the Georgics by H. YOUNG. 1s. 6d.

5. **Virgilii** Maronis Æneis. With Notes, Critical and Explanatory, by H. YOUNG. New Edition, revised and improved With copious Additional Notes by Rev. T. H. L. LEARY, D.C.L., formerly Scholar of Brasenose College, Oxford. 3s.

5* ——— Part 1. Books i.—vi., 1s. 6d.

5** ——— Part 2. Books vii.—xii., 2s.

6. **Horace;** Odes, Epode, and Carmen Sæculare. Notes by H. YOUNG. 1s. 6d.

7. **Horace;** Satires, Epistles, and Ars Poetica. Notes by W. BROWNRIGG SMITH, M.A., F.R.G.S. 1s. 6d.

8. **Sallustii** Crispi Catalina et Bellum Jugurthinum. Notes, Critical and Explanatory, by W. M. DONNE, B.A., Trin. Coll., Cam. 1s. 6d.

9. **Terentii** Andria et Heautontimorumenos. With Notes, Critical and Explanatory, by the Rev. JAMES DAVIES, M.A. 1s. 6d.

10. **Terentii** Adelphi, Hecyra, Phormio. Edited, with Notes, Critical and Explanatory, by the Rev. JAMES DAVIES, M.A. 2s.

11. **Terentii** Eunuchus, Comœdia. Notes, by Rev. J. DAVIES, M.A. 1s. 6d.

12. **Ciceronis** Oratio pro Sexto Roscio Amerino. Edited, with an Introduction, Analysis, and Notes, Explanatory and Critical, by the Rev. JAMES DAVIES, M.A. 1s. 6d.

13. **Ciceronis** Orationes in Catilinam, Verrem, et pro Archia. With Introduction, Analysis, and Notes, Explanatory and Critical, by Rev. T. H. L. LEARY, D.C.L. formerly Scholar of Brasenose College, Oxford. 1s. 6d.

14. **Ciceronis** Cato Major, Lælius, Brutus, sive de Senectute, de Amicitia, de Claris Oratoribus Dialogi. With Notes by W. BROWNRIGG SMITH, M.A., F.R.G.S. 2s.

16. **Livy:** History of Rome. Notes by H. YOUNG and W. B. SMITH, M.A. Part 1. Books i., ii., 1s. 6d.

16*. ——— Part 2. Books iii., iv., v., 1s. 6d.

17. ——— Part 3. Books xxi., xxii., 1s. 6d.

19. **Latin Verse Selections,** from Catullus, Tibullus, Propertius, and Ovid. Notes by W. B. DONNE, M.A., Trinity College, Cambridge. 2s.

20. **Latin Prose Selections,** from Varro, Columella, Vitruvius, Seneca, Quintilian, Florus, Velleius Paterculus, Valerius Maximus Suetonius, Apuleius, &c. Notes by W. B. DONNE, M.A. 2s.

21. **Juvenalis Satiræ.** With Prolegomena and Notes by T. H. S. ESCOTT, B.A., Lecturer on Logic at King's College, London. 2s.

GREEK.

14. **Greek Grammar**, in accordance with the Principles and Philological Researches of the most eminent Scholars of our own day. By HANS CLAUDE HAMILTON. 1s. 6d.

15,17. **Greek Lexicon.** Containing all the Words in General Use, with their Significations, Inflections, and Doubtful Quantities. By HENRY R. HAMILTON. Vol. 1. Greek-English, 2s. 6d.; Vol. 2. English-Greek, 2s. Or the Two Vols. in One, 4s. 6d.: cloth boards, 5s.

14,15. 17. **Greek Lexicon** (as above). Complete, with the GRAMMAR, in One Vol., cloth boards, 6s.

GREEK CLASSICS. With Explanatory Notes in English.

1. **Greek Delectus.** Containing Extracts from Classical Authors, with Genealogical Vocabularies and Explanatory Notes, by H. YOUNG. New Edition, with an improved and enlarged Supplementary Vocabulary, by JOHN HUTCHISON, M.A., of the High School, Glasgow. 1s. 6d.

2, 3. **Xenophon's Anabasis**; or, The Retreat of the Ten Thousand. Notes and a Geographical Register, by H. YOUNG. Part 1. Books i. to iii., 1s. Part 2. Books iv. to vii., 1s.

4. **Lucian's Select Dialogues.** The Text carefully revised, with Grammatical and Explanatory Notes, by H. YOUNG. 1s. 6d.

5-12. **Homer**, The Works of. According to the Text of BAEUMLEIN. With Notes, Critical and Explanatory, drawn from the best and latest Authorities, with Preliminary Observations and Appendices, by T. H. L. LEARY, M.A., D.C.L.

THE ILIAD:	Part 1. Books i. to vi., 1s. 6d.	Part 3. Books xiii. to xviii., 1s. 6d.
	Part 2. Books vii. to xii., 1s. 6d.	Part 4. Books xix. to xxiv., 1s. 6d.
THE ODYSSEY:	Part 1. Books i. to vi., 1s. 6d	Part 3. Books xiii. to xviii., 1s. 6d.
	Part 2. Books vii. to xii., 1s. 6d.	Part 4. Books xix. to xxiv., and Hymns, 2s.

13. **Plato's Dialogues**: The Apology of Socrates, the Crito, and the Phædo. From the Text of C. F. HERMANN. Edited with Notes, Critical and Explanatory, by the Rev. JAMES DAVIES, M.A. 2s.

14-17. **Herodotus**, The History of, chiefly after the Text of GAISFORD. With Preliminary Observations and Appendices, and Notes, Critical and Explanatory, by T. H. L. LEARY, M.A., D.C.L.
Part 1. Books i., ii. (The Clio and Euterpe), 2s.
Part 2. Books iii., iv. (The Thalia and Melpomene), 2s.
Part 3. Books v.-vii. (The Terpsichore, Erato, and Polymnia), 2s.
Part 4. Books viii., ix. (The Urania and Calliope) and Index, 1s. 6d.

18. **Sophocles**: Œdipus Tyrannus. Notes by H. YOUNG. 1s.

20. **Sophocles**: Antigone. From the Text of DINDORF. Notes, Critical and Explanatory, by the Rev. JOHN MILNER, B.A. 2s.

23. **Euripides**: Hecuba and Medea. Chiefly from the Text of DINDORF. With Notes, Critical and Explanatory, by W. BROWNRIGG SMITH, M.A., F.R.G.S. 1s. 6d.

26. **Euripides**: Alcestis. Chiefly from the Text of DINDORF. With Notes, Critical and Explanatory, by JOHN MILNER, B.A. 1s. 6d.

30. **Æschylus**: Prometheus Vinctus: The Prometheus Bound. From the Text of DINDORF. Edited, with English Notes, Critical and Explanatory, by the Rev. JAMES DAVIES, M.A. 1s.

32. **Æschylus**: Septem Contra Thebes: The Seven against Thebes. From the Text of DINDORF. Edited, with English Notes, Critical and Explanatory, by the Rev. JAMES DAVIES, M.A. 1s.

40. **Aristophanes**: Acharnians. Chiefly from the Text of C. H. WEISE. With Notes, by C. S. T. TOWNSHEND, M.A. 1s. 6d.

41. **Thucydides**: History of the Peloponnesian War. Notes by H. YOUNG. Book 1. 1s. 6d.

42. **Xenophon's Panegyric on Agesilaus.** Notes and Introduction by LL. F. W. JEWITT. 1s. 6d.

43. **Demosthenes.** The Oration on the Crown and the Philippics. With English Notes. By Rev. T. H. L. LEARY, D.C.L., formerly Scholar of Brasenose College, Oxford. 1s. 6d.

7, STATIONERS' HALL COURT, LONDON, E.C.
April, 1885.

A CATALOGUE OF BOOKS

INCLUDING MANY NEW AND STANDARD WORKS IN

ENGINEERING, MECHANICS, ARCHITECTURE, CARPENTRY, MINING, NAVAL ARCHITECTURE, SCIENCE, MATHEMATICS, THE INDUSTRIAL ARTS, MANUFACTURES, AGRICULTURE, GARDENING, ESTATE MANAGEMENT, &c.

PUBLISHED BY

CROSBY LOCKWOOD & CO.

CIVIL ENGINEERING, SURVEYING, etc.

The Water Supply of Cities and Towns.

A COMPREHENSIVE TREATISE on the WATER-SUPPLY OF CITIES AND TOWNS. By WILLIAM HUMBER, A-M. Inst. C.E., and M. Inst. M.E., Author of "Cast and Wrought Iron Bridge Construction," &c., &c. Illustrated with 50 Double Plates, 1 Single Plate, Coloured Frontispiece, and upwards of 250 Woodcuts, and containing 400 pages of Text. Imp. 4to, £6 6s. elegantly and substantially half-bound in morocco.

List of Contents.

I. Historical Sketch of some of the means that have been adopted for the Supply of Water to Cities and Towns.—II. Water and the Foreign Matter usually associated with it.—III. Rainfall and Evaporation.—IV. Springs and the water-bearing formations of various districts.—V. Measurement and Estimation of the flow of Water—VI. On the Selection of the Source of Supply.—VII. Wells.—VIII. Reservoirs.—IX. The Purification of Water.—X. Pumps.— XI. Pumping Machinery.— XII. Conduits.—XIII. Distribution of Water.—XIV. Meters, Service Pipes, and House Fittings.—XV. The Law and Economy of Water Works. XVI. Constant and Intermittent Supply.—XVII. Description of Plates. — Appendices, giving Tables of Rates of Supply, Velocities, &c. &c., together with Specifications of several Works illustrated, among which will be found Aberdeen, Bideford, Canterbury, Dundee Halifax, Lambeth, Rotherham, Dublin, and others.

"The most systematic and valuable work upon water supply hitherto produced in English, or in any other language. . . . Mr. Humber's work is characterised almost throughout by an exhaustiveness much more distinctive of French and German than of English technical treatises. —*Engineer*.

"We can congratulate Mr. Humber on having been able to give so large an amount of information on a subject so important as the water supply of cities and towns. The plates, fifty in number, are mostly drawings of executed works, and alone would have commanded the attention of every engineer whose practice may lie in this branch of the profession."—*Builder*.

Cast and Wrought Iron Bridge Construction.

A COMPLETE AND PRACTICAL TREATISE ON CAST AND WROUGHT IRON BRIDGE CONSTRUCTION, including Iron Foundations. In Three Parts—Theoretical, Practical, and Descriptive. By WILLIAM HUMBER, A-M. Inst. C.E., and M. Inst. M.E. Third Edition, Revised and much improved, with 115 Double Plates (20 of which now first appear in this edition), and numerous Additions to the Text. In Two Vols., imp. 4to, £6 16s. 6*d*. half-bound in morocco.

"A very valuable contribution to the standard literature of civil engineering. In addition to elevations, plans and sections, large scale details are given, which very much enhance the instructive worth of these illustrations. No engineer would willingly be without so valuable a fund of information."—*Civil Engineer and Architect's Journal*.

"Mr. Humber's stately volumes, lately issued—in which the most important bridges erected during the last five years, under the direction of the late Mr. Brunel, Sir W. Cubitt, Mr. Hawkshaw, Mr. Page, Mr. Fowler, Mr. Hemans, and others among our most eminent engineers, are drawn and specified in great detail."—*Engineer*.

B

HUMBER'S GREAT WORK ON MODERN ENGINEERING.

Complete in Four Volumes, imperial 4to, price £12 12s., half-morocco, each Volume sold separately as follows:—

A RECORD OF THE PROGRESS OF MODERN ENGINEERING. FIRST SERIES. Comprising Civil, Mechanical, Marine, Hydraulic, Railway, Bridge, and other Engineering Works, &c. By WILLIAM HUMBER, A-M. Inst. C.E., &c. Imp. 4to, with 36 Double Plates, drawn to a large scale, Photographic Portrait of John Hawkshaw, C.E., F.R.S., &c., and copious descriptive Letterpress, Specifications, &c., £3 3s. half-morocco.

List of the Plates and Diagrams.

Victoria Station and Roof, L. B. & S. C. R. (8 plates); Southport Pier (2 plates); Victoria Station and Roof, L. C. & D. and G. W. R. (6 plates); Roof of Cremorne Music Hall; Bridge over G. N. Railway; Roof of Station, Dutch Rhenish Rail (2 plates); Bridge over the Thames, West London Extension Railway (5 plates); Armour Plates: Suspension Bridge, Thames (4 plates); The Allen Engine; Suspension Bridge, Avon (3 plates); Underground Railway (3 plates).

"Handsomely lithographed and printed. It will find favour with many who desire to preserve in a permanent form copies of the plans and specifications prepared for the guidance of the contractors for many important engineering works."—*Engineer.*

HUMBER'S RECORD OF MODERN ENGINEERING. SECOND SERIES. Imp. 4to, with 36 Double Plates, Photographic Portrait of Robert Stephenson, C.E., M.P., F.R.S., &c., and copious descriptive Letterpress, Specifications, &c., £3 3s. half-morocco.

List of the Plates and Diagrams.

Birkenhead Docks, Low Water Basin (15 plates); Charing Cross Station Roof, C. C. Railway (3 plates); Digswell Viaduct, Great Northern Railway; Robbery Wood Viaduct, Great Northern Railway; Iron Permanent Way; Clydach Viaduct, Merthyr, Tredegar, and Abergavenny Railway; Ebbw Viaduct, Merthyr, Tredegar, and Abergavenny Railway; College Wood Viaduct, Cornwall Railway; Dublin Winter Palace Roof (3 plates); Bridge over the Thames, L. C. & D. Railway (6 plates); Albert Harbour, Greenock (4 plates).

"Mr. Humber has done the profession good and true service, by the fine collection of examples he has here brought before the profession and the public."—*Practical Mechanic's Journal.*

HUMBER'S RECORD OF MODERN ENGINEERING. THIRD SERIES. Imp. 4to, with 40 Double Plates, Photographic Portrait of J. R. M'Clean, Esq., late Pres. Inst. C.E., and copious descriptive Letterpress, Specifications, &c., £3 3s. half-morocco.

List of the Plates and Diagrams.

MAIN DRAINAGE, METROPOLIS.—*North Side.*—Map showing Interception of Sewers; Middle Level Sewer (2 plates); Outfall Sewer, Bridge over River Lea (3 plates); Outfall Sewer, Bridge over Marsh Lane, North Woolwich Railway, and Bow and Barking Railway Junction; Outfall Sewer, Bridge over Bow and Barking Railway (3 plates); Outfall Sewer, Bridge over East London Waterworks Feeder (2 plates); Outfall Sewer, Reservoir (2 plates); Outfall Sewer, Tumbling Bay and Outlet; Outfall Sewer, Penstocks. *South Side.*—Outfall Sewer, Bermondsey Branch (2 plates); Outfall Sewer, Reservoir and Outlet (4 plates); Outfall Sewer, Filth Hoist; Sections of Sewers (North and South Sides).

THAMES EMBANKMENT.—Section of River Wall; Steamboat Pier, Westminster (2 plates), Landing Stairs between Charing Cross and Waterloo Bridges; York Gate (2 plates); Overflow and Outlet at Savoy Street Sewer (3 plates); Steamboat Pier, Waterloo Bridge (3 plates); Junction of Sewers, Plans and Sections; Gullies, Plans and Sections; Rolling Stock; Granite and Iron Forts.

"The drawings have a constantly increasing value, and whoever desires to possess clear representations of the two great works carried out by our Metropolitan Board wil obtain Mr. Humber's volume."—*Engineer.*

HUMBER'S RECORD OF MODERN ENGINEERING. FOURTH SERIES. Imp. 4to, with 36 Double Plates, Photographic Portrait of John Fowler, Esq., late Pres. Inst. C.E., and copious descriptive Letterpress, Specifications, &c., £3 3s. half-morocco.

List of the Plates and Diagrams.

Abbey Mills Pumping Station, Main Drainage, Metropolis (4 plates); Barrow Docks (5 plates); Manquis Viaduct, Santiago and Valparaiso Railway (2 plates); Adam's Locomotive, St. Helen's Canal Railway (2 plates); Cannon Street Station Roof, Charing Cross Railway (3 plates); Road Bridge over the River Moka (2 plates); Telegraphic Apparatus for Mesopotamia; Viaduct over the River Wye, Midland Railway (3 plates); St. Germans Viaduct, Cornwall Railway (2 plates); Wrought-Iron Cylinder for Diving Bell; Millwall Docks (6 plates); Milroy's Patent Excavator; Metropolitan District Railway (6 plates); Harbours Ports, and Breakwaters (3 plates).

"We gladly welcome another year's issue of this valuable publication from the able pen of Mr. Humber. The accuracy and general excellence of this work are well known, while its usefulness in giving the measurements and details of some of the latest examples of engineering, as carried out by the most eminent men in the profession, cannot be too highly prized."—*Artizan.*

Trigonometrical Surveying.

AN OUTLINE OF THE METHOD OF CONDUCTING A TRIGONOMETRICAL SURVEY, for the Formation of Geographical and Topographical Maps and Plans, Military Reconnaissance, Levelling, &c., with Useful Problems, Formulæ, and Tables. By Lieut.-General FROME, R.E. Fourth Edition, Revised and partly Re-written by Captain CHARLES WARREN, R.E. With 19 Plates and 115 Woodcuts, royal 8vo, 16s. cloth.

Contents.—Chap. I. General Outline of the System of carrying on a Trigonometrical Survey.—Chap. II. Measurements of a Base Line.—Chap. III. Triangulation.—Chap. IV. Interior Filling-in of a Survey, either entirely or partially by Measurement.—Chap. V. Levelling and Contouring.—Chap. VI. Levelling by Barometer and Thermometric Hypsometer.—Chap. VII. Plotting, Penning-in, Copying, and Engraving Typographical Plans.—Chap. VIII. Modelling.—IX. Military Reconnaissance, and Hints on Sketching Ground, Colonial Surveying.—Chap. XI. Geodesical Operations connected with a Trigonometrical Survey.—Chap. XII. Practical Astronomy.—Problems, Tables, &c.

"The simple fact that a fourth edition has been called for is the best testimony to its merits. No words of praise from us can strengthen the position so well and so steadily maintained by this work. Captain Warren has revised the entire work, and made such additions as were necessary to bring every portion of the contents up to the present date."—*Broad Arrow.*

Oblique Bridges.

A PRACTICAL AND THEORETICAL ESSAY ON OBLIQUE BRIDGES. With 13 large Plates. By the late GEORGE WATSON BUCK, M.I.C.E. Third Edition, revised by his Son, J. H. WATSON BUCK, M.I.C.E.; and with the addition of Description to Diagrams for Facilitating the Construction of Oblique Bridges, by W. H. BARLOW, M.I.C.E. Royal 8vo, 12s. cloth.

"The standard text-book for all engineers regarding skew arches is Mr. Buck's treatise, and it would be impossible to consult a better."—*Engineer.*

"Mr. Buck's treatise is recognised as a standard text-book, and his treatment has divested the subject of many of the intricacies supposed to belong to it. As a guide to the engineer and architect, on a confessedly difficult subject, Mr. Buck's work is unsurpassed."—*Building News.*

Bridge Construction in Masonry, Timber and Iron.

EXAMPLES OF BRIDGE AND VIADUCT CONSTRUCTION OF MASONRY, TIMBER, AND IRON. Consisting of 46 Plates from the Contract Drawings or Admeasurement of select Works. By W. D. HASKOLL, C.E. Second Edition, with the addition of 554 Estimates, and the Practice of Setting out Works. Illustrated with 6 pages of Diagrams. Imp. 4to, £2 12s. 6*d*. half-morocco.

"A work of the present nature by a man of Mr. Haskoll's experience must prove invaluable. The tables of estimates will considerably enhance its value."—*Engineering.*

Earthwork.

EARTHWORK TABLES. Showing the Contents in Cubic Yards of Embankments, Cuttings, &c., of Heights or Depths up to an average of 80 feet. By JOSEPH BROADBENT, C.E., and FRANCIS CAMPIN, C.E. Crown 8vo, 5s. cloth.

"The way in which accuracy is attained, by a simple division of each cross section into three elements, two in which are constant and one variable, is ingenious."—*Athenæum.*

Barlow's Strength of Materials, enlarged.

A TREATISE ON THE STRENGTH OF MATERIALS; with Rules for Application in Architecture, the Construction of Suspension Bridges, Railways, &c. By PETER BARLOW, F.R.S. A New Edition, revised by his Sons, P. W. BARLOW, F.R.S., and W. H. BARLOW, F.R.S.; to which are added, Experiments by HODGKINSON, FAIRBAIRN, and KIRKALDY; and Formulæ for Calculating Girders, &c. Arranged and Edited by W. HUMBER, A-M. Inst. C.E. Demy 8vo, 400 pp., with 19 large Plates and numerous Woodcuts, 18s. cloth.

"Valuable alike to the student, tyro, and the experienced practitioner, it will always rank in future as it has hitherto done, as the standard treatise on that particular subject."—*Engineer.*

"A book which no engineer of any kind can afford to be without."—*Colliery Guardian.*

"There is no greater authority than Barlow."—*Building News.*

"The book is undoubtedly worthy of the highest commendation, and of an honourable place in the library of every engineer."—*Mining Journal.*

". . . As a scientific work of the first class, it deserves a foremost place on the bookshelves of every civil engineer and practical mechanic."—*English Mechanic.*

Survey Practice.

AID TO SURVEY PRACTICE, for Reference in Surveying, Levelling, Setting-out and in Route Surveys of Travellers by Land and Sea. With Tables, Illustrations, and Records. By LOWIS D'A. JACKSON, A.M.I.C.E., Author of "Hydraulic Manual," "Modern Metrology," &c. Large crown 8vo, 12s. 6d. cloth.

"Mr. Jackson has produced a valuable *vade-mecum* for the surveyor. We can recommend this book as containing an admirable supplement to the teaching of the accomplished surveyor."—*Athenæum.*

"We cannot recommend to the student who knows something of the mathematical principles of the subject a better course than to fortify his practice in the field under a competent surveyor with a study of Mr. Jackson's useful manual."—*Building News.*

"The author brings to his work a fortunate union of theory and practical experience which, aided by a clear and lucid style of writing, renders the book a very useful one."—*Builder.*

Levelling.

A TREATISE ON THE PRINCIPLES AND PRACTICE OF LEVELLING. Showing its Application to purposes of Railway and Civil Engineering, in the Construction of Roads; with Mr. TELFORD'S Rules for the same. By FREDERICK W. SIMMS, F.G.S., M. Inst. C.E. Seventh Edition, with the addition of LAW'S Practical Examples for Setting-out Railway Curves, and TRAUTWINE'S Field Practice of Laying-out Circular Curves. With 7 Plates and numerous Woodcuts, 8vo, 8s. 6d. cloth. *** TRAUTWINE on Curves, separate, 5s.

"The text-book on levelling in most of our engineering schools and colleges."—*Engineer.*

"The publishers have rendered a substantial service to the profession, especially to the younger members, by bringing out the present edition of Mr. Simms' useful work."—*Engineering.*

Tunnelling.

PRACTICAL TUNNELLING. Explaining in detail the Setting-out of the works, Shaft-sinking and Heading-driving, Ranging the Lines and Levelling underground, Sub-Excavating, Timbering, and the Construction of the Brickwork of Tunnels, with the amount of Labour required for, and the Cost of, the various portions of the work. By FREDERICK W. SIMMS, F.G.S., M. Inst. C.E. Third Edition, Revised and Extended by D. KINNEAR CLARK, M. Inst. C.E. Imp. 8vo, with 21 Folding Plates and numerous Wood Engravings, 30s. cloth.

"The estimation in which Mr. Simms' book on tunnelling has been held for over thirty years cannot be more truly expressed than in the words of the late Professor Rankine:—'The best source of information on the subject of tunnels is Mr. F. W. Simms' work on Practical Tunnelling.'"—*Architect.*

"It has been regarded from the first as a text-book of the subject. . . . . Mr. Clark has added immensely to the value of the book."—*Engineer.*

"The additional chapters by Mr. Clark, containing as they do numerous examples of modern practice, bring the book well up to date."—*Engineering.*

Statics, Graphic and Analytic.

GRAPHIC AND ANALYTIC STATICS, in Theory and Comparison: Their Practical Application to the Treatment of Stresses in Roofs, Solid Girders, Lattice, Bowstring and Suspension Bridges, Braced Iron Arches and Piers, and other Frameworks. To which is added a Chapter on Wind Pressures. By R. HUDSON GRAHAM, C.E. With numerous Examples, many taken from existing Structures. 8vo, 16s. cloth.

"Mr. Graham's book will find a place wherever graphic and analytic statics are used or studied. *Engineer.*

"This exhaustive treatise is admirably adapted for the architect and engineer, and will tend to wean the profession from a tedious and laboured mode of calculation. To prove the accuracy of the graphical demonstrations, the author compares them with the analytic formulæ given by Rankine."—*Building News.*

"The work is excellent from a practical point of view, and has evidently been prepared with much care. The directions for working are ample, and are illustrated by an abundance of well-selected examples. It is an excellent text-book for the practical draughtsman."—*Athenæum.*

Strains, Formulæ and Diagrams for Calculation of.

A HANDY BOOK FOR THE CALCULATION OF STRAINS IN GIRDERS AND SIMILAR STRUCTURES, AND THEIR STRENGTH. Consisting of Formulæ and Corresponding Diagrams, with numerous details for Practical Application, &c. By WILLIAM HUMBER, A-M. Inst. C.E., &c. Third Edition. Crown 8vo, nearly 100 Woodcuts and 3 Plates, 7s. 6d. cloth.

"The formulæ are neatly expressed, and the diagrams good."—*Athenæum.*

"We heartily commend this really *handy* book to our engineer and architect readers."—*English Mechanic.*

Hydraulic Tables.

HYDRAULIC TABLES, CO-EFFICIENTS, and FORMULÆ for finding the Discharge of Water from Orifices, Notches, Weirs, Pipes, and Rivers. With New Formulæ, Tables and General Information on Rainfall, Catchment-Basins, Drainage, Sewerage, Water Supply for Towns and Mill Power. By JOHN NEVILLE, Civil Engineer, M.R.I.A. Third Edition, carefully revised, with considerable Additions. Numerous Illustrations. Crown 8vo, 14*s.* cloth.

"Alike valuable to students and engineers in practice; its study will prevent the annoyance of avoidable failures, and assist them to select the readiest means of successfully carrying out any given work connected with hydraulic engineering."—*Mining Journal.*

"It is, of all English books on the subject, the one nearest to completion. . . . From the good arrangement of the matter, the clear explanations, and abundance of formulæ, the carefully calculated tables, and, above all, the thorough acquaintance with both theory and construction, which is displayed from first to last, the book will be found to be an acquisition."—*Architect.*

River Engineering.

RIVER BARS: The Causes of their Formation, and their Treatment by "Induced Tidal Scour." With a Description of the Successful Reduction by this Method of the Bar at Dublin. By I. J. MANN, Assist. Eng. to the Dublin Port and Docks Board. Royal 8vo, 7*s.* 6*d.* cloth.

"We recommend all interested in harbour works—and, indeed, those concerned in the improvement of rivers generally—to read Mr. Mann's interesting work on the treatment of river bars."—*Engineer.*

"The author's discussion on wave-action, currents, and scour is intelligent and interesting. . . a most valuable contribution to the history of this branch of engineering."—*Engineering and Mining Journal.*

Hydraulics.

HYDRAULIC MANUAL. Consisting of Working Tables and Explanatory Text. Intended as a Guide in Hydraulic Calculations and Field Operations. By LOWIS D'A. JACKSON. Fourth Edition, Rewritten and Enlarged. Large crown 8vo, 16*s.* cloth.

"The author has had a wide experience in hydraulic engineering, both in South America and in India, and has been a careful observer of the facts which have come under his notice, as well as a painstaking collector and critic of the results of the experiments of others; and from the great mass of material at his command he has constructed a manual which may be accepted as a trustworthy guide to this branch of the engineer's profession. We can heartily recommend this volume to all who desire to be acquainted with the latest development of this important subject."—*Engineering.*

"The most useful feature of this work is its freedom from what is superannuated, and its thorough adoption of recent experiments; the text is, in fact, in great part a short account of the great modern experiments."—*Nature.*

Tramways and their Working.

TRAMWAYS: THEIR CONSTRUCTION AND WORKING. Embracing a Comprehensive History of the System; with an exhaustive Analysis of the various Modes of Traction, including Horse-Power, Steam, Heated Water, and Compressed Air; a Description of the Varieties of Rolling Stock; and ample Details of Cost and Working Expenses: the Progress recently made in Tramway Construction, &c. &c. By D. KINNEAR CLARK, M. Inst. C.E. With over 200 Wood Engravings, and 13 Folding Plates. Two Vols., large crown 8vo, 30*s.* cloth.

"All interested in tramways must refer to it, as all railway engineers have turned to the author's work 'Railway Machinery.'"—*Engineer.*

"An exhaustive and practical work on tramways, in which the history of this kind of locomotion, and a description and cost of the various modes of laying tramways, are to be found."—*Building News.*

"The best form of rails, the best mode of construction, and the best mechanical appliances are so fairly indicated in the work under review, that any engineer about to construct a tramway will be enabled at once to obtain the practical information which will be of most service to him."—*Athenæum.*

Oblique Arches.

A PRACTICAL TREATISE ON THE CONSTRUCTION OF OBLIQUE ARCHES. By JOHN HART. Third Edition, with Plates. Imperial 8vo, 8*s.* cloth.

Strength of Girders.

GRAPHIC TABLE FOR FACILITATING THE COMPUTATION OF THE WEIGHTS OF WROUGHT IRON AND STEEL GIRDERS, &c., for Parliamentary and other Estimates. By J. H. WATSON BUCK, M. Inst. C.E. On a Sheet, 2*s.* 6*d.*

Tables for Setting-out Curves.

TABLES OF TANGENTIAL ANGLES AND MULTIPLES for Setting-out Curves from 5 to 200 Radius. By ALEXANDER BEAZELEY, M. Inst. C.E. Third Edition. Printed on 48 Cards, and sold in a cloth box, waistcoat-pocket size, 3*s.* 6*d.*

"Each table is printed on a small card, which, being placed on the theodolite, leaves the hands free to manipulate the instrument—no small advantage as regards the rapidity of work."—*Engineer*

"Very handy; a man may know that all his day's work must fall on two of these cards, which he puts into his own card-case, and leaves the rest behind."—*Athenæum.*

Engineering Fieldwork.

THE PRACTICE OF ENGINEERING FIELDWORK, applied to Land and Hydraulic, Hydrographic, and Submarine Surveying and Levelling. Second Edition, Revised, with considerable Additions, and a Supplement on Waterworks, Sewers, Sewage, and Irrigation. By W. DAVIS HASKOLL, C.E. Numerous Folding Plates. In One Volume, demy 8vo, £1 5*s.* cloth.

Large Tunnel Shafts.

THE CONSTRUCTION OF LARGE TUNNEL SHAFTS: A Practical and Theoretical Essay. By J. H. WATSON BUCK, M. Inst. C.E., Resident Engineer, London and North-Western Railway. Illustrated with Folding Plates, royal 8vo, 12*s.* cloth.

"Many of the methods given are of extreme practical value to the mason; and the observations on the form of arch, the rules for ordering the stone, and the construction of the templates will be found of considerable use. We commend the book to the engineering profession."—*Building News.*

"Will be regarded by civil engineers as of the utmost value, and calculated to save much time nd obviate many mistakes."—*Colliery Guardian.*

Field-Book for Engineers.

THE ENGINEER'S, MINING SURVEYOR'S, AND CONTRACTOR'S FIELD-BOOK. Consisting of a Series of Tables, with Rules, Explanations of Systems, and use of Theodolite for Traverse Surveying and Plotting the Work with minute accuracy by means of Straight Edge and Set Square only; Levelling with the Theodolite, Casting-out and Reducing Levels to Datum, and Plotting Sections in the ordinary manner; setting-out Curves with the Theodolite by Tangential Angles and Multiples, with Right and Left-hand Readings of the Instrument: Setting-out Curves without Theodolite, on the System of Tangential Angles by sets of Tangents and Offsets: and Earthwork Tables to 80 feet deep, calculated for every 6 inches in depth. By W. DAVIS HASKOLL, C.E. With numerous Woodcuts. Fourth Edition, Enlarged. Crown 8vo, 12*s.* cloth.

"The book is very handy, and the author might have added that the separate tables of sines and tangents to every minute will make it useful for many other purposes, the genuine traverse tables existing all the same."—*Athenæum.*

"Every person engaged in engineering field operations will estimate the importance of such a work and the amount of valuable time which will be saved by reference to a set of reliable tables prepared with the accuracy and fulness of those given in this volume."—*Railway News.*

Earthwork, Measurement and Calculation of.

A MANUAL ON EARTHWORK. By ALEX. J. S. GRAHAM, C.E. With numerous Diagrams. 18mo, 2*s.* 6*d.* cloth.

"A great amount of practical information, very admirably arranged, and available for rough estimates, as well as for the more exact calculations required in the engineer's and contractor's offices."—*Artizan.*

Strains.

THE STRAINS ON STRUCTURES OF IRONWORK; with Practical Remarks on Iron Construction. By F. W. SHEILDS, M. Inst. C.E. Second Edition, with 5 Plates. Royal 8vo, 5*s.* cloth.

"The student cannot find a better little book on this subject."—*Engineer.*

Strength of Cast Iron, etc.

A PRACTICAL ESSAY ON THE STRENGTH OF CAST IRON AND OTHER METALS. By THOMAS TREDGOLD, C.E. Fifth Edition, including HODGKINSON'S Experimental Researches. 8vo, 12*s.* cloth.

MECHANICS & MECHANICAL ENGINEERING.

Mechanic's Workshop Companion.

THE OPERATIVE MECHANIC'S WORKSHOP COMPANION, AND SCIENTIFIC GENTLEMAN'S PRACTICAL ASSISTANT. Comprising a great variety of the most useful Rules in Mechanical Science; with numerous Tables of Practical Data and Calculated Results. By W. TEMPLETON, Author of "The Engineer's Practical Assistant." Thirteenth Edition. With Tables for Operative Smiths, Millwrights, Engineers, &c., and Useful and Practical Rules in Hydraulics and Hydrodynamics, a variety of Experimental Results, and an extensive Table of Powers and Roots. 11 Plates. 12mo, 5*s.* bound.

"As a text-book of reference, in which mechanical and commercial demands are judiciously met, 'Templeton's Companion' stands unrivalled."—*Mechanic's Magazine.*

"It has met with great success in the engineering workshop, as we can testify; and there are a great many men who, in a great measure, owe their rise in life to this little book."—*Building News.*

Engineer's and Machinist's Assistant.

THE ENGINEER'S, MILLWRIGHT'S, and MACHINIST'S PRACTICAL ASSISTANT. Comprising a collection of Useful Tables, Rules and Data. Compiled and Arranged, with Original Matter, by WILLIAM TEMPLETON. Seventh Edition. Carefully revised, with Additions. 18mo, 2*s.* 6*d.* cloth. [*Just published.*

"With the utmost confidence we commend this book to the attention of our readers."—*Mechanic's Magazine.*

"A more suitable present to an apprentice to any of the mechanical trades could not possibly be made."—*Building News.*

Mechanics.

THE HANDBOOK OF MECHANICS. By DIONYSIUS LARDNER, D.C.L., formerly Professor of Natural Philosophy and Astronomy in University College, London. New Edition, Edited and considerably Enlarged by BENJAMIN LOEWY, F.R.A.S., &c. 378 Illustrations, post 8vo, 6*s.* cloth.

"The explanations throughout are studiously popular, and care has been taken to show the application of the various branches of physics to the industrial arts, and to the practical business of life."—*Mining Journal.*

Turning.

LATHE-WORK : A Practical Treatise on the Tools, Appliances, and Processes employed in the Art of Turning. By PAUL N. HASLUCK. Second Edition, thoroughly Revised, with a New Chapter on the Screw-cutting Lathe. Crown 8vo, 5*s.* cloth.

"Written by a man who knows, not only how work ought to be done, but who also knows how to do it, and how to convey his knowledge to others. To all turners this book would be valuable."—*Engineering.*

'We can safely recommend the work to young engineers. To the amateur it will simply be invaluable. To the student it will convey a great deal of useful information."—*Engineer.*

"A compact, succinct, and handy guide to lathe-work did not exist in our language until Mr. Hasluck, by the publication of this treatise, gave the turner a true *vade-mecum.*"—*House Decorator.*

Metal Turning.

THE METAL TURNER'S HANDBOOK. By PAUL N. HASLUCK. With over 100 Cuts. Crown 8vo, 1*s.* cloth.

Iron and Steel.

"IRON AND STEEL": A Work for the Forge, Foundry, Factory, and Office. Containing ready, useful, and trustworthy Information for Ironmasters and their Stock-takers; Managers of Bar, Rail, Plate, and Sheet Rolling Mills; Iron and Metal Founders; Iron Ship and Bridge Builders; Mechanical, Mining, and Consulting Engineers; Architects, Contractors, Builders, and Professional Draughtsmen. By CHARLES HOARE, Author of "The Slide Rule," &c. Eighth Edition, Revised throughout and considerably Enlarged. With folding Scales of "Foreign Measures compared with the English Foot," and "Fixed Scales of Squares, Cubes, and Roots, Areas, Decimal Equivalents, &c." Oblong 32mo, leather, elastic band, 6*s.*

For comprehensiveness the book has not its equal."—*Iron.*

One of the best of the pocket books, and a useful companion in other branches of work tha iron and steel."—*English Mechanic.*

Stone-working Machinery.

STONE-WORKING MACHINERY, and the Rapid and Economical Conversion of Stone. With Hints on the Arrangement and Management of Stone Works. By M. POWIS BALE, M.I.M.E., A.M.I.C.E. With numerous Illustrations. Large crown 8vo, 9*s.* cloth.

"The book should be in the hands of every mason or student of stone-work."—*Colliery Guardian.*

Engineer's Reference Book.

THE WORKS' MANAGER'S HANDBOOK OF MODERN RULES, TABLES, AND DATA. For Engineers, Millwrights, and Boiler Makers; Tool Makers, Machinists, and Metal Workers; Iron and Brass Founders, &c. By W. S. HUTTON, Civil and Mechanical Engineer. Second Edition, carefully revised, with Additions. In One handsome Volume, medium 8vo, price 15*s.* strongly bound. [*Just published.*

Contents:

Proportions and Rules for Modern Stationary and Locomotive Engines—Lancashire, Cornish, Vertical, Return Tube, and Portable Engine Boilers—Chimneys—Water-Wheels, Pumps, Pipes, Girders, Gearing, Shafting, and Millwork—Iron Foundry Work and Brass Work—Rules and Practical Data relating to the Strength and Weight of Metals and Materials—Iron and Brass Casting—Cutting Metals—Wheel Cutting—Screw Cutting—Wheel Gearing—Rope Gearing—Pulleys—Weight of Pulleys—Weight of Spur, Bevel, and Mortice Wheels—Warming and Ventilating—Weight of Iron, Steel, Brass, and various Metals and Materials.

Also, The Indicator and Indicator Diagrams—Various Memoranda for the Foundry and Workshop—Rules for the Weight of Castings—The New Patent Law and Costs of Patents—Legal Memoranda—List of French Words for English Engineering Terms—French and English Weights and Measures—And a variety of Modern Practical Information for Civil and Mechanical Engineers.

"The volume is an exceedingly useful one, brimful with engineers' notes, memoranda, and rules, and well worthy of being on every mechanical engineer's bookshelf. . . . There is valuable information on every page."—*Mechanical World.*

"The information is precisely that likely to be required in practice. . . . The work forms a desirable addition to the library, not only of the works manager, but of anyone connected with general engineering."—*Mining Journal.*

"A formidable mass of facts and figures, readily accessible through an elaborate index . . . . Such a volume will be found absolutely necessary as a book of reference in all sorts of 'works' connected with the metal trades. . . . Any ordinary foreman or workman can find all he wants in the crowded pages of this useful work."—*Ryland's Iron Trades Circular.*

Engineering Construction.

PATTERN-MAKING: A Practical Treatise, embracing the Main Types of Engineering Construction, and including Gearing, both Hand and Machine made, Engine Work, Sheaves and Pulleys, Pipes and Columns, Screws, Machine Parts, Pumps and Cocks, the Moulding of Patterns in Loam and Greensand, &c., together with the methods of Estimating the weight of Castings; to which is added an Appendix of Tables for Workshop Reference. By a FOREMAN PATTERN MAKER. With upwards of Three Hundred and Seventy Illustrations. Crown 8vo, 7*s.* 6*d.* cloth. [*Just published.*

Smith's Tables for Mechanics, etc.

TABLES, MEMORANDA, AND CALCULATED RESULTS, FOR MECHANICS, ENGINEERS, ARCHITECTS, BUILDERS, &c. Selected and Arranged by FRANCIS SMITH. Third Edition, Revised and Enlarged, 250 pp., waistcoat-pocket size, 1*s.* 6*d.* limp leather. [*Just published.*

"It would, perhaps, be as difficult to make a small pocket-book selection of notes and formulæ to suit ALL engineers as it would be to make a universal medicine; but Mr. Smith's waistcoat-pocket collection may be looked upon as a successful attempt."—*Engineer.*

"A veritable pocket treasury of knowledge."—*Iron.*

The High-Pressure Steam Engine.

THE HIGH-PRESSURE STEAM-ENGINE: An Exposition of its Comparative Merits and an Essay towards an Improved System of Construction. By DR. ERNST ALBAN. Translated from the German, with Notes, by DR. POLE, M. Inst. C.E., &c. With 28 Plates. 8vo, 16*s.* 6*d.* cloth.

"Goes thoroughly into the examination of the high-pressure engine, the boiler, and its appendages, and deserves a place in every scientific library."—*Steam Shipping Chronicle.*

Steam Boilers.

A TREATISE ON STEAM BOILERS: Their Strength, Construction, and Economical Working. By ROBERT WILSON, C.E., late Inspector, Manchester Steam Users' Association. Fifth Edition. 12mo, 6s. cloth.

"The best treatise that has ever been published on steam boilers."—*Engineer.*

"The author shows himself perfect master of his subject, and we heartily recommend all employing steam power to possess themselves of the work."—*Ryland's Iron Trade Circular.*

Boiler Making.

THE BOILER-MAKER'S READY RECKONER. With Examples of Practical Geometry and Templating, for the Use of Platers, Smiths and Riveters. By JOHN COURTNEY, Edited by D. K. CLARK, M.I.C.E. Second Edition, revised, with Additions, 12mo, 5s. half-bound.

"A reliable guide to the working boiler-maker."—*Iron.*

"Boiler-makers will readily recognise the value of this volume. . . . The tables are clearly printed, and so arranged that they can be referred to with the greatest facility, so that it cannot be doubted that they will be generally appreciated and much used."—*Mining Journal.*

Steam Engine.

TEXT-BOOK ON THE STEAM ENGINE. By T. M. GOODEVE, M.A., Barrister-at-Law, Author of "The Elements of Mechanism," &c. Sixth Edition. With numerous Illustrations. Crown 8vo, 6s. cloth.

"Professor Goodeve has given us a treatise on the steam engine which will bear comparison with anything written by Huxley or Maxwell, and we can award it no higher praise."—*Engineer.*

Steam.

THE SAFE USE OF STEAM. Containing Rules for Unprofessional Steam-users. By an ENGINEER. Fifth Edition. Sewed, 6*d.*

"If steam-users would but learn this little book by heart, boiler explosions would become sensations by their rarity."—*English Mechanic.*

Coal and Speed Tables.

A POCKET BOOK OF COAL AND SPEED TABLES, for Engineers and Steam-users. By NELSON FOLEY, Author of "Boiler Construction." Pocket-size, 3s. 6*d.* cloth; 4s. leather.

Contents:

Table 1. Decimals of Tons in cwts., qrs., lbs.—Table 2. Consumption per Day per I.H.P.—Table 3. Consumption per Hour per I.H.P.—Table 4. Consumption per Day per sq. ft. grate.—Table 5. Consumption per Hour per sq. ft. grate.—Table 6. Stowage of Coal and Composition.—Table 7. Knots per Hour (Measured Mile).—Table 8. Knots per Hour (Cloch and Cumbrae).—Table 9. Decimal Equivalents of Time.—Table 10. Knots per Hour in ft. per min.—Table 11. Constants for I.H.P.—Table 12. Decimals of Cwts. in lbs.—Table 13. Measures of Weight; also Miscellaneous Results—Combustion, Air required, Stoking, &c.—Time and Speed Examples.

Fire Engineering.

FIRES, FIRE-ENGINES, AND FIRE-BRIGADES. With a History of Fire-Engines, their Construction, Use, and Management; Remarks on Fire-Proof Buildings, and the Preservation of Life from Fire; Statistics of the Fire Appliances in English Towns; Foreign Fire Systems; Hints on Fire Brigades, &c. &c. By CHARLES F. T. YOUNG, C.E. With numerous Illustrations, 544 pp., demy 8vo, £1 4s. cloth.

"To such of our readers as are interested in the subject of fires and fire apparatus, we can most heartily commend this book. It is really the only English work we now have upon the subject."—*Engineering.*

"It displays much evidence of careful research; and Mr. Young has put his facts neatly together. It is evident enough that his acquaintance with the practical details of the construction of steam fire engines, old and new, and the conditions with which it is necessary they should comply, is accurate and full."—*Engineer.*

Gas Lighting.

COMMON SENSE FOR GAS-USERS: A Catechism of Gas-Lighting for Householders, Gasfitters, Millowners, Architects, Engineers, etc. By ROBERT WILSON, C.E., Author of "A Treatise on Steam Boilers." Second Edition. Crown 8vo, sewed, with Folding Plates and Wood Engravings, 2s. 6*d.*

"All gas-users will decidedly benefit, both in pocket and comfort, if they will avail themselves of Mr. Wilson's counsels."—*Engineering.*

THE POPULAR WORKS OF MICHAEL REYNOLDS.

(*Known as* "THE ENGINE DRIVER'S FRIEND").

Locomotive-Engine Driving.

LOCOMOTIVE-ENGINE DRIVING: A Practical Manual for Engineers in charge of Locomotive Engines. By MICHAEL REYNOLDS, Member of the Society of Engineers, formerly Locomotive Inspector L. B. and S. C. R. Sixth Edition. Including a KEY TO THE LOCOMOTIVE ENGINE. With Illustrations and Portrait of Author. Crown 8vo, 4*s.* 6*d.* cloth.

"Mr. Reynolds has supplied a want, and has supplied it well. We can confidently recommend the book, not only to the practical driver, but to everyone who takes an interest in the performance of locomotive engines."—*The Engineer.*

"Mr. Reynolds has opened a new chapter in the literature of the day. Of the practical utility of Mr. Reynolds's book we have to speak in terms of warm commendation."—*Athenæum.*

"Evidently the work of one who knows his subject thoroughly."—*Railway Service Gazette.*

"Were the cautions and rules given in the book to become part of the every-day working of our engine-drivers, we might have fewer distressing accidents to deplore."—*Scotsman.*

The Engineer, Fireman, and Engine-Boy.

THE MODEL LOCOMOTIVE ENGINEER, FIREMAN, and ENGINE-BOY. Comprising a Historical Notice of the Pioneer Locomotive Engines and their Inventors, with a project for the establishment of Certificates of Qualification in the Running Service of Railways. By MICHAEL REYNOLDS, Author of "Locomotive-Engine Driving." With numerous Illustrations and a fine Portrait of George Stephenson. Crown 8vo, 4*s.* 6*d.* cloth.

"From the technical knowledge of the author it will appeal to the railway man of to-day more forcibly than anything written by Dr. Smiles. . . . The volume contains information of a technical kind, and facts that every driver should be familiar with."—*English Mechanic.*

"We should be glad to see this book in the possession of everyone in the kingdom who has ever laid, or is to lay, hands on a locomotive engine."—*Iron.*

"Replete with information and graphic detail for the railway man."—*Railway Service Gazette.*

Stationary Engine Driving.

STATIONARY ENGINE DRIVING: A Practical Manual for Engineers in charge of Stationary Engines. By MICHAEL REYNOLDS. Second Edition, Enlarged. With Plates and Woodcuts. Crown 8vo, 4*s.* 6*d.* cloth.

"The author is thoroughly acquainted with his subjects, and his advice on the various points treated is clear and practical. . . . He has produced a manual which is an exceedingly useful one for the class for whom it is specially intended."—*Engineering.*

"Our author leaves no stone unturned. He is determined that his readers shall not only know something about the stationary engine, but all about it."—*Engineer.*

"An engineman who has mastered the contents of Mr. Reynolds's book will require but little actual experience with boilers and engines before he can be trusted to look after them."—*English Mechanic.*

"The book should be possessed by every intelligent and ambitious engineman."—*Builder.*

Continuous Railway Brakes.

CONTINUOUS RAILWAY BRAKES: A Practical Treatise on the several Systems in Use in the United Kingdom; their Construction and Performance. With copious Illustrations and numerous Tables. By MICHAEL REYNOLDS. Large crown 8vo, 9*s.* cloth.

"A popular explanation of the different brakes. It will be of great assistance in forming public opinion, and will be studied with benefit by those who take an interest in the brake. . . . It is a clear exposition of the brake question as it relates to the rival systems."—*English Mechanic.*

"Written with sufficient technical detail to enable the principle and relative connection of the various parts of each particular brake to be readily grasped."—*Mechanical World.*

"May be recommended to all who desire to study the subject of continuous brakes."—*Iron.*

Engine-Driving Life.

ENGINE-DRIVING LIFE; or, Stirring Adventures and Incidents in the Lives of Locomotive-Engine Drivers. By MICHAEL REYNOLDS. Eighth Thousand. Crown 8vo, 2*s.* cloth.

"The book from first to last is perfectly fascinating. Wilkie Collins' most thrilling conceptions are thrown into the shade by true incidents, endless in their variety, related in every page."—*North British Mail.*

"Anyone who wishes to get a real insight into railway life cannot do better than read 'Engine-Driving Life' for himself; and if he once takes it up he will find that the author's enthusiasm and real love of the engine-driving profession will carry him on till he has read every page."—*Saturday Review.*

ARCHITECTURE, BUILDING, etc.

Construction.

THE SCIENCE OF BUILDING: An Elementary Treatise on the Principles of Construction. By E. WYNDHAM TARN, M.A., Architect. Second Edition, Revised, with 58 Engravings. Crown 8vo, 7s. 6d. cloth.

"A very valuable book, which we strongly recommend to all students."—*Builder.*

"No architectural student should be without this handbook of constructional knowledge."—*Architect.*

Villa Architecture.

A HANDY BOOK OF VILLA ARCHITECTURE: Being a Series of Designs for Villa Residences in various Styles. With Outline Specifications and Estimates. By C. WICKES, Architect, Author of "The Spires and Towers of England," &c. 30 Plates, 4to, half-morocco, £1 1s.

*** Also an Enlarged Edition of the above. 61 Plates, with Outline Specifications, Estimates, &c. £2 2s. half-morocco.

"The whole of the designs bear evidence of their being the work of an artistic architect, and they will prove very valuable and suggestive."—*Building News.*

Useful Text-Book for Architects.

THE ARCHITECT'S GUIDE: Being a Text-Book of Useful Information for Architects, Engineers, Surveyors, Contractors, Clerks of Works, &c. &c. By FREDERICK ROGERS, Architect, Author of "Specifications for Practical Architecture," &c. Second Edition, Revised and Enlarged. With numerous Illustrations. Crown 8vo, 6s. cloth.

"As a text-book of useful information for architects, engineers, surveyors, &c., it would be hard to find a handier or more complete little volume."—*Standard.*

"A young architect could hardly have a better guide-book."—*Timber Trades Journal.*

Taylor and Cresy's Rome.

THE ARCHITECTURAL ANTIQUITIES OF ROME. By the late G. L. TAYLOR, Esq., F.R.I.B.A., and EDWARD CRESY, Esq. New Edition, thoroughly revised by the Rev. ALEXANDER TAYLOR, M.A. (son of the late G. L. Taylor, Esq.), Fellow of Queen's College, Oxford, and Chaplain of Gray's Inn. Large folio, with 130 Plates, half-bound, £3 3s.

N.B.—This is the only book which gives on a large scale, and with the precision of architectural measurement, the principal Monuments of Ancient Rome in plan, elevation, and detail.

"Taylor and Cresy's work has from its first publication been ranked among those professional books which cannot be bettered. . . . It would be difficult to find examples of drawings, even among those of the most painstaking students of Gothic, more thoroughly worked out than are the one hundred and thirty plates in this volume."—*Architect.*

Drawing for Builders and Students in Architecture.

PRACTICAL RULES ON DRAWING, for the Operative Builder and Young Student in Architecture. By GEORGE PYNE. With 14 Plates, 4to, 7s. 6d. boards.

Specifications for Practical Architecture.

SPECIFICATIONS FOR PRACTICAL ARCHITECTURE: A Guide to the Architect, Engineer, Surveyor, and Builder; with an Essay on the Structure and Science of Modern Buildings. By FREDERICK ROGERS, Architect. With numerous Illustrations, demy 8vo, 15s. cloth.

*** A volume of specifications of a practical character being greatly required, and the old standard work of Alfred Bartholomew being out of print, the author, on the basis of that work, has produced the above.—*Extract from Preface.*

The House-Owner's Estimator.

THE HOUSE-OWNER'S ESTIMATOR; or, What will it Cost to Build, Alter, or Repair? A Price Book adapted to the Use of Unprofessional People, as well as for the Architectural Surveyor and Builder. By the late JAMES D. SIMON, A.R.I.B.A. Edited and Revised by FRANCIS T. W. MILLER, A.R.I.B.A. With numerous Illustrations. Third Edition, Revised. Crown 8vo, 3s. 6d. cloth.

"In two years it will repay its cost a hundred times over."—*Field.*

"A very handy book."—*English Mechanic.*

Civil Architecture.

THE DECORATIVE PART OF CIVIL ARCHITECTURE. By Sir WILLIAM CHAMBERS, F.R.S. With Illustrations, Notes, and an Examination of Grecian Architecture, by JOSEPH GWILT, F.S.A. Edited by W. H. LEEDS. 66 Plates, 4to, 21s. cloth.

Designing, Measuring, and Valuing.

THE STUDENT'S GUIDE to the PRACTICE of MEASURING AND VALUING ARTIFICERS' WORKS. Containing Directions for taking Dimensions, Abstracting the same, and bringing the Quantities into Bill, with Tables of Constants, and copious Memoranda for the Valuation of Labour and Materials in the respective Trades of Bricklayer and Slater, Carpenter and Joiner, Painter and Glazier, Paperhanger, &c. With 8 Plates and 63 Woodcuts. Originally edited by EDWARD DOBSON, Architect. Fifth Edition, Revised, with considerable Additions on Mensuration and Construction, and a New Chapter on Dilapidations, Repairs, and Contracts, by E. WYNDHAM TARN, M.A. Crown 8vo, 9s.

"Well fulfils the promise of its title-page, and we can thoroughly recommend it to the class for whose use it has been compiled. Mr. Tarn's additions and revisions have much increased the usefulness of the work, and have especially augmented its value to students."—*Engineering*.

"The work has been carefully revised and edited by Mr. E. Wyndham Tarn, M.A., and comprises several valuable additions on construction, mensuration, dilapidations and repairs, and other matters. . . . This edition will be found the most complete treatise on the principles of measuring and valuing artificers' work that has yet been published."—*Building News*.

"Might be read and studied with advantage by almost everyone having any connection with building operations, from the architect downwards."—*Building World*.

Pocket Estimator.

THE POCKET ESTIMATOR for the BUILDING TRADES. Being an Easy Method of Estimating the various parts of a Building collectively, more especially applied to Carpenters' and Joiners' work. By A. C. BEATON, Author of "Quantities and Measurements." Third Edition, carefully revised, 33 Woodcuts, leather, waistcoat-pocket size, 1s. 6*d*.

"Contains a good deal of information not easily to be obtained from the ordinary price books. The prices given are accurate, and up to date."—*Building News*.

"This book is as complete as it is possible to make it."—*Building and Engineering Times*.

Builder's and Surveyor's Pocket Technical Guide.

THE POCKET TECHNICAL GUIDE AND MEASURER FOR BUILDERS AND SURVEYORS. Containing a Complete Explanation of the Terms used in Building Construction, Memoranda for Reference, Technical Directions for Measuring Work in all the Building Trades, with a Treatise on the Measurement of Timber, Complete Specifications, &c., &c. By A. C. BEATON. Second Edition, with 19 Woodcuts, leather, waistcoat-pocket size, 1s. 6*d*.

"An exceedingly handy pocket companion, thoroughly reliable."—*Builder's Weekly Reporter*.

"This neat little compendium contains all that is requisite in carrying out contracts for excavating, tiling, bricklaying, paving, &c."—*British Trade Journal*.

Handbook of Specifications.

THE HANDBOOK OF SPECIFICATIONS; or, Practical Guide to the Architect, Engineer, Surveyor, and Builder, in drawing up Specifications and Contracts for Works and Constructions. Illustrated by Precedents of Buildings actually executed by eminent Architects and Engineers. By Professor T. L. DONALDSON, P.R.I.B.A., &c. New Edition, in One large Vol., 8vo, with upwards of 1,000 pages of Text, and 33 Plates, £1 11*s*. 6*d*. cloth.

"In this work forty-four specifications of executed works are given, including the specifications for parts of the new Houses of Parliament, by Sir Charles Barry, and for the new Royal Exchange, by Mr. Tite, M.P. The latter, in particular, is a very complete and remarkable document. It embodies, to a great extent, as Mr. Donaldson mentions, 'the bill of quantities with the description of the works.' . . . It is valuable as a record, and more valuable still as a book of precedents. . . . Suffice it to say that Donaldson's 'Handbook of Specifications' must be bought by all architects."—*Builder*.

Boiler and Factory Chimneys.

BOILER AND FACTORY CHIMNEYS: Their Draught-power and Stability; with a Chapter on Lightning-Conductors. By ROBERT WILSON, C.E., Author of "Treatise on Steam Boilers." Cr. 8vo, 3s. 6*d*. cloth.

"A most valuable book of its kind, full of useful information."—*Local Government Chronicle*.

DECORATIVE ARTS, etc.

Woods and Marbles (Imitation of).

SCHOOL OF PAINTING FOR THE IMITATION OF WOODS AND MARBLES, as Taught and Practised by A. R. VAN DER BURG and P. VAN DER BURG, Directors of the Rotterdam Painting Institution. Royal folio, 18½ by 12½ in., Illustrated with 24 full-size Coloured Plates; also 12 plain Plates, comprising 154 Figures, price £2 12s. 6d.

List of Contents

Introductory Chapter — Tools required for Wood Painting—Observations on the different species of Wood: Walnut—Observations on Marble in general—Tools required for Marble Painting—St. Remi Marble: Preparation of the Paints: Process of Working—Wood Graining: Preparation of Stiff and Flat Brushes: Sketching different Grains and Knots: Glazing of Wood—Ash: Painting of Ash—Breche (Breccia) Marble: Breche Violette: Process of Working—Maple: Process of Working—The different species of White Marble: Methods of Working: Painting White Marble with Lac-dye: Painting White Marble with Poppy-paint—Mahogany: Methods of Working—Yellow Sienna Marble Process of Working—Juniper: Characteristics of the Natural Wood: Method of Imitation—Vert de Mer Marble: Description of the Marble: Process of Working—Oak: Description of the varieties of Oak: Manipulation of Oak-painting: Tools employed: Method of Working—Waulsort Marble: Varieties of the Marble: Process of Working—The Painting of Iron with Red Lead: How to make Putty: Out-door Work: Varnishing: Priming and Varnishing Woods and Marbles: Painting in General: Ceilings and Walls: Gilding: Transparencies, Flags, &c.

List of Plates.

1. Various Tools required for Wood Painting —2, 3. Walnut: Preliminary Stages of Graining and Finished Specimen — 4. Tools used for Marble Painting and Method of Manipulation—5, 6. St. Remi Marble: Earlier Operations and Finished Specimen—7. Methods of Sketching different Grains, Knots, &c.—8, 9. Ash: Preliminary Stages and Finished Specimen — 10. Methods of Sketching Marble Grains—11, 12. Breche Marble: Preliminary Stages of Working and Finished Specimen—13. Maple: Methods of Producing the different Grains—14, 15. Bird's-eye Maple: Preliminary Stages and Finished Specimen—16. Methods of Sketching the different Species of White Marble—17, 18. White Marble: Preliminary Stages of Process and Finished Specimen—19. Mahogany: Specimens of various Grains and Methods of Manipulation—20, 21. Mahogany: Earlier Stages and Finished Specimen—22, 23, 24. Sienna Marble: Varieties of Grain, Preliminary Stages and Finished Specimen—25, 26, 27. Juniper Wood: Methods of producing Grain, &c.: Preliminary Stages and Finished Specimen—28, 29, 30. Vert de Mer Marble: Varieties of Grain and Methods of Working Unfinished and Finished Specimens—31, 32, 33. Oak: Varieties of Grain, Tools Employed, and Methods of Manipulation, Preliminary Stages and Finished Specimen—34, 35, 36. Waulsort Marble: Varieties of Grain, Unfinished and Finished Specimens.

"A comprehensive guide to the art. The explanations of the processes, the manipulation and management of the colours, and the beautifully executed plates will not be the least valuable to the student who aims at making his work a faithful transcript of nature."—*Building News.*

"Students and novices are fortunate who are able to become the possessors of *so noble a work.*"—*Architect.*

Colour.

A GRAMMAR OF COLOURING. Applied to Decorative Painting and the Arts. By GEORGE FIELD. New Edition, adapted to the use of the Ornamental Painter and Designer. By ELLIS A. DAVIDSON. With New Coloured Diagrams and Engravings. 12mo, 3s. 6d. cloth boards.

"The book is a most useful *resume* of the properties of pigments."—*Builder.*

Glass Painting.

GLASS STAINING AND THE ART OF PAINTING ON GLASS. From the German of Dr. GESSERT and EMANUEL OTTO FROMBERG. With an Appendix on THE ART OF ENAMELLING. 12mo, 2s. 6d. cloth limp

Decoration.

ELEMENTARY DECORATION. A Guide to the Simpler Forms of Everyday Art, as applied to the Interior and Exterior Decoration of Dwelling Houses, &c. By JAMES W. FACEY, Jun. With 68 Cuts. 12mo, 2s. cloth limp.

"As a technical guide-book to the decorative painter it will be found reliable."—*Building News.*

House Painting, etc.

HOUSE PAINTING, GRAINING, MARBLING, AND SIGN WRITING, A Practical Manual of. By ELLIS A. DAVIDSON. Fourth Edition. With Coloured Plates and Wood Engravings. 12mo, 6s. cloth boards.

"A mass of information, of use to the amateur and of value to the practical man."—*English Mechanic.*

"Simply invaluable to the youngster entering upon this particular calling, and highly serviceable to the man who is practising it."—*Furniture Gazette.*

DELAMOTTE'S WORKS on ILLUMINATION & ALPHABETS.

A PRIMER OF THE ART OF ILLUMINATION, for the Use of Beginners: with a Rudimentary Treatise on the Art, Practical Directions for its exercise, and numerous Examples taken from Illuminated MSS., printed in Gold and Colours. By F. Delamotte. Small 4to, 9s. elegantly bound, cloth antique.

". . . . The examples of ancient MSS. recommended to the student, which, with much good sense, the author chooses from collections accessible to all, are selected with judgment and knowledge, as well as taste."—*Athenæum.*

ORNAMENTAL ALPHABETS, Ancient and Mediæval, from the Eighth Century, with Numerals; including Gothic, Church-Text, large and small, German, Italian, Arabesque, Initials for Illumination, Monograms, Crosses, &c., &c., for the use of Architectural and Engineering Draughtsmen, Missal Painters, Masons, Decorative Painters, Lithographers, Engravers, Carvers, &c., &c. Collected and Engraved by F. Delamotte, and printed in Colours. New and Cheaper Edition. Royal 8vo, oblong, 2s. 6d. ornamental boards.

"For those who insert enamelled sentences round gilded chalices, who blazon shop legends over shop-doors, who letter church walls with pithy sentences from the Decalogue, this book will be useful."—*Athenæum.*

EXAMPLES OF MODERN ALPHABETS, Plain and Ornamental; including German, Old English, Saxon, Italic, Perspective, Greek, Hebrew, Court Hand, Engrossing, Tuscan, Riband, Gothic, Rustic, and Arabesque; with several Original Designs, and an Analysis of the Roman and Old English Alphabets, large and small, and Numerals, for the use of Draughtsmen, Surveyors, Masons, Decorative Painters, Lithographers, Engravers, Carvers, &c. Collected and Engraved by F. Delamotte, and printed in Colours. New and Cheaper Edition. Royal 8vo, oblong, 2s. 6d. ornamental boards.

"There is comprised in it every possible shape into which the letters of the alphabet and numerals can be formed, and the talent which has been expended in the conception of the various plain and ornamental letters is wonderful."—*Standard.*

"This volume has borne the test of practical use, and is invariably spoken well of by those who possess it."—*Jeweller and Metal-worker.*

MEDIÆVAL ALPHABETS AND INITIALS FOR ILLUMINATORS. By F. Delamotte, Illuminator, Designer, and Engraver on Wood. Containing 21 Plates and Illuminated Title, printed in Gold and Colours. With an Introduction by J. Willis Brooks. Small 4to, 6s. cloth gilt.

"A volume in which the letters of the alphabet come forth glorified in gilding and all the colours of the prism interwoven and intertwined and intermingled."—*Sun.*

THE EMBROIDERER'S BOOK OF DESIGN. Containing Initials, Emblems, Cyphers, Monograms, Ornamental Borders, Ecclesiastical Devices, Mediæval and Modern Alphabets, and National Emblems. Collected by F. Delamotte, and printed in Colours. Oblong royal 8vo, 1s. 6d., ornamental wrapper.

"The designs are practical—not designs that cannot be done in embroidery; and the book will no doubt be found exceedingly useful in the lady's work-room and in schools."—*Newcastle Courant.*

"The book will be of great assistance to ladies and young children who are endowed with the art of plying the needle in this most ornamental and useful pretty work."—*East Anglian Times.*

Wood Carving.

INSTRUCTIONS IN WOOD-CARVING, for Amateurs; with Hints on Design. By A Lady. With Ten large Plates, 2s. 6d. in emblematic wrapper.

"The handicraft of the wood-carver, so well as a book can impart it, may be learnt from 'A Lady's' publication."—*Athenæum.*

"The directions given are plain and easily understood."—*English Mechanic.*

Letter Painting.

THE ART OF LETTER PAINTING MADE EASY. By James Greig Badenoch. With 12 full-page Engravings of Examples, 1s. cloth limp.

"The system is a simple one, but quite original, and well worth the careful attention of letter painters. It can be easily mastered and remembered."—*Building News.*

CARPENTRY, TIMBER, etc.

Tredgold's Carpentry, Enlarged by E. W. Tarn.

THE ELEMENTARY PRINCIPLES OF CARPENTRY. A Treatise on the Pressure and Equilibrium of Timber Framing, the Resistance of Timber, and the Construction of Floors, Arches, Bridges, Roofs, Uniting Iron and Stone with Timber, &c. To which is added an Essay on the Nature and Properties of Timber, &c., with Descriptions of the kinds of Wood used in Building; also numerous Tables of the Scantlings of Timber for different purposes, the Specific Gravities of Materials, &c. By THOMAS TREDGOLD, C.E. With an Appendix of Specimens of Various Roofs of Iron and Stone, Illustrated. Sixth Edition, thoroughly revised and considerably enlarged by E. WYNDHAM TARN, M.A., Author of "The Science of Building," &c. With 61 Plates, Portrait of the Author, and several Woodcuts. In one large vol., 4to, price £1 5*s.* cloth. [*Just published.*

"Ought to be in every architect's and every builder's library."—*Builder.*

"Tredgold's 'Elementary Principles of Carpentry' is, without doubt, the standard English authority upon the subject. Mr. Tarn, by supplementing the text of the author, adds much to the work, and makes it an indispensable addition to the library of the student, the architect, and the engineer."—*Building News.*

Woodworking Machinery.

WOODWORKING MACHINERY: Its Rise, Progress, and Construction. With Hints on the Management of Saw Mills and the Economical Conversion of Timber. Illustrated with Examples of Recent Designs by leading English, French, and American Engineers. By M. POWIS BALE, A.M. Inst. C.E., M.I.M.E. Large crown 8vo, 12*s.* 6*d.* cloth.

"Mr. Bale is evidently an expert on the subject, and he has collected so much information that his book is all-sufficient for builders and others engaged in the conversion of timber."—*Architect.*

"The most comprehensive compendium of wood-working machinery we have seen. The author is a thorough master of his subject."—*Building News.*

"Converters of timber, wholesale joiners, the members generally of the building trades, architects, and owners of and dealers in timber, owe Mr. Bale tribute to the value of the cost of his book. It is sound from end to end, well designed and well executed."—*Iron.*

"The appearance of this book at the present time will, we should think, give a considerable impetus to the onward march of the machinist engaged in the designing and manufacture of wood-working machines. It should be in the office of every wood-working factory."—*English Mechanic.*

Saw Mills.

SAW MILLS: Their Arrangement and Management, and the Economical Conversion of Timber. (Being a Companion Volume to "Woodworking Machinery.") By M. POWIS BALE, A.M. Inst. C.E., M.I.M.E. With numerous Illustrations. Crown 8vo, 10*s.* 6*d.* cloth.

"The author is favourably known by his former work on 'Woodworking Machinery,' of which we were able to speak approvingly. This is a companion volume, in which the *administration* of a large sawing establishment is discussed, and the subject examined from a financial standpoint. Hence the size, shape, order, and disposition of saw-mills and the like are gone into in detail, and the course of the timber is traced from its reception to its delivery in its converted state. We could not desire a more complete or practical treatise."—*Builder.*

"We highly recommend Mr. Bale's work to the attention and perusal of all those who are engaged in the art of wood conversion, or who are about building or remodelling saw-mills on improved principles."—*Building News.*

"Will be found of much value by that special class of readers for whose information it is designed. We recommend the book to those about to construct or to manage saw-mills."—*Athenæum.*

Underwood and Woodland Tables.

TABLES FOR PLANTING AND VALUING UNDERWOOD AND WOODLAND; also Lineal, Superficial, Cubical, Wages, Marketing, and Decimal Tables. Together with Tables for Converting Land-measure from one denomination to another, and Instructions for Measuring Round Timber. By RICHARD HORTON. 12mo, 2*s.* strongly bound in leather.

Carpentering.

THE CARPENTER'S NEW GUIDE; or, Book of Lines for Carpenters; comprising all the Elementary Principles essential for acquiring a knowledge of Carpentry. Founded on the late PETER NICHOLSON'S Standard Work. A New Edition, revised by ARTHUR ASHPITEL, F.S.A. Together with Practical Rules on Drawing, by GEORGE PYNE. With 74 Plates, 4to, £1 1*s.* cloth.

Timber Merchant's Companion.

THE TIMBER MERCHANT'S AND BUILDER'S COMPANION. Containing New and Copious Tables of the Reduced Weight and Measurement of Deals and Battens, of all sizes, from One to a Thousand Pieces, and the relative Price that each size bears per Lineal Foot to any given Price per Petersburg Standard Hundred; the Price per Cube Foot of Square Timber to any given Price per Load of 50 Feet; the proportionate Value of Deals and Battens by the Standard, to Square Timber by the Load of 50 Feet; the readiest mode of ascertaining the Price of Scantling per Lineal Foot of any size, to any given Figure per Cube Foot. Also a variety of other valuable information. By WILLIAM DOWSING, Timber Merchant. Third Edition, Revised and Corrected. Crown 8vo, 3s., cloth.

"Everything is as concise and clear as it can possibly be made. There can be no doubt that every timber merchant and builder ought to possess it."—*Hull Advertiser.*

"We are glad to see a third edition of these admirable tables, which for correctness and simplicity of arrangement leave nothing to be desired."—*Timber Trades Journal.*

Practical Timber Merchant.

THE PRACTICAL TIMBER MERCHANT. Being a Guide for the use of Building Contractors, Surveyors, Builders, &c., comprising useful Tables for all purposes connected with the Timber Trade, Marks of Wood, Essay on the Strength of Timber, Remarks on the Growth of Timber, &c. By W. RICHARDSON. Fcap. 8vo, 3s. 6d. cloth.

"This handy manual contains much valuable information for the use of timber merchants, builders, foresters, and all others connected with the growth, sale, and manufacture of timber."—*Journal of Forestry.*

"To timber merchants or users this compact treatise will be found very useful."—*Illustrated Carpenter.*

Timber Freight Book.

THE TIMBER MERCHANT'S, SAW MILLER'S, AND IMPORTER'S FREIGHT BOOK AND ASSISTANT. Comprising Rules, Tables, and Memoranda relating to the Timber Trade. By WILLIAM RICHARDSON, Timber Broker; together with a Chapter on "Speeds of Saw Mill Machinery," by M. POWIS BALE, M.I.M.E., &c. 12mo, 3s. 6d. cloth.

Tables for Packing-Case Makers.

PACKING-CASE TABLES; showing the number of Superficial Feet in Boxes or Packing-Cases, from six inches square and upwards. By W. RICHARDSON, Timber Broker. Second Edition. Oblong 4to, 3s. 6d. cloth.

"Will save much labour and calculation to makers and users of packing-cases."—*Grocer.*

"Invaluable labour-saving tables."—*Ironmonger*

Superficial Measurement.

THE TRADESMAN'S GUIDE TO SUPERFICIAL MEASUREMENT. Tables calculated from 1 to 200 inches in length, by 1 to 108 inches in breadth. For the use of Architects, Surveyors, Engineers, Timber Merchants, Builders, &c. By JAMES HAWKINGS. Third Edition. Fcap., 3s. 6d. cloth.

Forestry.

THE ELEMENTS OF FORESTRY. Designed to afford Information concerning the Planting and Care of Forest Trees for Ornament or Profit, with Suggestions upon the Creation and Care of Woodlands. By F. B. HOUGH. Large crown 8vo, 10s. cloth.

Timber Importer's Guide.

THE TIMBER IMPORTER'S, TIMBER MERCHANT'S AND BUILDER'S STANDARD GUIDE. By RICHARD E. GRANDY. Comprising an Analysis of Deal Standards, Home and Foreign, with Comparative Values and Tabular Arrangements for fixing Nett Landed Cost on Baltic and North American Deals, including all intermediate Expenses, Freight, Insurance, &c., &c.; together with copious Information for the Retailer and Builder. Second Edition, carefully revised and corrected. 12mo, 3s. 6d. cloth boards.

"Everything it pretends to be: built up gradually, it leads one from a forest to a treenail, and throws in, as a makeweight, a host of material concerning bricks, columns, cisterns, &c."—*English Mechanic.*

MINING AND MINING INDUSTRIES.

Mining in the United Kingdom.

BRITISH MINING: A Treatise on the History, Discovery, Practical Development, and Future Prospects of Metalliferous Mines in the United Kingdom. By ROBERT HUNT, F.R.S., Keeper of Mining Records; Editor of "Ure's Dictionary of Arts, Manufactures, and Mines," &c. Upwards of 950 pp., with 230 Illustrations. Super-royal 8vo, £3 3s. cloth.

Synopsis of Contents:

BOOK I. HISTORICAL SKETCH OF BRITISH MINING:—Chap. I. Mining Previous to the Roman Invasion.—II. Mining during the Roman Occupation.—III. Mining to the Eighteenth Century.—IV. Mining for Tin and Copper to the End of the Eighteenth Century.—V. Mining for Lead, Silver, &c., to the End of the Eighteenth Century.—VI. Gold, Plumbago, Iron Ore, and Sundries to the End of the Eighteenth Century

BOOK II. ON THE FORMATION OF METALLIFEROUS DEPOSITS.—Chap. I. The Rocks of Mining Districts, and the Distribution of Metalliferous Deposits.—II. Mechanics of Mineral Lodes, Faults, Cross Courses, &c.—III. The Laws relating to Mineral Deposits.—IV. Remarkable Phenomena observed in Metalliferous Ore Deposits.

BOOK III. PRACTICAL MINING.—Chap. I. Discovery of Mineral Lodes and the Opening of Mines.—II. Practical Operations for the Extraction of Metalliferous Ores.—III. Ventilation and Drainage of Mines, &c.—IV. Dressing Metalliferous Ores: Preparation for Smelter.—V. Discovery and Extraction of Iron Ores from Veins and other Deposits.

BOOK IV. THE FUTURE PROSPECTS OF BRITISH MINING.—Chap. I. Summary, Examination of the Probable Exhaustion of Metalliferous Minerals.—II. On the Limits of the Metalliferous Zone.—III. The Occurrence of Ores at Great Depths or in New Districts.—IV. Improvements and Economy in Working British Mines.—V. General Summary and Conclusion—Appendix—Glossary of Terms.

"One of the most valuable works of reference of modern times. Mr. Hunt, as keeper of mining records of the United Kingdom, has had opportunities for such a task not enjoyed by anyone else, and has evidently made the most of them. . . . The language and style adopted are good, and the treatment of the various subjects laborious, conscientious, and scientific."—*Engineering.*

"A mass of information not elsewhere available, and of the greatest value to those who may be interested in our great mineral industries."—*Engineer.*

"A sound, business-like collection of interesting facts. . . . The amount of information Mr. Hunt has brought together is enormous. . . . The volume appears likely to convey more instruction upon the subject than any work hitherto published."—*Mining Journal.*

"The work will be for the mining industry what Dr. Percy's celebrated treatise has been for the metallurgical—a book that cannot with advantage be omitted from the library."—*Iron and Coal Trades Review.*

"Probably no one in this country was better qualified than Mr. Hunt for undertaking such a work. Brought into frequent and close association during a long life-time with the principal guardians of our mineral and metallurgical industries, he enjoyed a position exceptionally favourable for collecting the necessary information. The use which he has made of his opportunities is sufficiently attested by the dense mass of information crowded into the handsome volume which has just been published. . . . In placing before the reader a sketch of the present position of British Mining, Mr. Hunt treats his subject so fully and illustrates it so amply that this section really forms a little treatise on practical mining. . . . The book is, in fact, a treasure-house of statistical information on mining subjects, and we know of no other work embodying so great a mass of matter of this kind. Were this the only merit of Mr. Hunt's volume it would be sufficient to render it indispensable in the library of everyone interested in the development of the mining and metallurgical industries of this country."—*Athenæum.*

"The literature of mining has hitherto possessed no work approaching in importance to that which has just been published. There is much in Mr. Hunt's valuable work that every shareholder in a mine should read with close attention. The entire subject of practical mining—from the first search for the lode to the latest stages of dressing the ore—is dealt with in a masterly manner."—*Academy.*

Coal and Iron.

THE COAL AND IRON INDUSTRIES OF THE UNITED KINGDOM. Comprising a Description of the Coal Fields, and of the Principal Seams of Coal, with Returns of their Produce and its Distribution, and Analyses of Special Varieties. Also an Account of the occurrence of Iron Ores in Veins or Seams; Analyses of each Variety; and a History of the Rise and Progress of Pig Iron Manufacture since the year 1740, exhibiting the Economies introduced in the Blast Furnaces for its Production and Improvement. By RICHARD MEADE, Assistant Keeper of Mining Records. With Maps of the Coal Fields and Ironstone Deposits of the United Kingdom. 8vo, £1 8s. cloth.

"The book is one which must find a place on the shelves of all interested in coal and iron production, and in the iron, steel, and other metallurgical industries."—*Engineer.*

"Of this book we may unreservedly say that it is the best of its class which we have ever met. . . . A book of reference which no one engaged in the iron or coal trades should omit from his library."—*Iron and Coal Trades' Review.*

"An exhaustive treatise and a valuable work of reference. . . . The amount of labour which the preparation of the work has involved must have been enormous."—*Mining Journal.*

C

Metalliferous Minerals and Mining.

TREATISE ON METALLIFEROUS MINERALS AND MINING. By D. C. DAVIES, F.G.S., Mining Engineer, &c., Author of "A Treatise on Slate and Slate Quarrying." Illustrated with numerous Wood Engravings. Second Edition, carefully Revised. Crown 8vo, 12*s.* 6*d.* cloth.

"Neither the practical miner nor the general reader interested in mines, can have a better book for his companion and his guide."—*Mining Journal.*

"A book that will not only be useful to the geologist, the practical miner, and the metallurgist; but also very interesting to the general public."—*Iron.*

"As a history of the present state of mining throughout the world this book has a real value, and it supplies an actual want, for no such information has hitherto been brought together within such limited space."—*Athenæum.*

Earthy Minerals and Mining.

A TREATISE ON EARTHY AND OTHER MINERALS AND MINING. By D. C. DAVIES, F.G.S. Uniform with, and forming a Companion Volume to, the same Author's "Metalliferous Minerals and Mining." With 76 Wood Engravings. Crown 8vo, 12*s.* 6*d.* cloth.

Summary of Contents:

PART I. Silica—Alumina—Lime—Magnesia—Glucina—Zirconia—Thoria—with some of their combinations. PART II. Chloride of Sodium (Common Salt)—Nitrate of Soda—Borax—Baryta—Gypsum—Alum Shale—Phosphate of Lime. PART III. Carbon and Compounds of Carbon—Sulphur. PART IV. Arsenic—Cobalt—Molybdenum—Antimony and Manganese—Classified List of Mineral Substances.

"It is essentially a practical work, intended primarily for the use of practical men. . . . We do not remember to have met with any English work on mining matters that contains the same amount of information packed in equally convenient form."—*Academy.*

Underground Pumping Machinery.

MINE DRAINAGE. Being a Complete and Practical Treatise on Direct-Acting Underground Steam Pumping Machinery, with a Description of a large number of the best known Engines, their General Utility and the Special Sphere of their Action, the Mode of their Application, and their merits compared with other forms of Pumping Machinery. By STEPHEN MICHELL. 8vo, 15*s.* cloth.

"Will be highly esteemed by colliery owners and lessees, mining engineers, and students generally who require to be acquainted with the best means of securing the drainage of mines. It is a most valuable work, and stands almost alone in the literature of steam pumping machinery."—*Colliery Guardian.*

Mining Tools.

A MANUAL OF MINING TOOLS. For the Use of Mine Managers, Agents, Students, &c. By WILLIAM MORGANS, Lecturer on Practical Mining at the Bristol School of Mines. 12mo, 3*s.* cloth boards.

ATLAS OF ENGRAVINGS to Illustrate the above, containing 235 Illustrations of Mining Tools, drawn to scale. 4to, 6*s.* cloth boards.

"Students in the science of mining, and overmen, captains, managers, and viewers may gain practical knowledge and useful hints by the study of Mr. Morgans' manual."—*Colliery Guardian.*

Coal Mining.

COAL AND COAL MINING: A Rudimentary Treatise on. By WARINGTON W. SMYTH, M.A., F.R.S., &c., Chief Inspector of the Mines of the Crown. New Edition, Revised and Corrected. With numerous Illustrations. 12mo, 4*s.* cloth boards.

"As an outline is given of every known coal-field in this and other countries, as well as of the principal methods of working, the book will doubtless interest a very large number of readers."—*Mining Journal.*

Mining Surveying.

THE MINERAL SURVEYOR AND VALUER'S COMPLETE GUIDE. By WILLIAM LINTERN, Mining and Civil Engineer. With Four Plates of Diagrams, Plans, &c. 12mo, 4*s.* cloth boards.

"Contains much valuable information given in a small compass, and which, as far as we have tested it, is thoroughly trustworthy."—*Iron and Coal Trades Review.*

Subterraneous Surveying.

SUBTERRANEOUS SURVEYING, Elementary and Practical Treatise on; with and without the Magnetic Needle. By THOMAS FENWICK, Surveyor of Mines, and THOMAS BAKER, C.E. Illustrated. 12mo, 3*s.* cloth.

NAVAL ARCHITECTURE, NAVIGATION, etc.

Pocket-Book for Naval Architects and Shipbuilders.

THE NAVAL ARCHITECT'S AND SHIPBUILDER'S POCKET-BOOK of Formulæ, Rules, and Tables, and Marine Engineer's and Surveyor's Handy Book of Reference. By CLEMENT MACKROW, Member of the Institution of Naval Architects, Naval Draughtsman. Third Edition, Revised. With numerous Diagrams, &c. Fcap., 12s. 6*d*. strongly bound in leather.

"Should be used by all who are engaged in the construction or design of vessels. . . . Will be found to contain the most useful tables and formulæ required by shipbuilders, carefully collected from the best authorities, and put together in a popular and simple form."—*Engineer.*

"The professional shipbuilder has now, in a convenient and accessible form, reliable data for solving many of the numerous problems that present themselves in the course of his work."—*Iron.*

"There is scarcely a subject on which a naval architect or shipbuilder can require to refresh his memory which will not be found within the covers of Mr. Mackrow's book."—*English Mechanic.*

Pocket-Book for Marine Engineers.

A POCKET-BOOK OF USEFUL TABLES AND FORMULÆ FOR MARINE ENGINEERS. By FRANK PROCTOR, A.I.N.A. Third Edition. Royal 32mo, leather, gilt edges, with strap, 4s.

"We recommend it to our readers as going far to supply a long-felt want."—*Naval Science.*

"A most useful companion to all marine engineers."—*United Service Gazette.*

Grantham's Iron Shipbuilding.

ON IRON SHIPBUILDING. With Practical Examples and Details. By JOHN GRANTHAM, M. Inst. C.E., &c. Fifth Edition. Imp. 4to, boards, enlarged to 40 Plates, including the latest Examples. Together with separate Text, also considerably enlarged. 12mo, cloth limp, price £2 2s. complete.

"Mr. Grantham's work is of great interest. . . . It is also valuable as a record of the progress of iron shipbuilding. . . . It will, we are confident, command an extensive circulation among shipbuilders in general. . . . The text-book on which the examination in iron shipbuilding of candidates for promotion in the dockyards will be mainly based."—*Engineering.*

Lighthouses.

EUROPEAN LIGHTHOUSE SYSTEMS. Being a Report of a Tour of Inspection made in 1873. By Major GEORGE H. ELLIOT, Corps of Engineers, U.S.A. Illustrated by 51 Engravings and 31 Woodcuts. 8vo, 21s. cloth.

Navigation (Practical), with Tables.

PRACTICAL NAVIGATION. Consisting of the Sailor's Sea-Book, by JAMES GREENWOOD and W. H. ROSSER; together with the requisite Mathematical and Nautical Tables for the Working of the Problems, by HENRY LAW, C.E., and Professor J. R. YOUNG. Illustrated. 12mo, 7s. strongly half-bound.

Storms.

STORMS: Their Nature, Classification, and Laws; with the Means of Predicting them by their Embodiments, the Clouds. By WILLIAM BLASIUS. With Coloured Plates and numerous Wood Engravings. Crown 8vo, 10s. 6*d*. cloth.

"A very readable book. . . . The fresh facts contained in its pages, collected with evident care, form a useful repository to meteorologists in the study of atmospherical disturbances . . . The book will repay perusal as being the production of one who gives evidence of acute observation."—*Nature.*

The following books on NAVAL ARCHITECTURE, etc., *are published in* WEALE'S RUDIMENTARY SERIES.

MASTING, MAST-MAKING, AND RIGGING OF SHIPS. By ROBERT KIPPING, N.A. Fourteenth Edition. 12mo, 2s. 6*d*. cloth boards.

SAILS AND SAIL-MAKING. Tenth Edition, Enlarged, with an Appendix. By ROBERT KIPPING, N.A. Illustrated. 12mo, 3s. cloth boards.

NAVAL ARCHITECTURE. By JAMES PEAKE. Fourth Edition, with Plates and Diagrams. 12mo, 4s. cloth boards.

NATURAL PHILOSOPHY AND SCIENCE.

Electricity.

A MANUAL OF ELECTRICITY: Including Galvanism, Magnetism, Dia-Magnetism, Electro-Dynamics, Magno-Electricity, and the Electric Telegraph. By HENRY M. NOAD, Ph.D., F.R.S., F.C.S. Fourth Edition. With 500 Woodcuts. 8vo, £1 4s. cloth.

"The accounts given of electricity and galvanism are not only complete in a scientific sense, but, which is a rarer thing, are popular and interesting."—*Lancet.*

"Among the numerous writers on the attractive and fascinating subject of electricity, the author of the present volume has occupied our best attention. It is worthy of a place in the library of every public institution, and we have no doubt it will be deservedly patronised by the scientific community."—*Mining Journal.*

Text Book of Electricity.

THE STUDENT'S TEXT-BOOK OF ELECTRICITY. By HENRY M. NOAD, Ph.D., F.R.S., F.C.S. New Edition, carefully Revised. With an Introduction and Additional Chapters, by W. H. PREECE, M.I.C.E., Vice-President of the Society of Telegraph Engineers, &c. With 470 Illustrations. Crown 8vo, 12s. 6d. cloth.

"The original plan of this book has been carefully adhered to so as to make it a reflex of the existing state of electrical science, adapted for students. . . . Discovery seems to have progressed with marvellous strides; nevertheless it has now apparently ceased, and practical applications have commenced their career; and it is to give a faithful account of these that this fresh edition of Dr. Noad's valuable text-book is launched forth."—*Extract from Introduction by W. H. Preece, Esq.*

"We can recommend Dr. Noad's book for clear style, great range of subject, a good index, and a plethora of woodcuts. Such collections as the present are indispensable."—*Athenæum.*

"An admirable text-book for every student—beginner or advanced—of electricity."—*Engineering.*

"A most elaborate compilation of the facts of electricity and magnetism."—*Popular Science Review.*

"Dr. Noad's text-book has earned for itself the reputation of a truly scientific manual for the student of electricity, and we gladly hail this new amended edition, which brings it once more to the front. Mr. Preece as reviser, with the assistance of Mr. H. R. Kempe and Mr. J. P. Edwards, has added all the practical results of recent invention and research to the admirable theoretical expositions of the author, so that the book is about as complete and advanced as it is possible for any book to be within the limits of a text-book."—*Telegraphic Journal.*

Dr. Lardner's School Handbooks.

NATURAL PHILOSOPHY FOR SCHOOLS. By Dr. LARDNER. 328 Illustrations. Sixth Edition. One Vol., 3s. 6d. cloth.

"A very convenient class-book for junior students in private schools. It is intended to convey, in clear and precise terms, general notions of all the principal divisions of Physical Science."—*British Quarterly Review.*

ANIMAL PHYSIOLOGY FOR SCHOOLS. By Dr. LARDNER. With 190 Illustrations. Second Edition. One Vol., 3s. 6d. cloth.

"Clearly written, well arranged, and excellently illustrated."—*Gardener's Chronicle.*

Dr. Lardner's Electric Telegraph.

THE ELECTRIC TELEGRAPH. By Dr. LARDNER. New Edition. Revised and Re-written by E. B. BRIGHT, F.R.A.S. 140 Illustrations. Small 8vo, 2s. 6d. cloth.

"One of the most readable books extant on the Electric Telegraph."—*English Mechanic.*

Field Fortification.

A TREATISE ON FIELD FORTIFICATION, THE ATTACK OF FORTRESSES, MILITARY MINING, AND RECONNOITRING. By Colonel I. S. MACAULAY, late Professor of Fortification in the R.M.A., Woolwich. Sixth Edition, crown 8vo, cloth; with separate Atlas of 12 Plates, 12s. complete.

Lightning.

THE ACTION OF LIGHTNING, and the Means of Defending Life and Property from its Effects. By Major A. PARNELL, R.E. 12mo, 7s. 6d. cloth.

"Major Parnell has written an original work on a scientific subject of unusual interest; and he has prefaced his arguments by a patient and almost exhaustive citation of the best writers on the subject in the English language."—*Athenæum.*

Geology and Genesis.

THE TWIN RECORDS OF CREATION; or, Geology and Genesis: their Perfect Harmony and Wonderful Concord. By GEORGE W. VICTOR LE VAUX. Numerous Illustrations. Fcap. 8vo, 5s. cloth.

"A valuable contribution to the evidences of revelation, and disposes very conclusively of the arguments of those who would set God's Works against God's Word. No real difficulty is shirked, and no sophistry is left unexposed."—*The Rock.*

"The remarkable peculiarity of this author is that he combines an unbounded admiration of science with an unbounded admiration of the Written Record. The two impulses are balanced to a nicety; and the consequence is that difficulties which to minds less evenly poised would be serious find immediate solutions of the happiest kinds."—*London Review.*

The Blowpipe.

THE BLOWPIPE IN CHEMISTRY, MINERALOGY, AND GEOLOGY. Containing all known Methods of Anhydrous Analysis, many Working Examples, and Instructions for Making Apparatus. By Lieut.-Colonel W. A. Ross, R.A., F.G.S. With 120 Illustrations. Crown 8vo, 3s. 6d. cloth.

Contents:

CHAP. I. Manufacture of Blowing Apparatus. II. Construction of Pyrological Lamps.—III. Supports and Apparatus.—IV. On Auxiliary Apparatus.—V. On the Structure and Management of Pyrocones.—VI. On Pyrological Reagents.—VII. On Reagents and Simple Mineral Analyses.—VIII. First Operations: Aluminium-plate Reactions of Metals and Alloys.—IX. On Pyrological Mineralogy and a New Specific Gravitometer.—X. Inner Calcium-pyroborate Balls, "Chemical Water," &c.—XI. Rationale of Outer and Inner Ball Formation in Boric Acid before the Blowpipe.—XII. Frieberg Qualitative Examples.

"The student who goes conscientiously through the course of experimentation here laid down will gain a better insight into inorganic chemistry and mineralogy than if he had 'got up' any of the best text-books of the day, and passed any number of examinations in their contents."—*Chemical News.*

The Military Sciences.

AIDE-MEMOIRE TO THE MILITARY SCIENCES. Framed from Contributions of Officers and others connected with the different Services. Originally edited by a Committee of the Corps of Royal Engineers. Second Edition, most carefully revised by an Officer of the Corps, with many Additions; containing nearly 350 Engravings and many hundred Woodcuts. Three Vols., royal 8vo, extra cloth boards, and lettered, £4 10s.

"A compendious encyclopædia of military knowledge, to which we are greatly indebted."—*Edinburgh Review.*

"The most comprehensive work of reference to the military and collateral sciences.'—*Volunteer Service Gazette.*

Astronomy.

ASTRONOMY. By the late Rev. ROBERT MAIN, M.A., F.R.S., formerly Radcliffe Observer at Oxford. Third Edition, Revised and Corrected to the present time, by WILLIAM THYNNE LYNN, B.A., F.R.A.S., formerly of the Royal Observatory, Greenwich. 12mo, 2s. cloth limp.

"A sound and simple treatise, very carefully edited, and a capital book for beginners."—*Knowledge.*

"The present edition seems to have been carefully and accurately brought down to the requirements of the present time by Mr. Lynn."—*Educational Times.*

Geology.

GEOLOGY, Physical and Historical. Consisting of "Physical Geology," which sets forth the leading Principles of the Science; and "Historical Geology," which treats of the Mineral and Organic Conditions of the Earth at each successive epoch, especial reference being made to the British Series of Rocks. By RALPH TATE, A.L.S., F.G.S., &c., &c. With over 250 Illustrations. 12mo, 5s. cloth boards.

"The fulness of the matter has elevated the book into a manual. Its information is exhaustive and well arranged."—*School Board Chronicle.*

Conchology.

MANUAL OF THE MOLLUSCA: A Treatise on Recent and Fossil Shells. By Dr. S. P. WOODWARD, A.L.S. With Appendix by RALPH TATE, A.L.S., F.G.S. With numerous Plates and 300 Woodcuts. Handsomely bound in cloth boards, 7s. 6d.

"A most valuable storehouse of conchological and geological information."—*Hardwicke's Science Gossip.*

Dr. LARDNER'S HANDBOOKS of NATURAL PHILOSOPHY.

**** The following five volumes, though each is complete in itself, and to be purchased separately, form* A COMPLETE COURSE OF NATURAL PHILOSOPHY. *The style is studiously popular. It has been the author's aim to supply Manuals for the Student, the Engineer, the Artisan, and the superior classes in Schools.*

THE HANDBOOK OF MECHANICS. Enlarged and almost re-written by BENJAMIN LOEWY, F.R.A.S. With 378 Illustrations. Post 8vo, 6s. cloth.

"The perspicuity of the original has been retained, and chapters which had become obsolete have been replaced by others of more modern character. The explanations throughout are studiously popular, and care has been taken to show the application of the various branches of physics to the industrial arts, and to the practical business of life."—*Mining Journal.*

"Mr. Loewy has carefully revised the book, and brought it up to modern requirements."—*Nature.*

"Natural philosophy has had few exponents more able or better skilled in the art of popularising the subject than Dr. Lardner; and Mr. Loewy is doing good service in fitting this treatise and the others of the series, for use at the present time."—*Scotsman.*

THE HANDBOOK OF HYDROSTATICS AND PNEUMATICS. New Edition, Revised and Enlarged by BENJAMIN LOEWY, F.R.A.S. With 236 Illustrations. Post 8vo, 5s. cloth.

"For those 'who desire to attain an accurate knowledge of physical science without the profound methods of mathematical investigation,' this work is not merely intended, but well adapted."—*Chemical News.*

"The volume before us has been carefully edited, augmented to nearly twice the bulk of the former edition, and all the most recent matter has been added. . . . It is a valuable text-book."—*Nature.*

"Candidates for pass examinations will find it, we think, specially suited to their requirements."—*English Mechanic.*

THE HANDBOOK OF HEAT. Edited and almost entirely re written by BENJAMIN LOEWY, F.R.A.S., &c. 117 Illustrations. Post 8vo, 6s. cloth.

"The style is always clear and precise, and conveys instruction without leaving any cloudiness or lurking doubts behind."—*Engineering.*

"A most exhaustive book on the subject on which it treats, and is so arranged that it can be understood by all who desire to attain an accurate knowledge of physical science. . . . Mr. Loewy has included all the latest discoveries in the varied laws and effects of heat."—*Standard.*

"A complete and handy text-book for the use of students and general readers."—*English Mechanic.*

THE HANDBOOK OF OPTICS. By DIONYSIUS LARDNER, D.C.L., formerly Professor of Natural Philosophy and Astronomy in University College, London. New Edition. Edited by T. OLVER HARDING, B.A. Lond., of University College, London. With 298 Illustrations. Small 8vo, 448 pages, 5s. cloth.

"Written by one of the ablest English scientific writers, beautifully and elaborately illustrated."—*Mechanics' Magazine.*

THE HANDBOOK OF ELECTRICITY, MAGNETISM, AND ACOUSTICS. By Dr. LARDNER. New Edition. Edited by GEORGE CAREY FOSTER, B.A., F.C.S. With 400 Illustrations. Small 8vo, 5s. cloth.

"The book could not have been entrusted to anyone better calculated to preserve the terse and lucid style of Lardner, while correcting his errors and bringing up his work to the present state of cientific knowledge."—*Popular Science Review.*

Dr. Lardner's Handbook of Astronomy.

THE HANDBOOK OF ASTRONOMY. Forming a Companion to the "Handbook of Natural Philosophy." By DIONYSIUS LARDNER, D.C.L., formerly Professor of Natural Philosophy and Astronomy in University College, London. Fourth Edition. Revised and Edited by EDWIN DUNKIN, F.R.A.S., Royal Observatory, Greenwich. With 38 Plates and upwards of 100 Woodcuts. In One Vol., small 8vo, 550 pages, 9s. 6d. cloth.

"Probably no other book contains the same amount of information in so compendious and well-arranged a form—certainly none at the price at which this is offered to the public."—*Athenæum.*

"We can do no other than pronounce this work a most valuable manual of astronomy, and we strongly recommend it to all who wish to acquire a general—but at the same time correct—acquaintance with this sublime science."—*Quarterly Journal of Science.*

"One of the most deservedly popular books on the subject . . . We would recommend not only the student of the elementary principles of the science, but he who aims at mastering the higher and mathematical branches of astronomy, not to be without this work beside him."—*Practical Magazine.*

DR. LARDNER'S MUSEUM OF SCIENCE AND ART.

THE MUSEUM OF SCIENCE AND ART. Edited by DIONYSIUS LARDNER, D.C.L., formerly Professor of Natural Philosophy and Astronomy in University College, London. With upwards of 1,200 Engravings on Wood. In 6 Double Volumes, £1 1s., in a new and elegant cloth binding; or handsomely bound in half-morocco, 31s. 6d.

Contents:

The Planets: Are they Inhabited Worlds?—Weather Prognostics—Popular Fallacies in Questions of Physical Science—Latitudes and Longitudes—Lunar Influences—Meteoric Stones and Shooting Stars—Railway Accidents—Light—Common Things: Air—Locomotion in the United States—Cometary Influences—Common Things: Water—The Potter's Art—Common Things: Fire—Locomotion and Transport, their Influence and Progress—The Moon—Common Things: The Earth—The Electric Telegraph—Terrestrial Heat—The Sun—Earthquakes and Volcanoes—Barometer, Safety Lamp, and Whitworth's Micrometric Apparatus—Steam—The Steam Engine—The Eye—The Atmosphere—Time—Common Things: Pumps—Common Things: Spectacles, the Kaleidoscope—Clocks and Watches—Microscopic Drawing and Engraving—Locomotive—Thermometer—New Planets: Leverrier and Adams's Planet—Magnitude and Minuteness—Common Things: The Almanack—Optical Images—How to observe the Heavens—Common Things: The Looking-glass—Stellar Universe—The Tides—Colour—Common Things: Man—Magnifying Glasses—Instinct and Intelligence—The Solar Microscope—The Camera Lucida—The Magic Lantern—The Camera Obscura—The Microscope—The White Ants: Their Manners and Habits—The Surface of the Earth, or First Notions of Geography—Science and Poetry—The Bee—Steam Navigation—Electro-Motive Power—Thunder, Lightning, and the Aurora Borealis—The Printing Press—The Crust of the Earth—Comets—The Stereoscope—The Pre-Adamite Earth—Eclipses—Sound.

Opinions of the Press.

"This series, besides affording popular but sound instruction on scientific subjects, with which the humblest man in the country ought to be acquainted, also undertakes that teaching of 'Common Things' which every well-wisher of his kind is anxious to promote. Many thousand copies of this serviceable publication have been printed, in the belief and hope that the desire for instruction and improvement widely prevails; and we have no fear that such enlightened faith will meet with disappointment."—*Times.*

"A cheap and interesting publ'cation, alike informing and attractive. The papers combine subjects of importance and great scientific knowledge, considerable inductive powers, and a popular style of treatment."—*Spectator.*

"The 'Museum of Science and Art' is the most valuable contribution that has ever been made to the Scientific Instruction of every class of society."—Sir DAVID BREWSTER, in the *North British Review.*

"Whether we consider the liberality and beauty of the illustrations, the charm of the writing, or the durable interest of the matter, we must express our belief that there is hardly to be found among the new books one that would be welcomed by people of so many ages and classes as a valuable present."—*Examiner.*

*** *Separate books formed from the above, suitable for Workmen's Libraries, Science Classes, &c.*

Common Things Explained. Containing Air, Earth, Fire, Water, Time, Man, the Eye, Locomotion, Colour, Clocks and Watches, &c. 233 Illustrations, cloth gilt, 5s.

The Microscope. Containing Optical Images, Magnifying Glasses, Origin and Description of the Microscope, Microscopic Objects, the Solar Microscope, Microscopic Drawing and Engraving, &c. 147 Illustrations, cloth gilt, 2s.

Popular Geology. Containing Earthquakes and Volcanoes, the Crust of the Earth, &c. 201 Illustrations, cloth gilt, 2s. 6d.

Popular Physics. Containing Magnitude and Minuteness, the Atmosphere, Meteoric Stones, Popular Fallacies, Weather Prognostics, the Thermometer, the Barometer, Sound, &c. 85 Illustrations, cloth gilt, 2s. 6d.

Steam and its Uses. Including the Steam Engine, the Locomotive, and Steam Navigation. 89 Illustrations, cloth gilt, 2s.

Popular Astronomy. Containing How to observe the Heavens—The Earth, Sun, Moon, Planets, Light, Comets, Eclipses, Astronomical Influences, &c. 182 Illustrations, 4s. 6d.

The Bee and White Ants: Their Manners and Habits. With Illustrations of Animal Instinct and Intelligence. 135 Illustrations, cloth gilt, 2s.

The Electric Telegraph Popularised. To render intelligible to all who can Read, irrespective of any previous Scientific Acquirements, the various forms of Telegraphy in Actual Operation. 100 Illustrations, cloth gilt, 1s. 6d.

MATHEMATICS, GEOMETRY, TABLES, etc.

Practical Mathematics.

MATHEMATICS FOR PRACTICAL MEN. Being a Common-place Book of Pure and Mixed Mathematics. Designed chiefly for the Use of Civil Engineers, Architects, and Surveyors. Part I. PURE MATHEMATICS: comprising Arithmetic, Algebra, Geometry, Mensuration, Trigonometry, Conic Sections, Properties of Curves. Part II. MIXED MATHEMATICS: comprising Mechanics in general Statics, Dynamics, Hydrostatics, Hydrodynamics, Pneumatics, Mechanical Agents, Strength of Materials. With an Appendix of copious Logarithmic and other Tables. By OLINTHUS GREGORY, LL.D., F.R.A.S., Enlarged by HENRY LAW, C.E. 4th Edition, carefully Revised by J. R. YOUNG, formerly Professor of Mathematics, Belfast College. With 13 Plates, 8vo, £1 1s. cloth.

"The engineer or architect will here find ready to his hand rules for solving nearly every mathematical difficulty that may arise in his practice. The rules are in all cases explained by means of examples, in which every step of the process is clearly worked out."—*Builder.*

"One of the most serviceable books for practical mechanics. . . . Professor Young has modernised the notation throughout, introduced a few paragraphs here and there, and corrected the numerous typographical errors which had escaped the eyes of the former Editor. The book is now as complete as it is possible to make it. It is an instructive book for the student, and a Text-book for him who, having once mastered the subjects it treats of, needs occasionally to refresh his memory upon them."—*Building News.*

"As a standard work on mathematics it has not been excelled."—*Artizan.*

Metrical Units and Systems, etc.

MODERN METROLOGY: A Manual of the Metrical Units and Systems of the Present Century. With an Appendix containing a proposed English System. By LOWIS D'A. JACKSON, A.M. Inst. C.E., Author of "Aid to Survey Practice," &c. Large crown 8vo, 12s. 6d. cloth.

"The author has brought together much valuable and interesting information. . . . The main object of the work appears to be the discussion of a remedy for the evils of the complex systems of weights and measures which are unfortunately still in use in this country. To provide such a remedy is a serious task, and one well worthy of the attention of a great statesman such as Mr. Gladstone, to whom the work is inscribed. . . . We cannot but recommend the work to the consideration of all interested in the practical reform of our weights and measures."—*Nature.*

"For the large collection of measures brought together, the author supplies the French scientific equivalents, in terms of the metrical system. He also gives throughout a double set of English equivalents, the first of which he calls the 'Commercial Measures,' and the second the 'Scientific Value.' . . . There is no doubt as to the great amount of labour that must have been devoted to the calculation; and the juxtaposition of the two values affords an easy means of checking the work by comparison."—*Athenæum.*

"For exhaustive tables of equivalent weights and measures of all sorts, and for clear demonstrations of the effects of the various systems that have been proposed or adopted, Mr. Jackson's treatise is without a rival."—*Academy.*

The Metric System.

A SERIES OF METRIC TABLES, in which the British Standard Measures and Weights are compared with those of the Metric System at present in Use on the Continent. By C. H. DOWLING, C.E. Second Edition, Revised and Enlarged. 8vo, 10s. 6d. strongly bound.

"Their accuracy has been certified by Professor Airy, the Astronomer-Royal."—*Builder.*

"Mr. Dowling's Tables, which are well put together, come just in time as a ready-reckoner for the conversion of one system into the other."—*Athenæum*

Geometry for the Architect, Engineer, etc.

PRACTICAL GEOMETRY, for the Architect, Engineer and Mechanic. Giving Rules for the Delineation and Application of various Geometrical Lines, Figures and Curves. By E. W. TARN, M.A., Architect, Author of "The Science of Building," &c. Second Edition. With Appendices on Diagrams of Strains and Isometrical Projection. With 172 Illustrations, demy 8vo, 9s. cloth.

"No book with the same objects in view has ever been published in which the clearness of the rules laid down and the illustrative diagrams have been so satisfactory."—*Scotsman.*

"This is a manual for the practical man, whether architect, engineer, or mechanic. . . . The object of the author being to avoid all abstruse formulæ or complicated methods, and to enable persons with but a moderate knowledge of geometry to work out the problems required."—*English Mechanic.*

Comprehensive Weight Calculator.

THE WEIGHT CALCULATOR. Being a Series of Tables upon a New and Comprehensive Plan, exhibiting at One Reference the exact Value of any Weight from 1 lb. to 15 tons, at 300 Progressive Rates, from 1*d.* to 168*s.* per cwt., and containing 186,000 Direct Answers, which, with their Combinations, consisting of a single addition (mostly to be performed at sight), will afford an aggregate of 10,266,000 Answers; the whole being calculated and designed to ensure correctness and promote despatch. By HENRY HARBEN, Accountant, Sheffield, Author of "The Discount Guide." An entirely New Edition, carefully revised. Royal 8vo, strongly half-bound, £1 5*s.*

"A practical and useful work of reference for men of business generally; it is the best of the kind we have seen. We have frequently been asked if such a work as this could be obtained, and therefore refer to it with pleasure."—*Ironmonger.*

"Of priceless value to business men. Its accuracy and completeness have secured for it a reputation which renders it quite unnecessary for us to say one word in its praise. It is a necessary book in all mercantile offices."—*Sheffield Independent.*

"An enormous amount of labour must have been bestowed upon the preparation of the tables, but the result is a series which gives the answers sought more readily than any of its predecessors." *Mining Journal.*

Comprehensive Discount Guide.

THE DISCOUNT GUIDE. Comprising several Series of Tables for the use of Merchants, Manufacturers, Ironmongers, and others, by which may be ascertained the exact Profit arising from any mode of using Discounts, either in the Purchase or Sale of Goods, and the method of either Altering a Rate of Discount or Advancing a Price, so as to produce, by one operation, a sum that will realise any required profit after allowing one or more Discounts: to which are added Tables of Profit or Advance from 1¼ to 90 per cent., Tables of Discount from 1¼ to 98¾ per cent., and Tables of Commission, &c., from ⅛ to 10 per cent. By HENRY HARBEN, Accountant, Author of "The Weight Calculator." New Edition, carefully Revised and Corrected. Demy 8vo, 544 pp. half-bound, £1 5*s.*

"All these tables are well arranged and clearly printed; and the collection will be found of great value in those businesses for which the book has been especially compiled."—*Engineering.*

"A book such as this can only be appreciated by business men, to whom the saving of time means saving of money. We have the high authority of Professor J. R. Young that the tables throughout the work are constructed upon strictly accurate principles. The work is a model of typographical clearness, and must prove of great value to merchants, manufacturers, and general traders."—*British Trade Journal.*

"Much time and labour will be saved by the use of this book—even to the most expert arithmetician. The great practical utility of the 'Discount Guide' will no doubt make it a standard work of reference."—*London Commercial Record.*

Iron and Metal Trades' Calculator.

THE IRON AND METAL TRADES' COMPANION. Being a Calculator, containing a Series of Tables upon a New and Comprehensive Plan, for expeditiously ascertaining the Value of any Goods bought or sold by Weight, from 1*s.* per cwt. to 112*s.* per cwt., and from one farthing per pound to one shilling per pound. Each Table extends from one pound to 100 tons. To which are appended Rules on Decimals, Square and Cube Root, Mensuration of Superficies and Solids, &c.; also Tables of Weights of Materials, and other Useful Memoranda. By THOMAS DOWNIE. Strongly bound in leather, 396 pp., 9*s.*

"A most useful set of tables, and will supply a want, for nothing like them before existed."—*Building News.*

"Will save the possessor the trouble of making numerous intricate calculations. Although specially adapted to the iron and metal trades, the tables contained in this handy little companion will be found useful in every other business in which merchandise is bought and sold by weight."—*Railway News.*

Practical Geometry.

THE GEOMETRY OF COMPASSES; or, Problems Resolved by the mere Description of Circles and the use of Coloured Diagrams and Symbols. By OLIVER BYRNE. Coloured Plates. Crown 8vo, 3*s.* 6*d.* cloth.

"A very useful work, which will be valued by all who are pursuing the useful and fascinating study of geometry."—*Iron.*

"The treatise is a good one, and remarkable—like all Mr. Byrne's contributions to the science of geometry—for the lucid character of its teaching."—*Building News.*

"The problems in this useful book are cleverly worked out by beautifully coloured and uncoloured diagrams. It will no doubt be extensively circulated. We highly recommend it."—*Cambridge Express.*

INDUSTRIAL AND USEFUL ARTS.

Soap-making.

THE ART OF SOAP-MAKING: A Practical Handbook of the Manufacture of Hard and Soft Soaps, Toilet Soaps, &c. Including many New Processes, and a Chapter on the Recovery of Glycerine from Waste Leys. By ALEXANDER WATT, Author of "Electro-Metallurgy Practically Treated," &c. With numerous Illustrations. Crown 8vo, 9*s.* cloth.

"The work will prove very useful, not merely to the technological student, but to the practical soapboiler who wishes to understand the theory of his art."—*Chemical News.*

"It is really an excellent example of a technical manual, entering, as it does, thoroughly and exhaustively both into the theory and practice of soap manufacture. The book is well and honestly done, and deserves the considerable circulation with which it will doubtless meet."—*Knowledge.*

"Mr. Watt's book is a thoroughly practical treatise on an art which has almost no literature in our language. We congratulate the author on the success of his endeavour to fill a void in English technical literature."—*Nature.*

". . . . Clearly and concisely written, and appears to be comprehensive and complete."—*Engineering.*

Leather Manufacture.

THE ART OF LEATHER MANUFACTURE. Being a Practical Handbook, in which the Operations of Tanning, Currying, and Leather Dressing are fully Described, and the Principles of Tanning Explained, and many Recent Processes introduced; as also Methods for the Estimation of Tannin, and a Description of the Arts of Glue Boiling, Gut Dressing, &c. By ALEXANDER WATT, Author of "Soap-Making," "Electro-Metallurgy," &c. With numerous Illustrations. Crown 8vo, 12*s.* 6*d.* cloth. [*Just published.*

"Every item of use and interest to the leather trade has been touched upon, and the descriptions and explanations of the various processes are exhaustively given."—*Tanners' and Curriers' Journal.*

"A most lucid and readable book upon difficult and intricate subjects. Every known process of tanning, from the most primitive to the most recent, is fully and accurately described."—*Scottish Leather Trader.*

Boot and Shoe Making.

THE ART OF BOOT AND SHOE-MAKING. A Practical Handbook, including Measurement, Last-Fitting, Cutting-Out, Closing and Making, with a Description of the most approved Machinery employed. By JOHN B. LENO, late Editor of *St. Crispin*, and *The Boot and Shoe-Maker*. With numerous Illustrations. Crown 8vo, 5*s.* cloth. [*Just published.*

"A very complete account of the art and science of bootmaking, which includes all that need be said about leathers and other materials, as well as about hand-tools and the various machines that have latterly been introduced to supplement or supersede the old-fashioned handiwork."—*Weekly Dispatch.*

Dentistry.

MECHANICAL DENTISTRY: A Practical Treatise on the Construction of the various kinds of Artificial Dentures. Comprising also Useful Formulæ, Tables and Receipts for Gold Plate, Clasps, Solders, &c. &c. By CHARLES HUNTER. Second Edition, Revised. With upwards of 100 Wood Engravings. Crown 8vo, 7*s.* 6*d.* cloth.

"The work is very practical."—*Monthly Review of Dental Surgery.*

"An authoritative treatise. . . . We can strongly recommend Mr. Hunter's treatise to all students preparing for the profession of dentistry, as well as to every mechanical dentist."—*Dublin Journal of Medical Science.*

"A work in a concise form that few could read without gaining information from."—*British Journal of Dental Science.*

"The best book on the subject with which we are acquainted."—*Medical Press and Circular.*

Brewing.

A HANDBOOK FOR YOUNG BREWERS. By HERBERT EDWARDS WRIGHT, B.A. Crown 8vo, 3*s.* 6*d.* cloth.

"This little volume, containing such a large amount of good sense in so small a compass, ought to recommend itself to every brewery pupil, and many who have passed that stage."—*Brewers' Guardian.*

"The book is very clearly written, and the author has successfully brought his scientific knowledge to bear upon the various processes and details of brewing. To the young student of brewing the reading of such a book as this is calculated to do good, for it will lead him to inquire not only what is to be done, but why it should be done"—*Brewer.*

Electroplating, etc.

ELECTROPLATING: A Practical Handbook. By J. W. URQUHART, C.E. With numerous Illustrations. Crown 8vo, 5s. cloth.

"The volume is without a rival in its particular sphere, and the lucid style in which it is written commends it to those amateurs and experimental electrotypers who have but slight, if any, knowledge of the processes of the art to which they turn their attention."—*Design and Work.*

"The information given appears to be based on direct personal knowledge. . . . Its science is sound and the style is always clear."—*Athenæum.*

Electrotyping, etc.

ELECTROTYPING: The Reproduction and Multiplication of Printing Surfaces and Works of Art by the Electro-deposition of Metals. By J. W. URQUHART, C.E. Crown 8vo, 5s. cloth.

"The book is so thoroughly practical that it assumes to start with an entire ignorance on the reader's part of electricity. He is, therefore, conducted through its leading laws, then through the metals used by electrotypers, the apparatus, and the depositing processes, up to the final preparation of the work."—*Art Journal.*

"In this work the author enters systematically and thoroughly into every department of the process, in the style of one who combines theory with practice. We can recommend this treatise, not merely to amateurs, but to those actually engaged in the trade."—*Chemical News.*

Electric Lighting.

ELECTRIC LIGHT: Its Production and Use. Embodying Plain Directions for the Treatment of Voltaic Batteries, Electric Lamps, and Dynamo-Electric Machines. By J. W. URQUHART, C.E., Author of "Electroplating: A Practical Handbook." Edited by F. C. WEBB, M.I.C.E., M.S.T.E. Second Edition, revised, with large Additions and 128 Illusts. 7s. 6d. cloth.

"The book is by far the best that we have yet met with on the subject."—*Athenæum.*

"It is the only work at present available which gives, in language intelligible for the most part to the ordinary reader, a general but concise history of the means which have been adopted up to the present time in producing the electric light. . . . A chapter on the comparative cost of the electric light and gas contains much valuable and interesting information."—*Metropolitan.*

"The book contains a general account of the means adopted in producing the electric light, not only as obtained from voltaic or galvanic batteries, but treats at length of the dynamo-electric machine in several of its forms. . . . An important addition to the literature of the electric light. Students of the subject should not fail to read it."—*Colliery Guardian.*

Electro-Metallurgy.

ELECTRO-METALLURGY; Practically Treated. By ALEXANDER WATT, F.R.S.S.A. Eighth Edition, Revised, with Additional Matter and Illustrations, including the most recent Processes. 12mo, 3s. 6d. cloth boards.

"From this book both amateur and artisan may learn everything necessary for the successful prosecution of electroplating."—*Iron.*

"A practical treatise for the use of those who desire to work in the art of electro-deposition as a business."—*English Mechanic.*

Silversmiths' Work.

THE SILVERSMITH'S HANDBOOK. Containing full Instructions for the Alloying and Working of Silver, including the different modes of Refining and Melting the Metal, its Solders, the Preparation of Imitation Alloys, Methods of Manipulation, Prevention of Waste, Instructions for Improving and Finishing the Surface of the Work, together with other useful Information and Memoranda. By GEORGE E. GEE, Jeweller, &c. Second Edition, Revised, with numerous Illustrations. 12mo, 3s. 6d. cloth boards. [*Just published.*

"The chief merit of the work is its practical character. . . . The workers in the trade will speedily discover its merits when they sit down to study it."—*English Mechanic.*

"This work forms a valuable sequel to the author's 'Goldsmith's Handbook,' and supplies a want long felt in the silver trade."—*Silversmiths' Trade Journal.*

Goldsmiths' Work.

THE GOLDSMITH'S HANDBOOK. Containing full Instructions in the Art of Alloying, Melting, Reducing, Colouring, Collecting and Refining. The processes of Manipulation, Recovery of Waste, Chemical and Physical Properties of Gold, with a New System of Mixing its Alloys; Solders, Enamels, and other useful Rules and Recipes, &c. By GEORGE E. GEE. Second Edition, considerably enlarged. 12mo, 3s. 6d. cloth boards.

"A good, sound, technical educator, and will be generally accepted as an authority. It gives full particulars for mixing alloys and enamels, is essentially a book for the workshop, and exactly fulfils the purpose intended."—*Horological Journal.*

"The best work yet printed on its subject for a reasonable price. We have no doubt that it will speedily become a standard book which few will care to be without."—*Jeweller and Metalworker.*

CHEMICAL MANUFACTURES & COMMERCE.

Alkali Trade, Manufacture of Sulphuric Acid, etc.

A MANUAL OF THE ALKALI TRADE, including the Manufacture of Sulphuric Acid, Sulphate of Soda, and Bleaching Powder. By JOHN LOMAS, Alkali Manufacturer, Newcastle-upon-Tyne and London. With 232 Illustrations and Working Drawings, and containing 386 pages of Text. Super-royal 8vo, £2 12*s.* 6*d.* cloth.

*** This work provides (1) a Complete Handbook for intending Alkali and Sulphuric Acid Manufacturers, and for those already in the field who desire to improve their plant, or to become practically acquainted with the latest processes and developments of the trade: (2) a Handy Volume which Manufacturers can put into the hands of their Managers and Foremen as a useful guide in their daily rounds of duty.

Synopsis of Contents:

Chap. I. Choice of Site and General Plan of Works.—II. Sulphuric Acid.—III. Recovery of the Nitrogen Compounds, and Treatment of Small Pyrites.—IV. The Salt Cake Process.—V. Legislation upon the Noxious Vapours Question.—VI. The Hargreaves' and Jones' Processes.—VII. The Balling Process.—VIII. Lixiviation and Salting Down.—IX. Carbonating or Finishing.—X. Soda Crystals.—XI. Refined Alkali.—XII. Caustic Soda.—XIII. Bi-carbonate of Soda.—XIV. Bleaching Powder.—XV. Utilisation of Tank Waste.—XVI. General Remarks—Four Appendices treating of Yields, Sulphuric Acid Calculations, Anemometers, and Foreign Legislation upon the Noxious Vapours Question.

"The author has given the fullest, most practical, and, to all concerned in the alkali trade, most valuable mass of information that, to our knowledge, has been published in any language."—*Engineer.*

"This book is written by a manufacturer for manufacturers. The working details of the most approved forms of apparatus are given, and these are accompanied by no less than 232 wood engravings, all of which may be used for the purposes of construction. Every step in the manufacture is very fully described in this manual, and each improvement explained. Everything which tends to introduce economy into the technical details of this trade receives the fullest attention."—*Athenæum.*

"The author is not one of those clever compilers who, on short notice, will 'read up' any conceivable subject, but a practical man in the best sense of the word. We find here not merely a sound and luminous explanation of the chemical principles of the trade, but a notice of numerous matters which have a most important bearing on the successful conduct of alkali works, but which are generally overlooked by even the most experienced technological authors."—*Chemical Review.*

Commercial Chemical Analysis.

THE COMMERCIAL HANDBOOK OF CHEMICAL ANALYSIS; or, Practical Instructions for the determination of the Intrinsic or Commercial Value of Substances used in Manufactures, in Trades, and in the Arts. By A. NORMANDY, Author of "Practical Introduction to Rose's Chemistry," and Editor of Rose's "Treatise on Chemical Analysis." New Edition, Enlarged and to a great extent re-written, by HENRY M. NOAD, Ph.D., F.R.S. With numerous Illustrations. Crown 8vo, 12*s.* 6*d.* cloth.

"We recommend this book to the careful perusal of everyone; it may be truly affirmed to be of universal interest, and we strongly recommend it to our readers as a guide, alike indispensable to the housewife as to the pharmaceutical practitioner."—*Medical Times.*

"Essential to the analysts appointed under the new Act. The most recent results are given, and the work is well edited and carefully written."—*Nature.*

Dye-Wares and Colours.

THE MANUAL OF COLOURS AND DYE-WARES: Their Properties, Applications, Valuation, Impurities, and Sophistications. For the use of Dyers, Printers, Drysalters, Brokers, &c. By J. W. SLATER. Second Edition, Revised and greatly Enlarged. Crown 8vo, 7*s.* 6*d.* cloth.

*** This book contains a description of about Six Hundred Colours, Chemicals, and Drugs used in the Tinctorial Arts, and their Sources, Applications, and possible Impurities.

"A complete encyclopædia of the *materia tinctoria*. The information given respecting each article is full and precise, and the methods of determining the value of articles such as these, so liable to sophistication, are given with clearness, and are practical as well as valuable."—*Chemist and Druggist.*

"Practical dyers, &c., will welcome the work in its improved form. There is no other work in the language which covers precisely the same ground. To technological students preparing for examinations in dyeing and printing it will prove exceedingly useful."—*Chemical News.*

AGRICULTURE, LAND MANAGEMENT, etc.

Youatt and Burn's Complete Grazier.

THE COMPLETE GRAZIER, and FARMER'S and CATTLE-BREEDER'S ASSISTANT. A Compendium of Husbandry; especially in the departments connected with the Breeding, Rearing, Feeding, and General Management of Stock; the Management of the Dairy, &c. With Directions for the Culture and Management of Grass Land, of Grain and Root Crops, the Arrangement of Farm Offices, the use of Implements and Machines, and on Draining, Irrigation, Warping, &c.; and the Application and Relative Value of Manures. By WILLIAM YOUATT, Esq., V.S. Twelfth Edition, very considerably enlarged and brought up to the present requirements of Agricultural Practice by ROBERT SCOTT BURN, Author of "Outlines of Modern Farming," "Landed Estates Management," "Farm Management," "The Lessons of My Farm," &c. One large 8vo Volume, 860 pp., with 244 Illustrations, £1 1s. half-bound.

"The standard and text-book with the farmer and grazier."—*Farmers' Magazine.*

"A treatise which will remain a standard work on the subject as long as British agriculture endures."—*Mark Lane Express* (First Notice).

"The book deals with all departments of agriculture, and contains an immense amount of valuable information. It is, in fact, an encyclopædia of agriculture put into readable form, and it is the only work equally comprehensive brought down to present date. It is excellently printed on thick paper, and strongly bound, and deserves a place in the library of every agriculturist."—*Mark Lane Express* (Second Notice).

"Of great value to the farmer, more especially to the young cattle breeder and feeder. . . . This esteemed work is well worthy of a place in the libraries of agriculturists."—*North British Agriculturist.*

"A valuable repertory of intelligence for all who make agriculture a pursuit, and especially for those who aim at keeping pace with the improvements of the age. . . . The new matter is of so valuable a nature that the volume is now almost entitled to be considered as a distinct work.'—*Bell's Messenger.*

Modern Farming.

OUTLINES OF MODERN FARMING. By R. SCOTT BURN. Soils, Manures, and Crops—Farming and Farming Economy—Cattle, Sheep, and Horses—Management of the Dairy, Pigs and Poultry—Utilisation of Town-Sewage, Irrigation, &c. Sixth Edition. In One Vol., 1,250 pp., half-bound, profusely Illustrated, 12s.

"The aim of the author has been to make his work at once comprehensive and trustworthy, and in this aim he has succeeded to a degree which entitles him to much credit."—*Morning Advertiser.*

"Eminently calculated to enlighten the agricultural community on the varied subjects of which it treats, and hence it should find a place in every farmer's library."—*City Press.*

"No farmer should be without this book."—*Banbury Guardian.*

Agricultural Engineering.

THE COMPLETE TEXT-BOOK OF FARM ENGINEERING. Comprising Practical Treatises on Draining and Embanking; Irrigation and Water Supply; Farm Roads, Fences, and Gates; Farm Buildings, Barn Implements, and Machines; Field Implements and Machines; and Agricultural Surveying, Levelling, &c. By Prof. JOHN SCOTT, Editor of the *Farmers' Gazette*, late Professor of Agriculture and Rural Economy at the Royal Agricultural College, Cirencester, &c., &c. In One Vol., 1,150 pages, wih 600 Illustrations, 12s. half-bound. [*Just published.*

"A copy of this work should be treasured up in every library where the owner thereof is in any way connected with land."—*Farm and Home.*

"Written with great care, as well as with knowledge and ability. The author has done his work well; we have found him a very trustworthy guide wherever we have tested his statements. The volume will be of great value to agricultural students, and we have much pleasure in recommending it."—*Mark Lane Express.*

"For a young agriculturist we know of no handy volume so likely to be more usefully studied."—*Bell's Weekly Messenger.*

Amateur Farming.

THE LESSONS OF MY FARM: A Book for Amateur Agriculturists. Being an Introduction to Farm Practice. By ROBERT SCOTT BURN. With numerous Illustrations.

[*A New and Enlarged Edition in preparation.*

A Text-Book of English Agriculture.

THE FIELDS OF GREAT BRITAIN: A Text-Book of Agriculture, adapted to the Syllabus of the Science and Art Department. For Elementary and Advanced Students. By HUGH CLEMENTS (Board of Trade). 18mo, 2s. 6d. cloth.

"A most comprehensive volume, giving a mass of information."—*Agricultural Economist.*

"It is a long time since we have seen a book which has pleased us more, or which contains such a vast and useful fund of knowledge."—*Educational Times.*

Agricultural Data.

NOTE BOOK of AGRICULTURAL FACTS and FIGURES, for Farmers and Farm Students. By PRIMROSE McCONNELL, Fellow of the Highland and Agricultural Society; late Professor of Agriculture, Glasgow Veterinary College. Royal 32mo oblong, leather, with strap, 4s.

"It is full of very valuable information. Farmers' sons and other youths who wish to become farmers at home or abroad, might, even before their school education is completed, become familiar with the facts and figures furnished in this interesting and valuable little book."—*Aberdeen Free Press.*

Hudson's Land Valuer's Pocket-Book.

THE LAND VALUER'S BEST ASSISTANT: Being Tables on a very much Improved Plan, for Calculating the Value of Estates. With Tables for reducing Scotch, Irish, and Provincial Customary Acres to Statute Measure, &c. By R. HUDSON, C.E. New Edition. Royal 32mo, leather, gilt edges, elastic band, 4s.

"This new edition includes tables for ascertaining the value of leases for any term of years; and for showing how to lay out plots of ground of certain acres in forms, square, round, &c., with valuable rules for ascertaining the probable worth of standing timber to any amount; and is of incalculable value to the country gentleman and professional man."—*Farmers' Journal.*

Ewart's Land Improver's Pocket-Book.

THE LAND IMPROVER'S POCKET-BOOK OF FORMULÆ, TABLES and MEMORANDA required in any Computation relating to the Permanent Improvement of Landed Property. By JOHN EWART, Land Surveyor and Agricultural Engineer. Royal 32mo, oblong, leather, gilt edges, with elastic band, 4s.

"A compendious and handy little volume."—*Spectator.*

Complete Agricultural Surveyor's Pocket-Book.

THE LAND VALUER'S AND LAND IMPROVER'S COMPLETE POCKET-BOOK. Consisting of the above Two Works bound together. Leather, gilt edges, with strap, 7s. 6d.

"We consider Hudson's book to be the best ready-reckoner on matters relating to the valuation of land and crops we have ever seen, and its combination with Mr. Ewart's work greatly enhances the value and usefulness of the latter-mentioned. . . . It is most useful as a manual for reference."—*North of England Farmer.*

Potato Culture.

POTATOES: How to Grow and Show them. A Practical Guide to the Cultivation and General Treatment of the Potato. By JAMES PINK. With Illustrations. Second Edition. Crown 8vo, 2s. cloth.

"A well-written little volume. The author gives good practical instructions under both divisions of his subject."—*Agricultural Gazette.*

GARDENING, FLORICULTURE, etc.

Early Fruits, Flowers and Vegetables.

THE FORCING GARDEN: or, How to Grow Early Fruits, Flowers, and Vegetables. With Plans, and Estimates for Building Glass-houses, Pits and Frames. Containing also Original Plans for Double Glazing, a New Method of Growing the Gooseberry under Glass, &c., &c., and on Ventilation, Protecting Vine Borders, &c. With Illustrations. By SAMUEL WOOD. Crown 8vo, 3s. 6d. cloth.

"A good book, and fairly fills a place that was in some degree vacant. The book is written with great care, and contains a great deal of valuable teaching."—*Gardeners' Magazine.*

"Mr. Wood's book is an original and exhaustive answer to the question 'How to Grow Early Fruits, Flowers and Vegetables?'"—*Land and Water.*

Good Gardening.

A PLAIN GUIDE TO GOOD GARDENING; or, How to Grow Vegetables, Fruits, and Flowers. With Practical Notes on Soils, Manures, Seeds, Planting, Laying-out of Gardens and Grounds, &c. By S. WOOD. With numerous Illustrations. Third Edition. Crown 8vo, 5s. cloth.

"A very good book, and one to be highly recommended as a practical guide. The practical directions are excellent."—*Athenæum*.

"May be recommended to young gardeners, cottagers, and specially to amateurs, for the plain, simple, and trustworthy information it gives on common matters too often neglected."—*Gardeners' Chronicle*.

Gainful Gardening.

MULTUM-IN-PARVO GARDENING; or, How to make One Acre of Land produce £620 a-year by the Cultivation of Fruits and Vegetables; also, How to Grow Flowers in Three Glass Houses, so as to realise £176 per annum clear Profit. By SAMUEL WOOD, Author of "Good Gardening," &c. Fourth Edition, revised. With Wood Engravings. Crown 8vo, 2s. cloth.

"We are bound to recommend it as not only suited to the case of the amateur and gentleman's gardener, but to the market grower."—*Gardeners' Magazine*.

"Of all the practical guides to the amateur, as well as being invaluable to most gardeners, Mr Wood's book is the most accurate and concise."—*Horticultural Record*.

Gardening for Ladies.

THE LADIES' MULTUM-IN-PARVO FLOWER GARDEN, and Amateur's Complete Guide. With Illustrations. By SAMUEL WOOD. Crown 8vo, 3s. 6d. cloth.

"This volume contains a good deal of sound, common-sense instruction."—*Florist*.

"Full of shrewd hints and useful instructions, based on a lifetime of experience."—*Scotsman*.

Receipts for Gardeners.

GARDEN RECEIPTS. Edited by CHARLES W. QUIN. 12mo, 1s. 6d. cloth limp.

"A useful and handy book, containing a good deal of valuable information."—*Athenæum*.

Kitchen Gardening.

THE KITCHEN AND MARKET GARDEN. By Contributors to "The Garden." Compiled by C. W. SHAW, Editor of "Gardening Illustrated." 12mo, 3s. 6d. cloth boards.

"The most valuable compendium of kitchen and market-garden work published."—*Farmer*.

Cottage Gardening.

COTTAGE GARDENING; or, Flowers, Fruits, and Vegetables for Small Gardens. By E. HOBDAY. 12mo, 1s. 6d. cloth limp.

"Definite instructions as to the cultivation of small gardens."—*Scotsman*.

"Contains much useful information at a small charge."—*Glasgow Herald*.

AUCTIONEERING, ESTATE AGENCY, etc.

Auctioneer's Assistant.

THE APPRAISER, AUCTIONEER, BROKER, HOUSE AND ESTATE AGENT AND VALUER'S POCKET ASSISTANT, for the Valuation for Purchase, Sale, or Renewal of Leases, Annuities and Reversions, and of property generally; with Prices for Inventories, &c. By JOHN WHEELER, Valuer, &c. Fifth Edition, Re-written and greatly Extended by C. NORRIS, Surveyor, Valuer, &c. Royal 32mo, 5s. cloth.

"A neat and concise book of reference, containing an admirable and clearly-arranged list of prices for inventories, and a very practical guide to determine the value of furniture, &c."—*Standard*

"Cram full of valuable information of practical value. It is a trustworthy and compendious guide to all sorts of valuation."—*Insurance Agent*.

Auctioneering.

AUCTIONEERS: Their Duties and Liabilities. By ROBERT SQUIBBS, Auctioneer. Demy 8vo, 10s. 6d. cloth.

"The position and duties of auctioneers are treated compendiously and clearly."—*Builder*.

"Every auctioneer ought to possess a copy of this excellent work."—*Ironmonger*.

"Of great value to the profession. . . . We readily welcome this book."—*Estates Gazette*.

House Property.

HANDBOOK OF HOUSE PROPERTY: A Popular and Practical Guide to the Purchase, Mortgage, Tenancy, and Compulsory Sale of Houses and Land. By E. L. TARBUCK, Architect and Surveyor. Third Edition, 12mo, 3*s*. 6*d*. cloth.

"The advice is thoroughly practical."—*Law Journal.*

"This is a well-written and thoughtful work. We commend the work to the careful study of all interested in questions affecting houses and land."—*Land Agents' Record.*

Inwood's Estate Tables.

TABLES FOR THE PURCHASING OF ESTATES, Freehold, Copyhold, or Leasehold; Annuities, Advowsons, &c., and for the Renewing of Leases held under Cathedral Churches, Colleges, or other Corporate bodies, for Terms of Years certain, and for Lives; also for Valuing Reversionary Estates, Deferred Annuities, Next Presentations, &c.: together with SMART'S Five Tables of Compound Interest, and an Extension of the same to Lower and Intermediate Rates. By W. INWOOD. 22nd Edition, with considerable Additions, and new and valuable Tables of Logarithms for the more Difficult Computations of the Interest of Money, Discount, Annuities, &c., by M. FEDOR THOMAN, of the Société Crédit Mobilier of Paris. 12mo, 8*s*. cloth.

"Those interested in the purchase and sale of estates, and in the adjustment of compensation cases, as well as in transactions in annuities, life insurances, &c., will find the present edition of eminent service."—*Engineering.*

"'Inwood's Tables' still maintain a most enviable reputation. The new issue has been enriched by large additional contributions by M. Fedor Thoman, whose carefully arranged Tables cannot fail to be of the utmost utility."—*Mining Journal.*

How to Invest.

HINTS FOR INVESTORS: Being an Explanation of the Mode of Transacting Business on the Stock Exchange. To which are added Comments on the Fluctuations and Table of Quarterly Average prices of Consols since 1759. Also a Copy of the London Daily Stock and Share List. By WALTER M. PLAYFORD, Sworn Broker. Crown 8vo, 2*s*. cloth.

"A clearly-written book, by one who evidently knows the sort of information which the investor is likely to want."—*Lloyd's News.*

"An invaluable guide to investors and speculators."—*Bullionist.*

A Complete Epitome of the Laws of this Country.

EVERY MAN'S OWN LAWYER: A Handy-book of the Principles of Law and Equity. By A BARRISTER. Twenty-second Edition. Carefully revised and brought down to the end of the last Session, including Summaries of the Latest Statute Laws. With Notes and References to the Authorities. Crown 8vo, price 6*s*. 8*d*. (saved at every consultation), strongly bound in cloth.

Comprising THE RIGHTS AND WRONGS OF INDIVIDUALS—MERCANTILE AND COMMERCIAL LAW—CRIMINAL LAW—PARISH LAW—COUNTY COURT LAW—GAME AND FISHERY LAWS—POOR MEN'S LAWSUITS—THE LAWS OF BANKRUPTCY—BETS AND WAGERS—CHEQUES, BILLS, AND NOTES—CONTRACTS AND AGREEMENTS—COPYRIGHT—ELECTIONS AND REGISTRATION—INSURANCE—LIBEL AND SLANDER—MARRIAGE AND DIVORCE—MERCHANT SHIPPING—MORTGAGES—SETTLEMENTS—STOCK EXCHANGE PRACTICE—TRADE MARKS AND PATENTS—TRESPASS—NUISANCES, &c.—TRANSFER OF LAND, &c.—WARRANTY—WILLS AND AGREEMENTS, &c. &c.

Also, Law for Landlord and Tenant—Master and Servant—Workmen and Apprentices—Heirs—Devisees and Legatees—Husband and Wife—Executors and Trustees—Guardian and Ward—Married Women and Infants—Partners and Agents—Lender, Borrower and Sureties—Debtor and Creditor—Purchaser and Vendor—Companies and Associations—Friendly Societies—Clergymen—Churchwardens—Medical Practitioners, &c.—Bankers—Farmers—Contractors—Stock and Share Brokers—Sportsmen—Gamekeepers—Farriers and Horse Dealers—Auctioneers—House Agents—Innkeepers, &c.—Bakers—Millers, &c.—Pawnbrokers—Surveyors—Railways and Carriers—Constables—Seamen—Soldiers, &c. &c.

Opinions of the Press.

"*No Englishman ought to be without this book.* . . . Any person perfectly uninformed on legal matters, who may require sound information on unknown law points, will, by reference to this book, acquire the necessary information, and thus on many occasions save the expense and loss of time of a visit to a lawyer."—*Engineer.*

"It is a complete code of English Law, written in plain language, which all can understand. . . . . Should be in the hands of every business man, and all who wish to abolish lawyers' bills."—*Weekly Times.*

"A useful and concise epitome of the law, compiled with considerable care."—*Law Magazine.*

"What it professes to be—a complete epitome of the laws of this country, thoroughly intelligible to non-professional readers. The book is a handy one to have in readiness when some knotty point requires ready solution."—*Bell's Life.*